IMAGES
of America

SIX FLAGS GREAT ADVENTURE

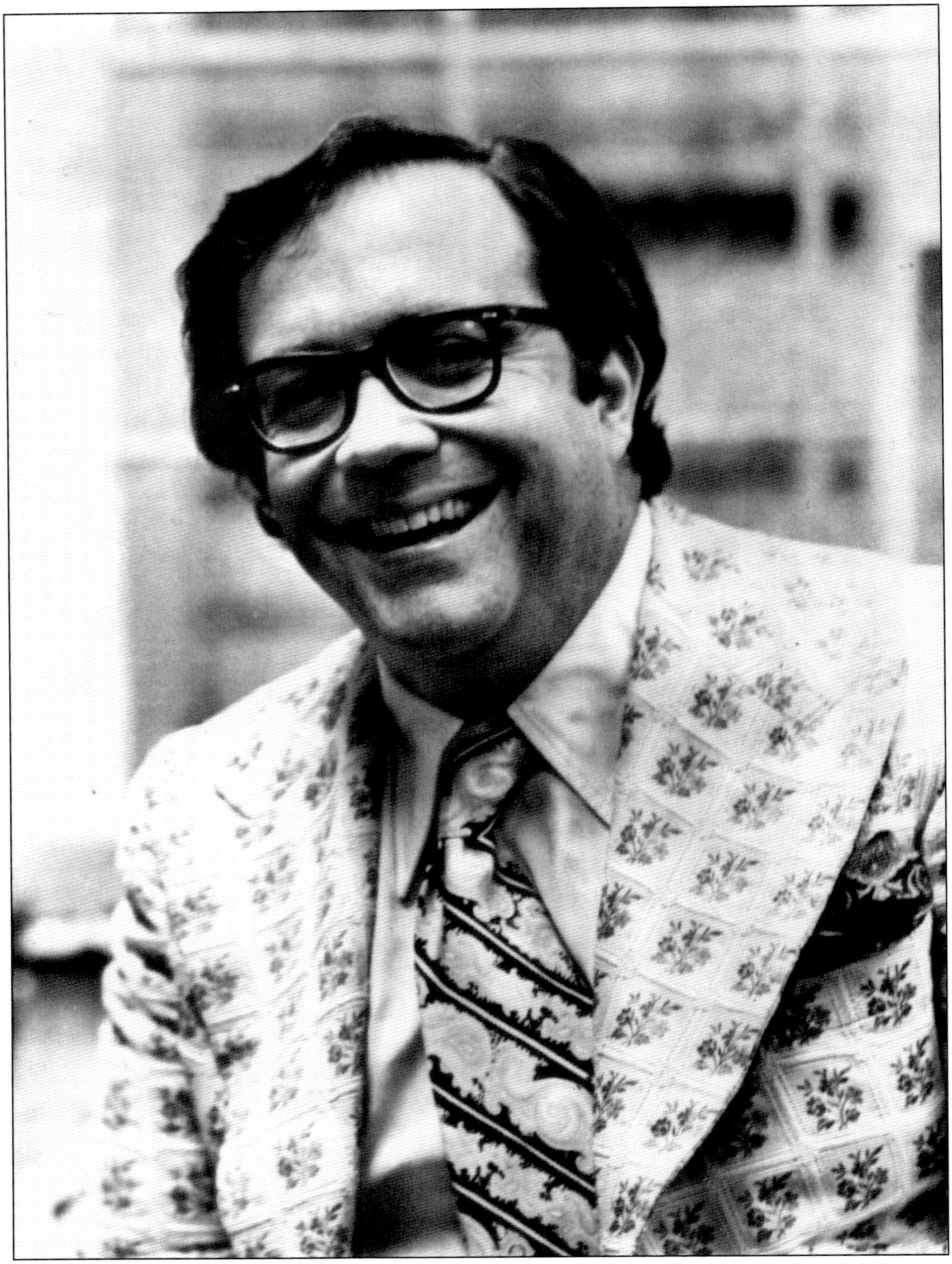

Warner LeRoy was the creative visionary behind Great Adventure. The son of *Wizard of Oz* director Mervyn LeRoy, Warner grew up around the fantastic movie sets of Hollywood and became a famous New York City restaurateur, best known for the spectacular Tavern on the Green, Maxwell's Plum, and the Russian Tea Room. (Courtesy of GreatAdventureHistory.com collection.)

On the cover: Riders splash down on Great Adventure's Log Flume (now known as the Saw Mill Log Flume), one of the park's original attractions and still a family favorite after 35 years. (Courtesy of Six Flags Great Adventure.)

IMAGES
of America

SIX FLAGS GREAT ADVENTURE

Harry Applegate and Thomas Benton

ARCADIA
PUBLISHING

ISBN 978-0-7385-6569-9

Published by Arcadia Publishing
Charleston, South Carolina

Printed in the United States of America

Library of Congress Control Number: 2009925362

For all general information contact Arcadia Publishing at:
Telephone 843-853-2070
Fax 843-853-0044
E-mail sales@arcadiapublishing.com
For customer service and orders:
Toll-Free 1-888-313-2665

Visit us on the Internet at www.arcadiapublishing.com

CONTENTS

ACKNOWLEDGMENTS

We would like to thank all the people who helped in the compilation of this book, beginning with Six Flags Great Adventure's incredibly supportive staff who have been great enthusiasts of this project. Special thanks to park president Mark Kane and Angel Aristone and Jenn Lawton from the public relations department. They shared their pictures and knowledge of the park with us and expanded our knowledge of Great Adventure along the way.

We have been fortunate enough to come to know many of the great employees throughout our more than 35 years of Great Adventures and thank them for all their contributions making the park the amazing place that it has been.

A special thank-you to Brian Wyant for his assistance with the editing of the thousands of pictures that made the book possible and adding his perspective.

Thank you to the members of our Web site, GreatAdventureHistory.com, for their support and encouragement as we chronicle the park's colorful past and bright future.

Also, special thanks to our families who have indulged our love of Great Adventure and put up with our devotion to the park as we make our hundreds of visits and add to our collections of park memorabilia from eBay, flea markets, and garage sales.

Unless otherwise noted, all images appear courtesy of Six Flags Great Adventure.

INTRODUCTION

Great Adventure was designed as a mix of natural beauty and Hollywood fantasy, creating a larger-than-life park that matched the dreams of its larger-than-life creator, Warner LeRoy.

Growing up in Hollywood as the son of Mervyn LeRoy, producer and director of many classic films, including *The Wizard of Oz*, Warner was raised among the Tinseltown royalty. Named after Jack Warner, head of Warner Brothers studio, he grew up in an atmosphere of magic and wonder where anything could happen.

Warner had a flair for spectacle and came into fame of his own with his restaurant and nightclub projects in New York City, which included the famous Maxwell's Plum, and the transformations of Tavern on the Green and the Russian Tea Room into the landmarks they are today.

Warner partnered with the Hardwicke Companies, developer of wildlife park projects, to create a huge new concept in theme parks, Great Adventure. The early 1970s was a boom time for the theme park industry, with operators like Six Flags perfecting the model of the regional park, combining Disney-style theme elements with thrilling rides. Great Adventure was originally planned to surpass other regional parks in size and scope and to compete with Walt Disney World as a vacation destination, with year-round activities.

Original proposals for Great Adventure included many themed areas, a drive through Safari park, hotels, sports venues, and recreational activities of all kinds. Every aspect of Great Adventure was planned to be the biggest and best of its kind. The ideal piece of property was found for building the park, located in the geographical center of New Jersey, midway between New York City and Philadelphia, with millions of people living within a short drive. The land was full of lakes and woodlands, which provided the most spectacular setting for a park complex.

The cost of bringing Warner's originally envisioned dreams to life exceeded the funds available from the developers, so plans needed to be scaled back. Many of the proposed themed areas were combined to create the Enchanted Forest theme park and Safari park, which opened in July 1974.

Even before opening the park, plans for expansion were put into place. These included spectacular water shows, polar bear exhibits, additional rides, shows, and other attractions. However, the park faced some financial setbacks and, with the departure of Warner LeRoy, some changes in ownership over the first three years.

The Six Flags Corporation purchased Great Adventure in 1977, investing in improvements and expansions over the next several decades, making the park bigger and more exciting. Six Flags introduced more thrilling rides from the start and kept the park at the forefront of the theme park industry. Those constant advances brought millions of guests to the park, with Six

Flags Great Adventure at one point being ranked as the most attended seasonal theme park in the world.

Over the years, the park has been home to many mascots of all shapes and sizes, beginning with a crew of unique characters created just for Great Adventure. Later the madcap cast of characters would be joined by Pac Man and Ms. Pac Man in the early 1980s with the video game craze, followed by the popular Shirt Tales in 1983. With the acquisition of Six Flags Great America in 1984, Six Flags also acquired the rights to the Looney Tunes characters, and Bugs Bunny and all his friends have called the park home ever since. In 2007, the kids' sensation from Down Under, the Wiggles, also came to Six Flags Great Adventure, opening the first Wiggles World–themed area in the United States.

In the early 1990s, Time Warner purchased Six Flags and brought the magic of the movies into the parks. Just as other media companies were building movie studio theme parks, Warner Brothers looked to Six Flags as a way of expanding its market presence and creating synergy. If you liked the movie, you would love the ride; if you liked the ride, you would love the movie. A big part of that was bringing the DC Comics superheroes, including Batman, Robin, Superman, Wonder Woman, the Flash, and Green Lantern, into the parks, along with their foes. The Batman franchise spawned Batman: The Ride, which became an instant classic.

The park has always been known for breaking records and offering state-of-the-art attractions. Upon opening in 1974, those records included the world's largest drive-through safari outside Africa, the biggest hot-air balloon, tallest fountain water jet, the longest log flume ride, and the world's largest teepee. More recent records have included the world's steepest wooden roller coaster drop and, of course, the world's tallest and fastest roller coaster, Kingda Ka.

Animals have been a huge part of the success of Six Flags Great Adventure. The Six Flags Wild Safari Animal Park has been the home to thousands of animals, roaming large habitats that went beyond the scope of any zoo. Millions of guests have visited the Wild Safari since 1974, and it remains one of the park's best and most unique features.

The popularity of the animals has also extended into the theme park, with the dolphin and sea lion shows delighting guests of all ages since the park opened. The Golden Kingdom introduced the park guests to the world of tigers with the elaborate Temple of the Tiger, as well as smaller animals like kinkajous and capuchin monkey.

Always innovating and changing, the park has seen many rides come and go over time. Although some of the unique attractions may be gone from the park now and updated with newer forms of entertainment, they are not forgotten. For millions of guests over the years, Six Flags Great Adventure holds a special place in their hearts, remembering some of the best moments of their lives. Whether it was getting up the courage to ride the newest roller coaster as a child, going on a first date at the park as a teenager, or sharing special times as a family, the park has always been a magical place. This is the amazing history of Six Flags Great Adventure.

One

A Dream Comes True

Warner LeRoy's vision for Great Adventure was to create a spectacle like no other with a mix of fantastic architecture and every imaginable form of entertainment, including rides, shows, sports, animals, and nature. The park's site was chosen both for its proximity to the huge population centers of the New York and Philadelphia metropolitan areas, being nearly equidistant from both, and for the natural beauty of the property. The acres of woods and lakes with natural small hills made the land the perfect choice for developing a park.

The original vision for Great Adventure was to build eight unique areas on the property, including theme parks (the Enchanted Forest, Neptune's Kingdom, and Over the Rainbow), Dream Street shopping district, Safari, Sports and Games complex, beach and boating area, and Wild Country campground, still leaving room for hotels and resorts. The various areas of the complex were to be connected with numerous styles of transportation, including monorails, trains, boats, Skyrides, and vehicles of all shapes and sizes.

The dreams of LeRoy were larger than life , and the budget required to make them a reality was beyond the available funding at the time, so many of the concepts were modified and combined with the idea that the park would expand and add more with each season.

LeRoy teamed up with the Hardwicke Companies, which had developed safari parks in the past. Refined final plans came together for the project, with the Safari being built as originally proposed and the Enchanted Forest theme park becoming a conglomeration of the best aspects of the three park concepts from the original proposals.

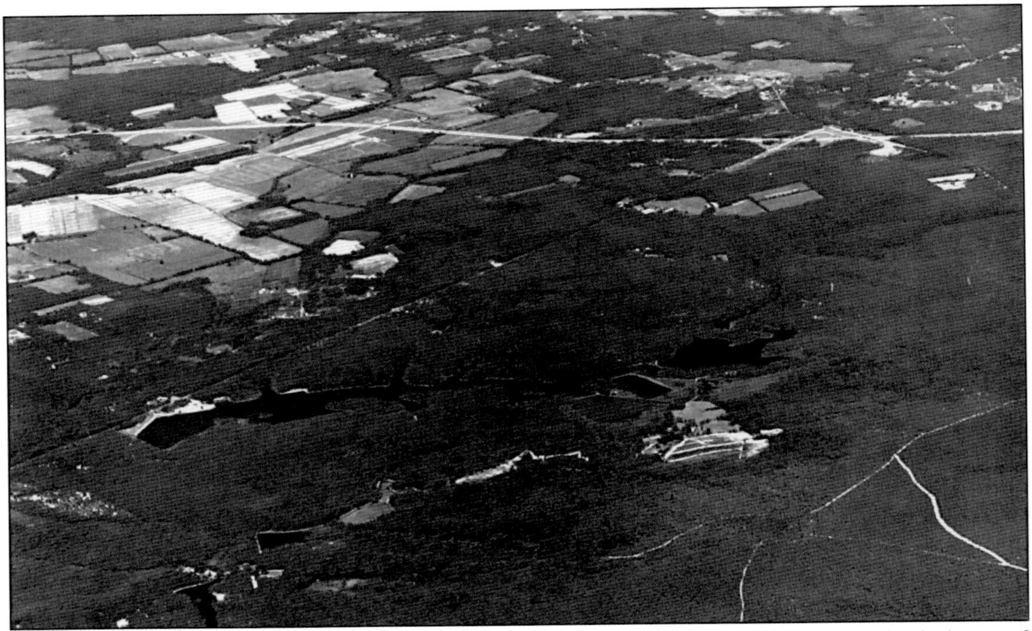

The site chosen for Great Adventure was 2,200 acres of privately owned land, which featured scenic lakes, gentle rolling hills, and unspoiled woodlands in Jackson Township. This aerial photograph from 1972 shows the entire plot of land and the existing lakes prior to the start of construction. (GreatAdventureHistory.com collection.)

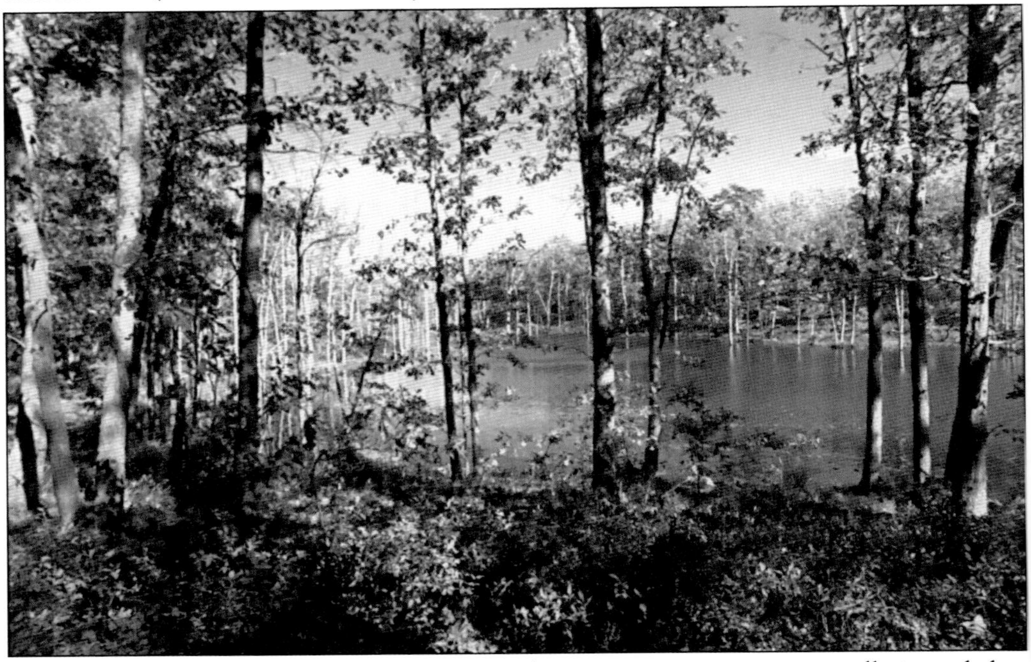

The beautiful man-made lakes on the Great Adventure property were originally intended to serve as part of the park's transportation network and are to this day one of the property's best features. The series of lakes would later be used for fireworks, waterskiing, and stunt shows. (GreatAdventureHistory.com collection.)

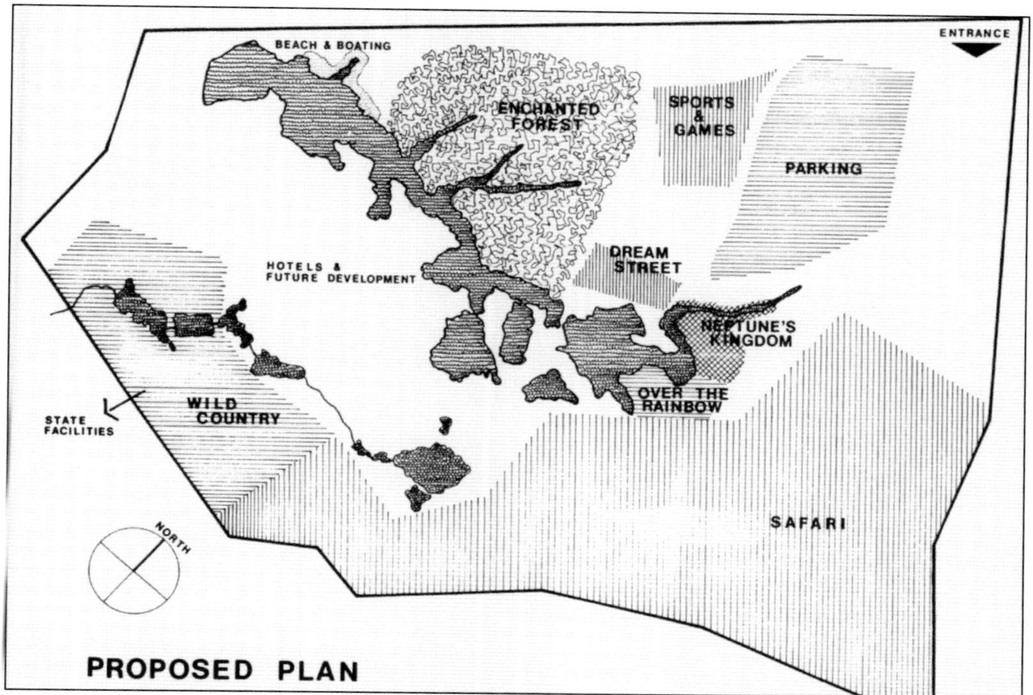

Plans for the 2,200 acres included multiple theme parks, recreational facilities, campgrounds, and hotels. Two of the major areas that never went beyond concepts were the Sports and Games area, which was to be home to all kinds of sporting venues, and Wild Country, which was to be a rustic campground described as "A camping and wilderness area containing several thousand campsites along with cabins and tents." (GreatAdventureHistory.com collection.)

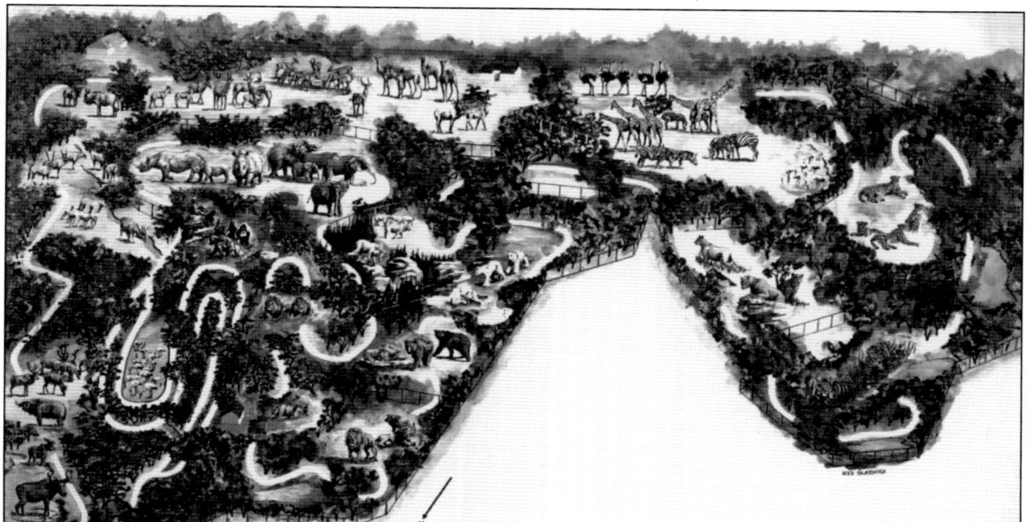

The most unique feature of Great Adventure was the animal park, designed as the largest drive-through safari outside Africa, featuring animals from six continents. Original plans called for the Safari to be nearly 10 miles long with 12 themed sections housing immense herds of wildlife. (GreatAdventureHistory.com collection.)

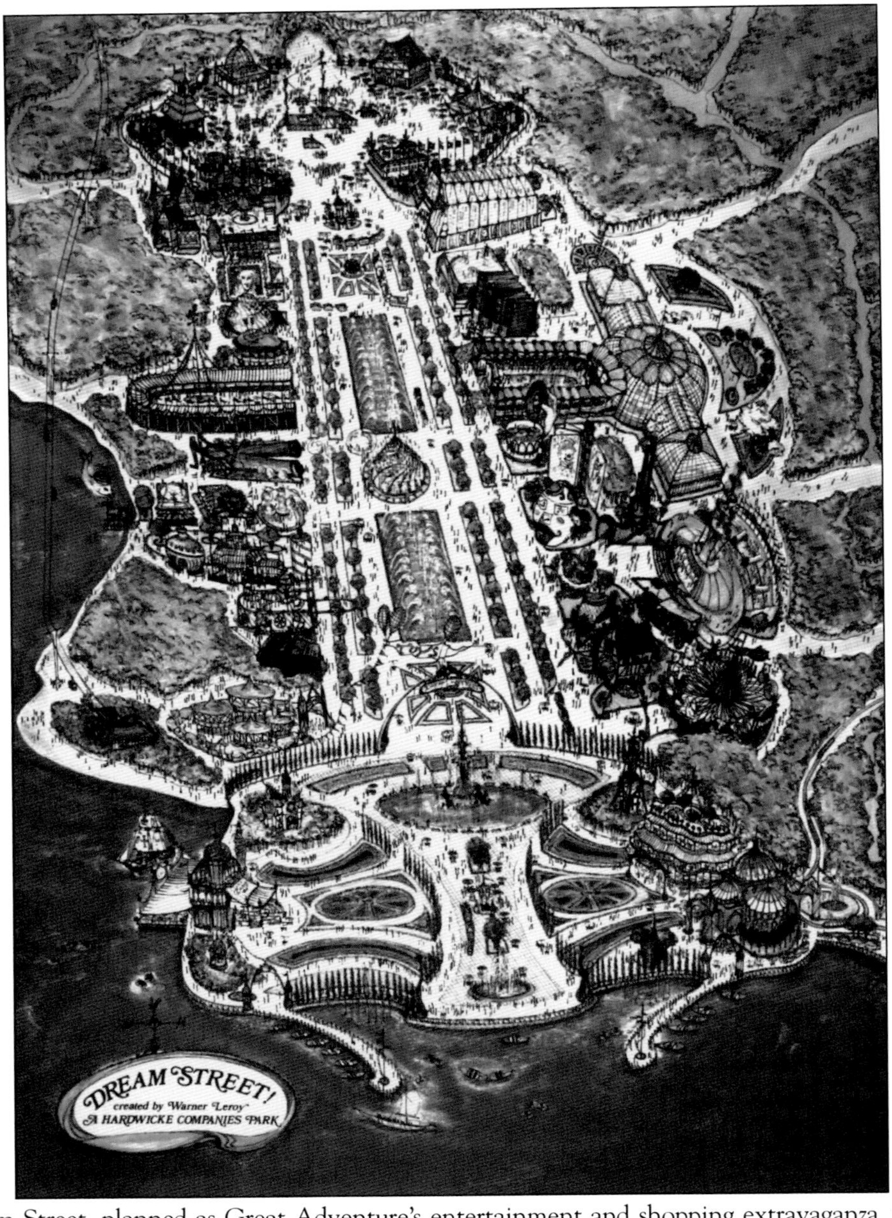

Dream Street, planned as Great Adventure's entertainment and shopping extravaganza, was to be the home of themed retail and dining experiences. A wide street of fountains and gardens with multitudes of flowers would lead to shops and restaurants designed to look like the things they sold and served. It was planned that entertainers would be everywhere, including clowns, jugglers, musicians, and fairy tale characters. Many of the stores were to feature working craftsmen, workshops, and factories, where patrons could watch the merchandise being produced. The centrally located Dream Street was also to serve as the hub of Great Adventure, with transportation to the other themed areas. The site for Dream Street was to be located along the shore of the property's largest lake. The concept of Dream Street would be incorporated in a scaled-down version when the final plans for the park were drawn up. (GreatAdventureHistory.com collection.)

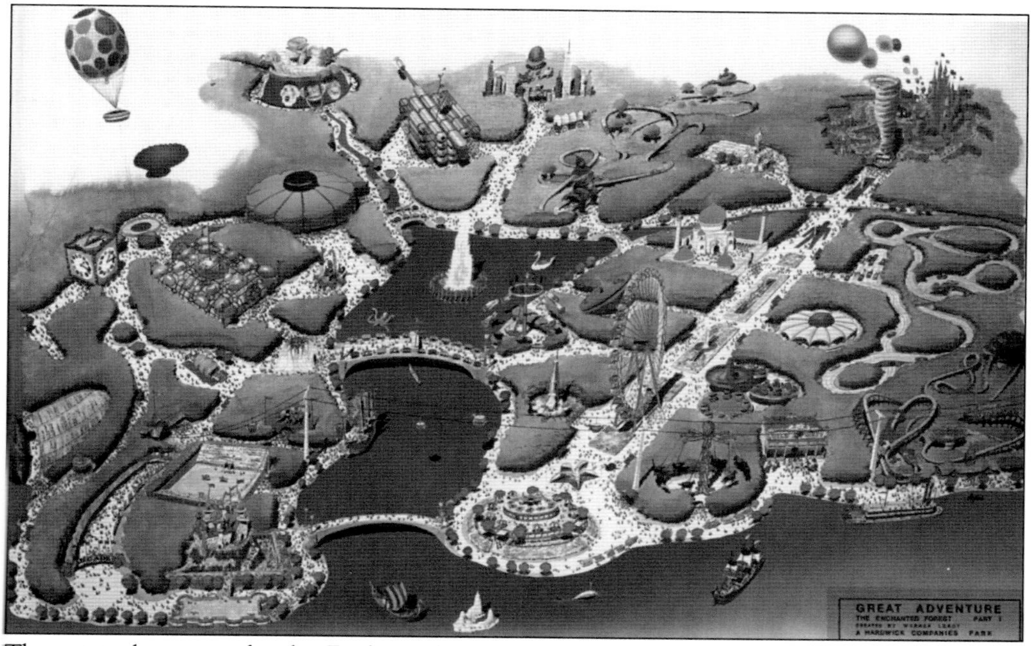

The original concept for the Enchanted Forest theme park was a magic land of unique rides, games, shows, and restaurants. Among the planned attractions were the Cave of the Oracle, the Arabian Knights, a revolving restaurant, a walk-in clock, a Transylvanian Banquet Hall, and Alice in Wonderland– and Wizard of Oz–themed dark rides. (GreatAdventureHistory.com collection.)

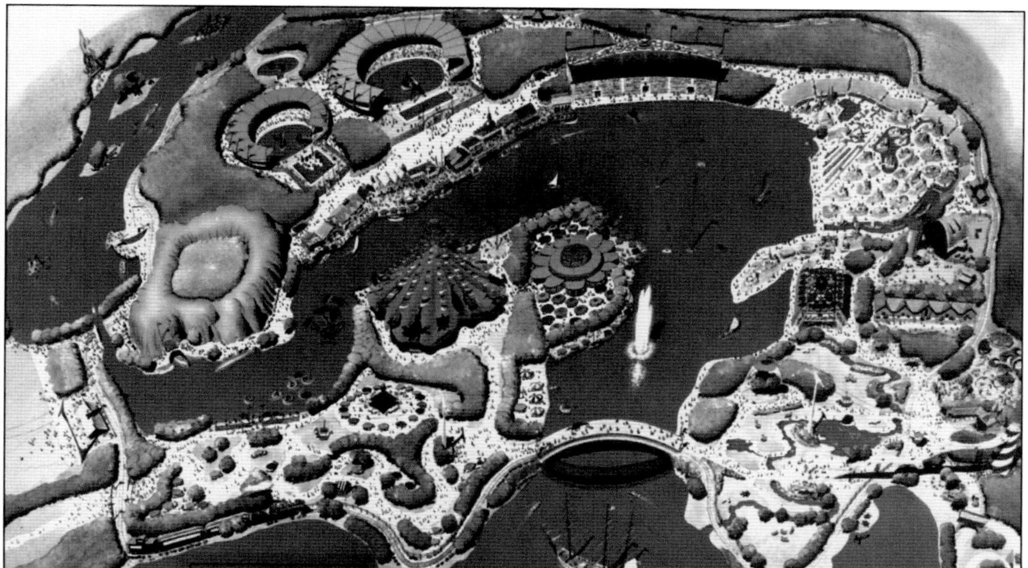

Neptune's Kingdom and Over the Rainbow were to have been the home to incredible marine life shows and exhibits along with fanciful gardens that featured tame animals and miniature villages, along with several children's attractions. A 200-foot bridge resembling a rainbow was to have connected the two peninsulas. (GreatAdventureHistory.com collection.)

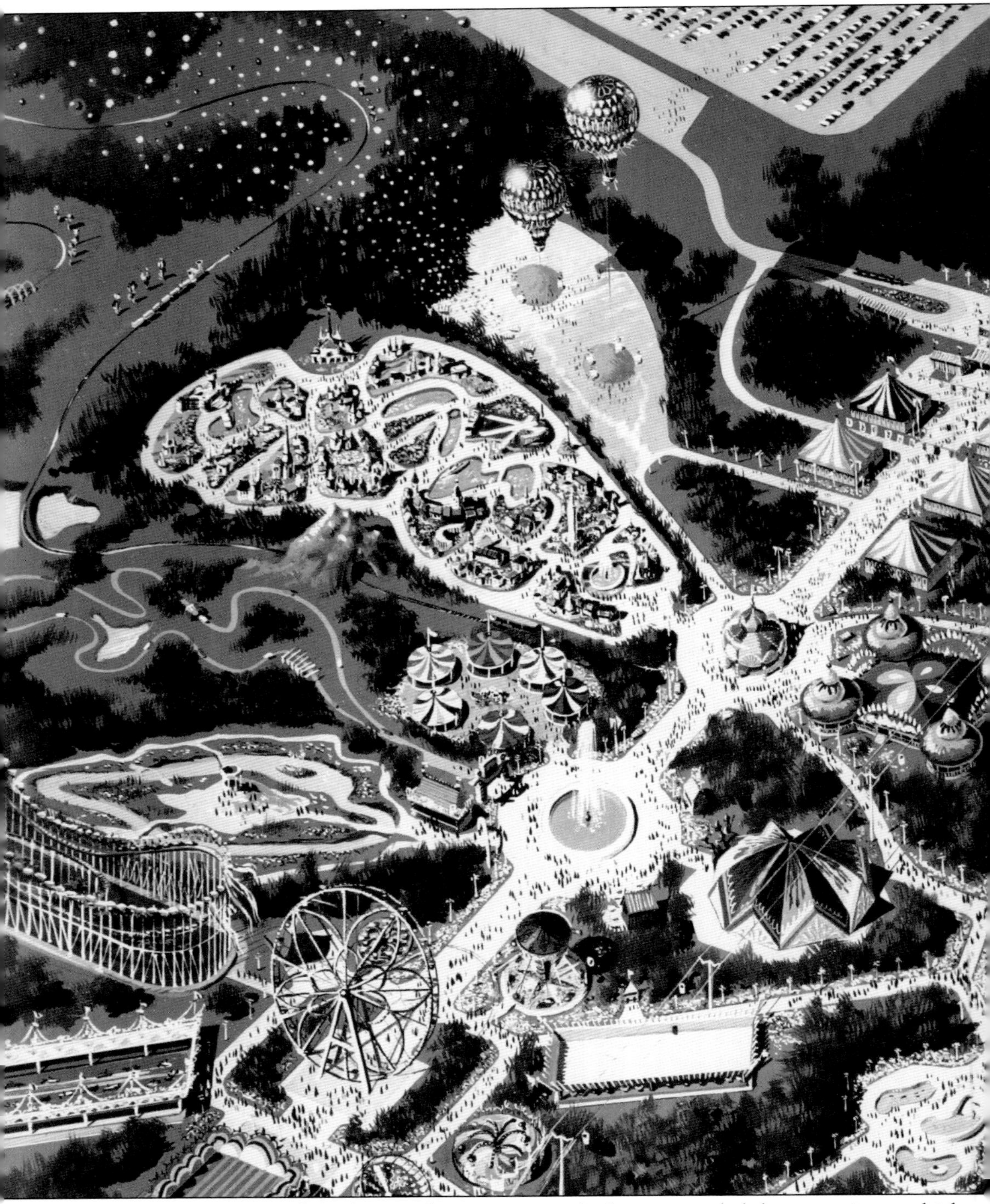

Time constraints and budgetary limitations resulted in a scaled-down project, which combined the best elements of the original plans into a single theme park. The resulting design of the Enchanted Forest occupied the land originally planned for Dream Street and Neptune's Kingdom. This rendering is one of the final designs and is quite similar to what

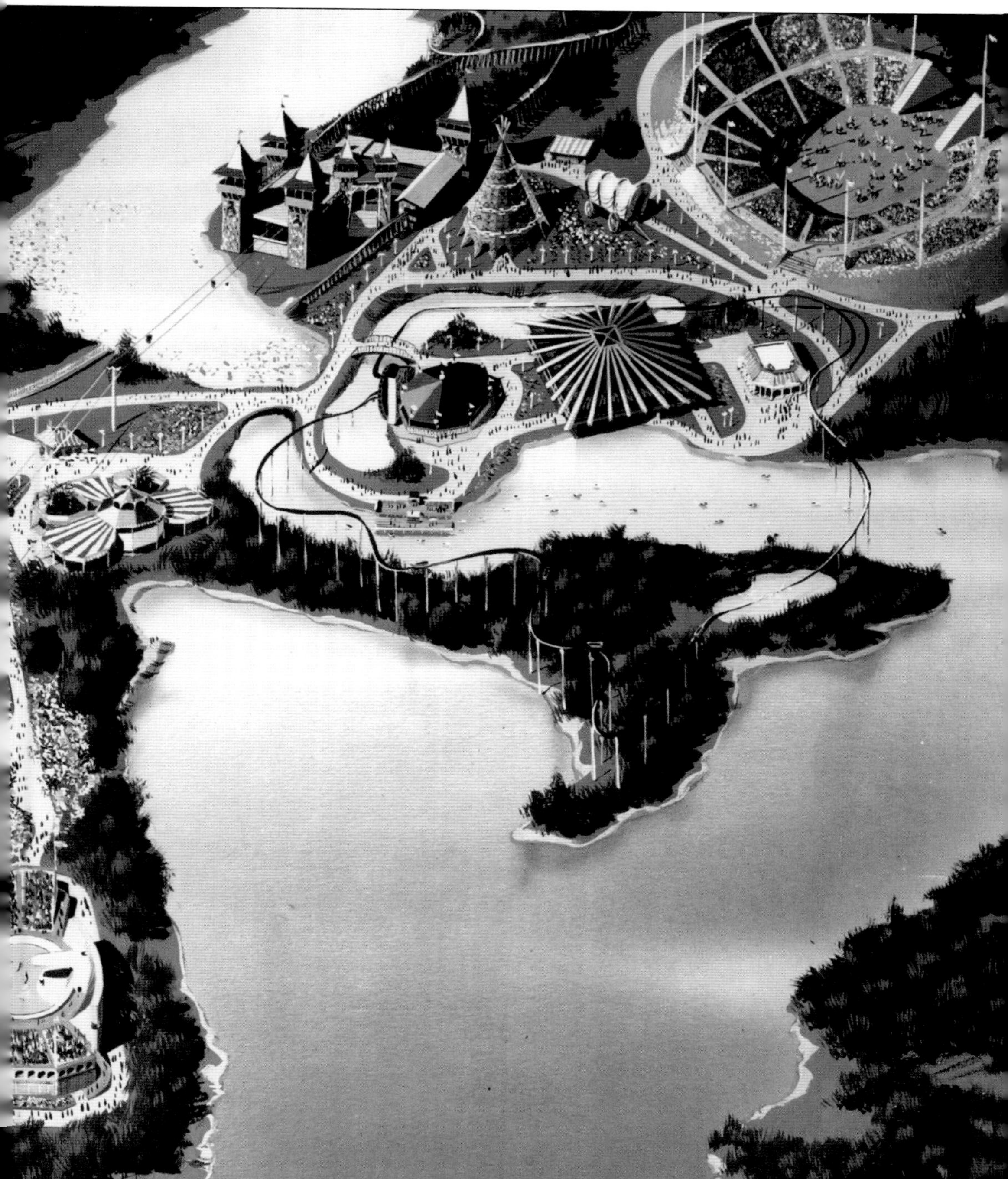

was eventually constructed. Two planned structures shown in the rendering that never materialized are a fifth Dream Street tent and the park's fourth major indoor restaurant, a large faceted building situated between the fountain and the Aqua Spectacle stadium. (GreatAdventureHistory.com collection.)

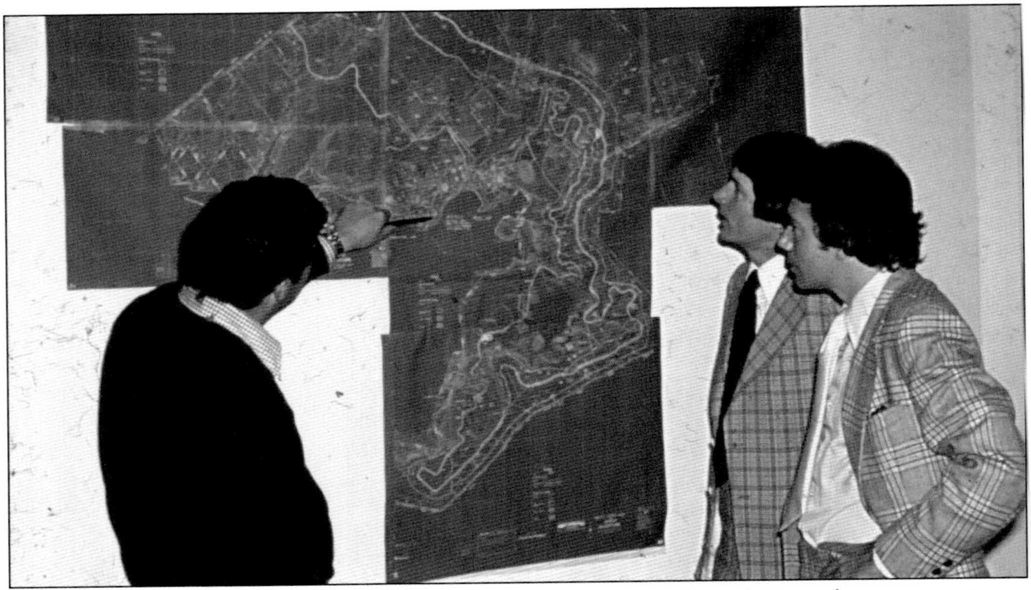

Prior to any construction, a detailed ecological survey was conducted. From day one, great care was taken to preserve as many trees as possible with individual trees being marked for careful preservation in an effort to minimize any impact on the natural beauty of the land. As Warner LeRoy stated, "this plan of action has resulted in producing an enchanted forest environment, right in keeping with Great Adventure's theme." (GreatAdventureHistory.com collection.)

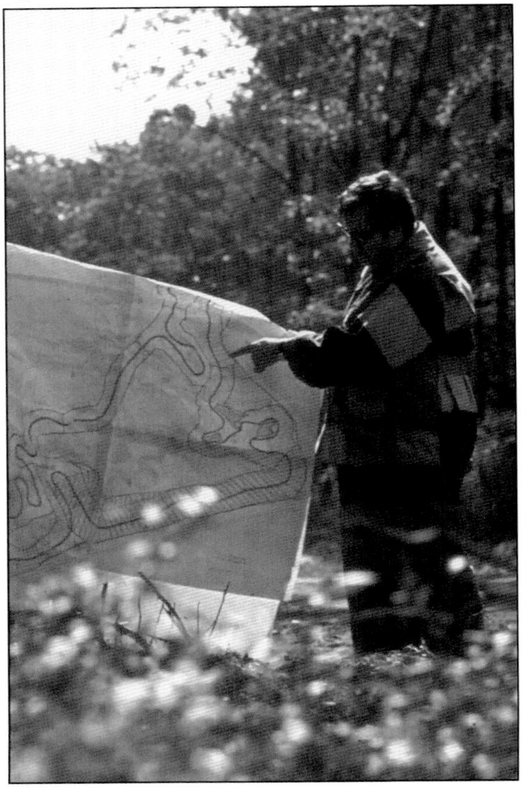

Warner LeRoy stands in the Safari with a map of the proposed layout in hand as clearing and construction has begun. Before any construction began, animal experts were brought in to decide which areas would best resemble the animals' natural habitats. The greatest change in the landscape involved removing stands of trees to create the grassy plains for the herd animals. (GreatAdventureHistory.com collection.)

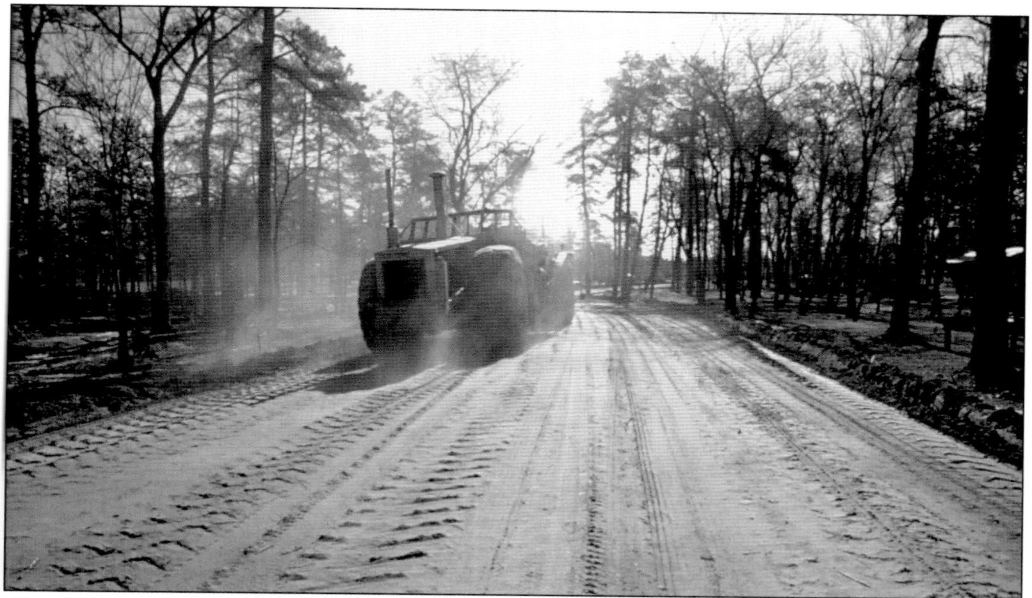

The Safari road is starting to take shape through what had been a heavily forested area. The four-and-a-half-mile-long, three-lane Safari road would wind through the various sections with a few major elevation changes along the way as the natural hills were incorporated into the animal habitats. (GreatAdventureHistory.com collection.)

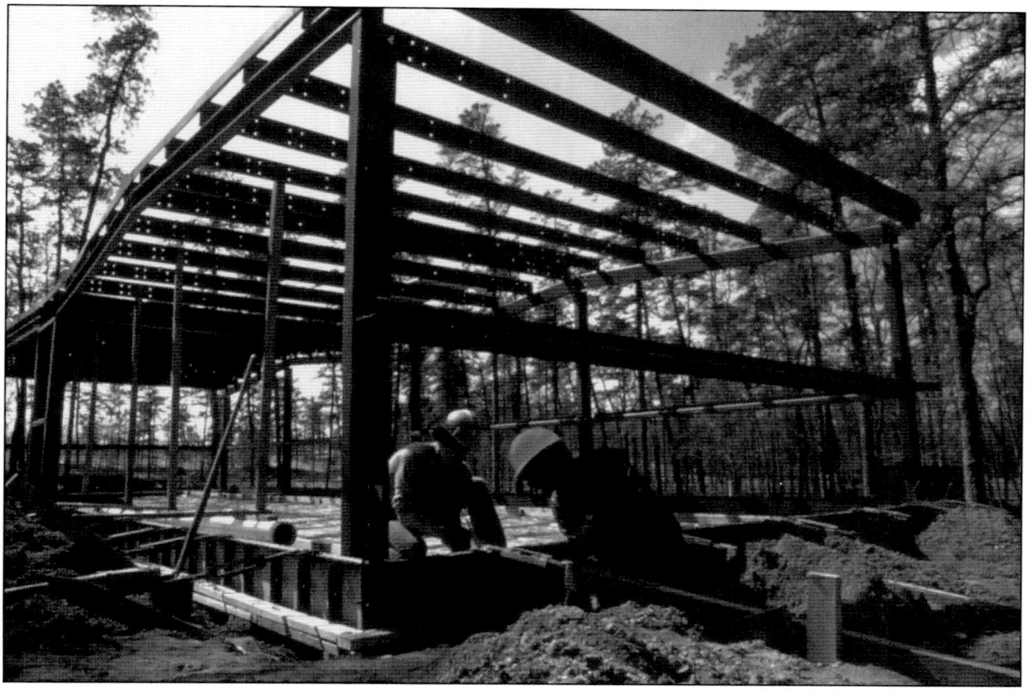

To prepare for the arrival of more than 1,200 animals, barns and other care facilities were constructed so the animals could adapt to the New Jersey climate. Each facility was specifically designed for the various shapes and sizes of animals and tailored to their needs with some including heated floors and other creature comforts. (GreatAdventureHistory.com collection.)

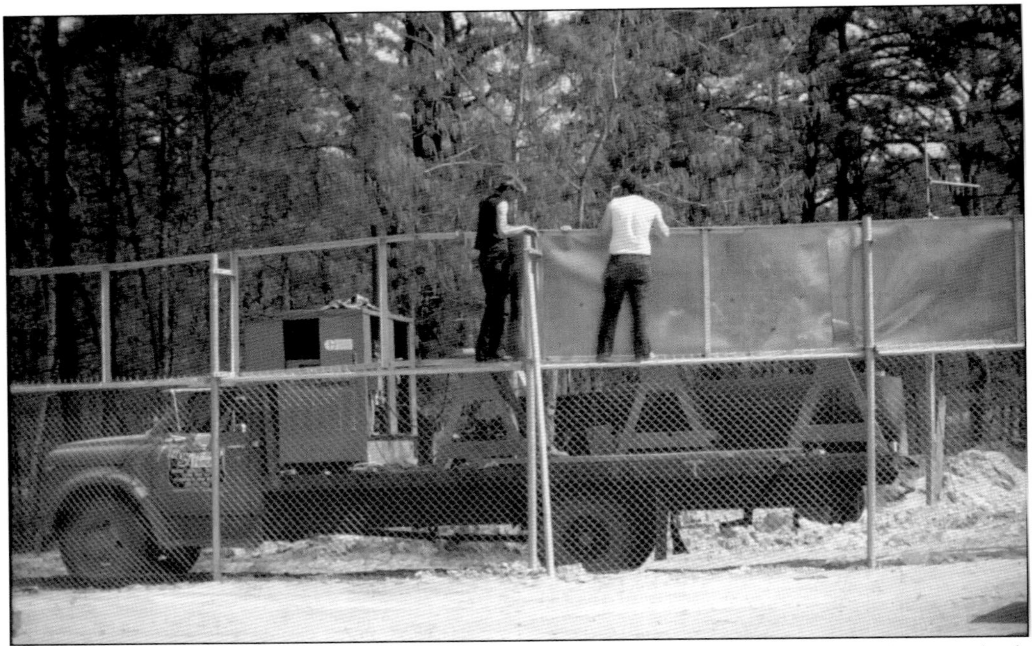

Prior to the arrival of some of the more dangerous animals such as the bears and big cats, high fences with metal panels that could not be climbed needed to be installed all around the Safari perimeter. To keep them as unobtrusive as possible, these necessary elements were painted green to help them blend in with the surrounding trees. (GreatAdventureHistory.com collection.)

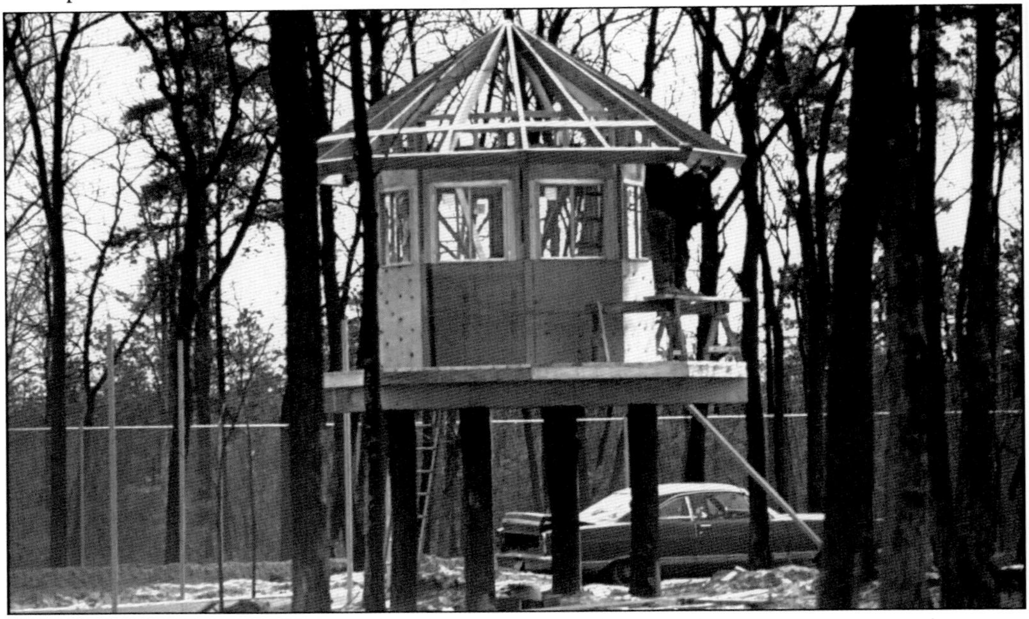

Two guard towers were constructed at the entrance and exit to the carnivorous animal section. These towers housed an attendant who would let cars into an air lock configuration, opening gates at either end to let cars through while keeping in the more dangerous animals. These elevated structures gave the wardens an unobstructed view of the animals to ensure they did not slip between the gates. (GreatAdventureHistory.com collection.)

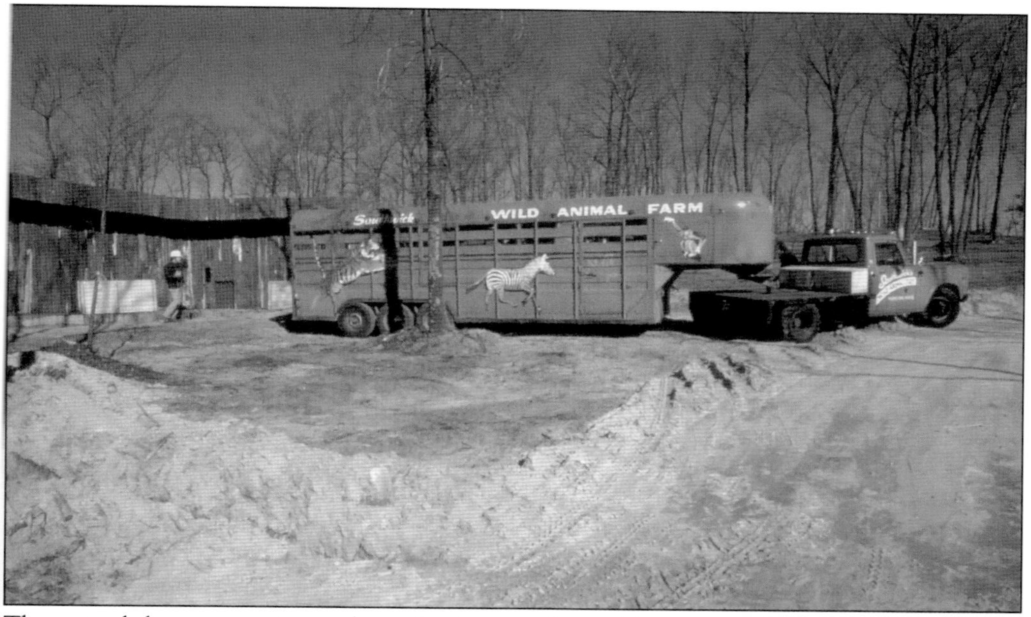

The animals began to arrive at the park via specially modified livestock trailers as opening day drew near. Brought in from their native habitats as well as from other safari parks, many were transferred from other facilities throughout North America, including some owned by the park's financier, Hardwicke Companies. (GreatAdventureHistory.com collection.)

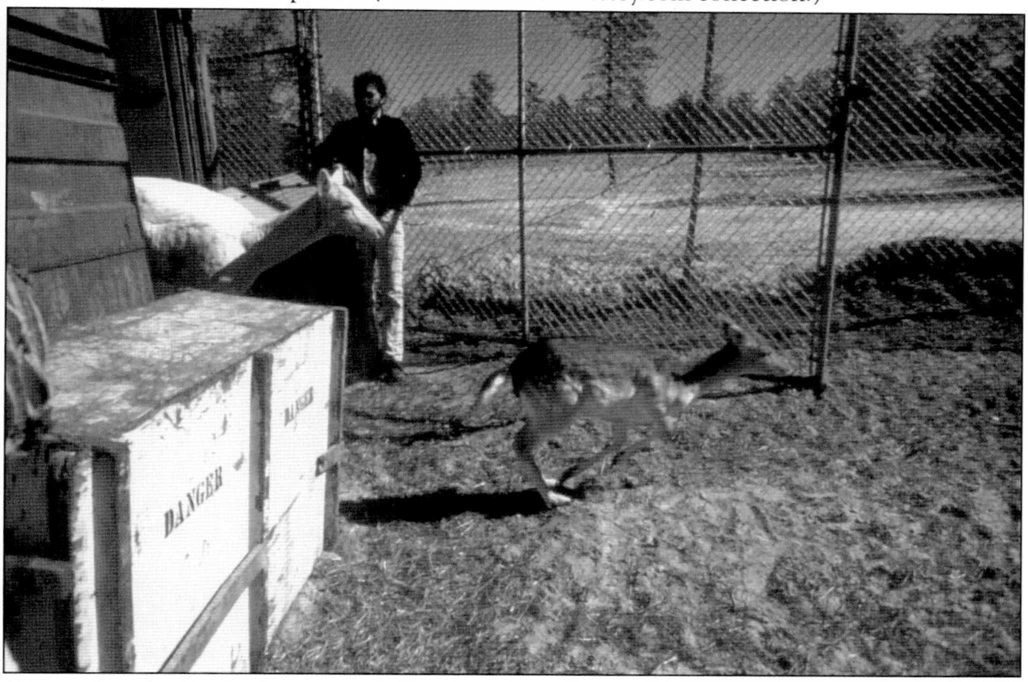

The newly arrived animals were carefully released into their new homes and given time to acclimate to their surroundings before the first park guests arrived. Moving animals the size of elephants and giraffes and as dangerous as lions and tigers was a difficult task expertly accomplished by the park's staff of veterinarians and animal handlers. (GreatAdventureHistory.com collection.)

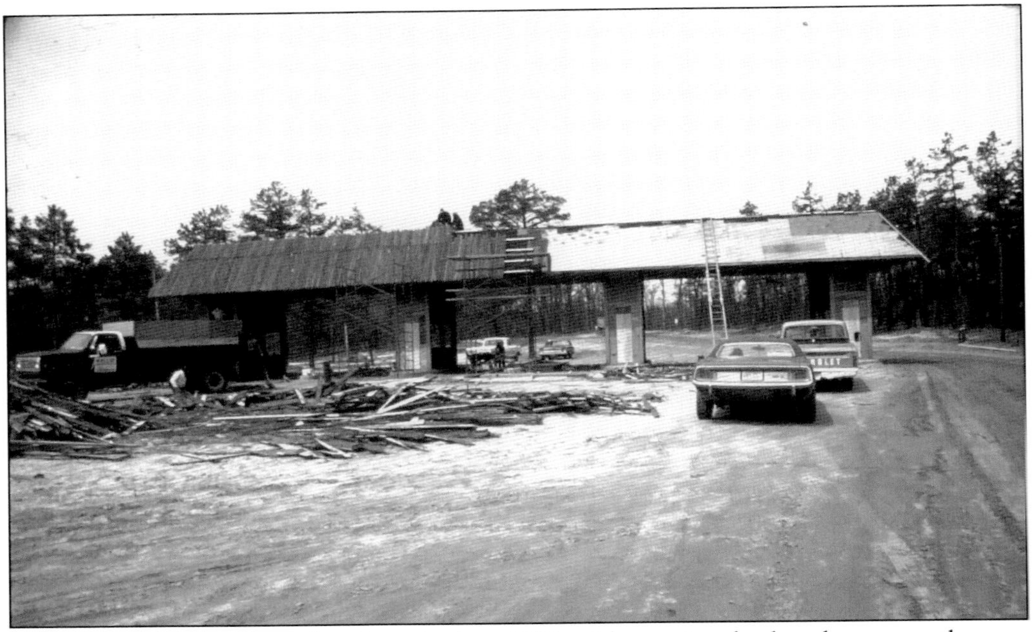

The Safari entrance plaza takes shape in June 1974, with opening day less than a month away. Tasks from paving roads to small decorative details still need to be completed, along with the installation of the wire for the radio broadcast narration, which was run down the middle of the road. (GreatAdventureHistory.com collection.)

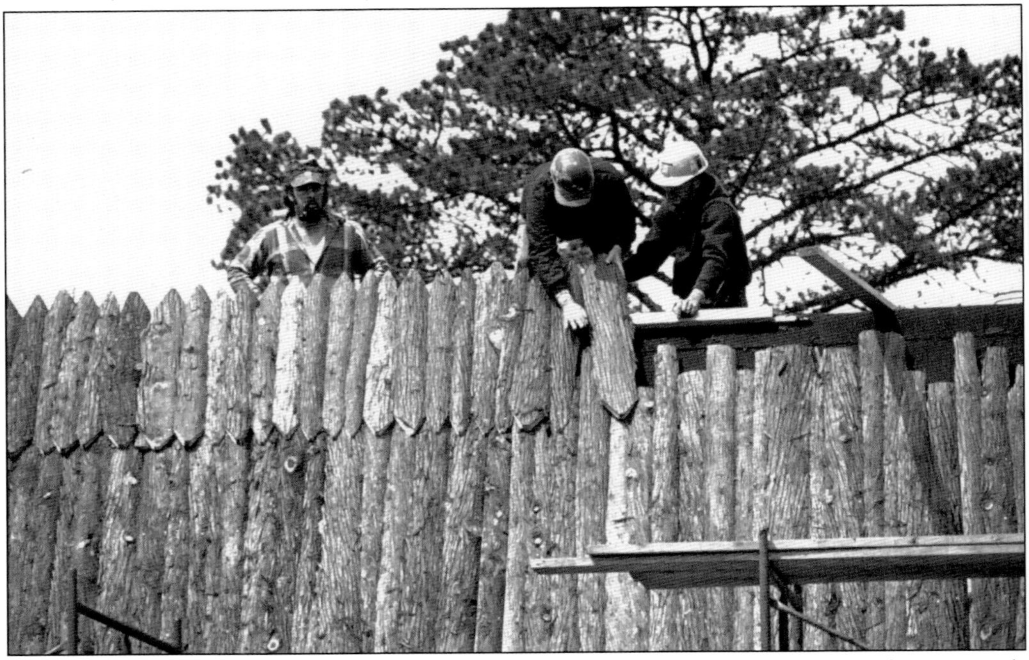

Great care was taken to give the Safari structures a rustic look, with siding and roofing materials of split logs applied to the buildings to help make them part of the natural environment. From the entrance gates to all the animal barns and feeders, everything was sheathed with the same style of log siding. (GreatAdventureHistory.com collection.)

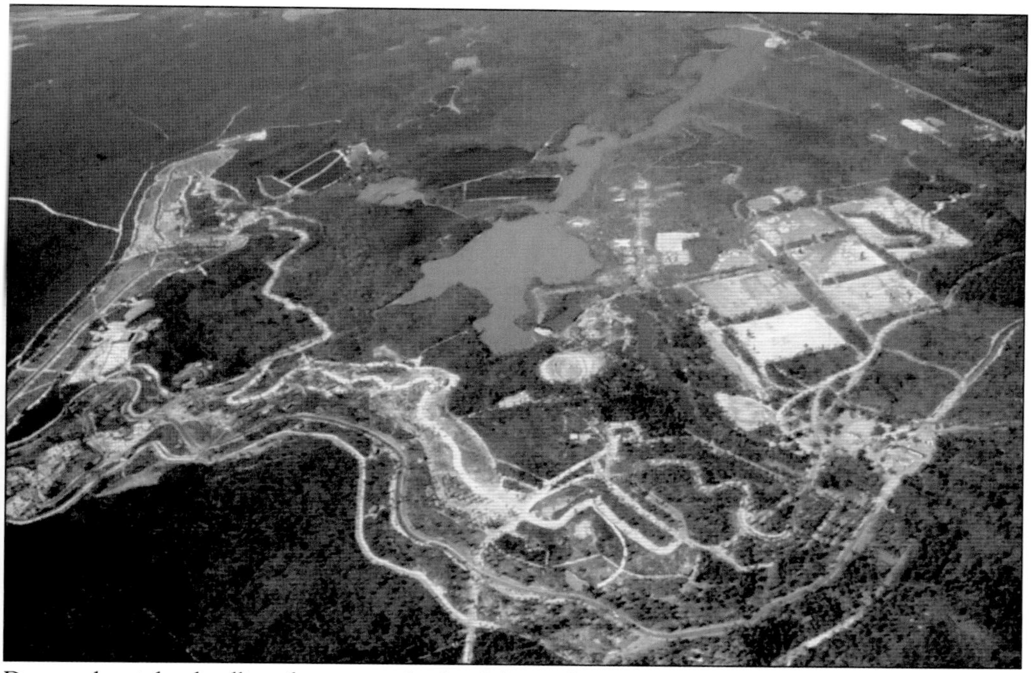

Due to the tight deadline for getting both of the parks open, construction was taking place all over the property simultaneously through the spring of 1974. The Enchanted Forest theme park and Safari utilized the talents of hundreds of construction workers, craftsmen, and other artisans in order to meet the July 1 opening date. (GreatAdventureHistory.com collection.)

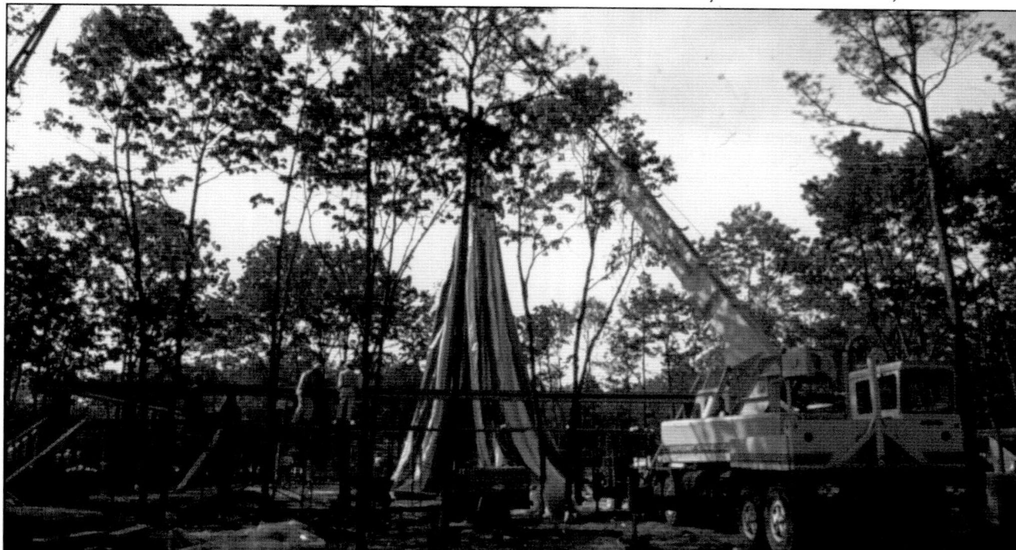

Some of the most recognizable structures in the park were the four colorful tent buildings that served as the gift shops at the front gate. These simple structures featured canvas roofs over steel frames, creating strong but lightweight buildings that could be assembled quickly. Each tent's interior covered 5,000 square feet, while their festive exteriors maximized visual impact. (GreatAdventureHistory.com collection.)

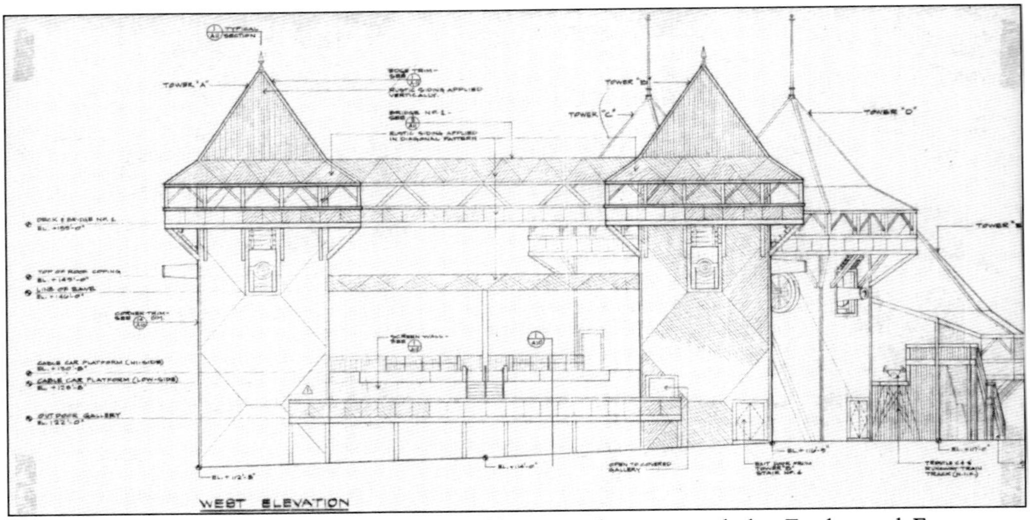

One of the first park structures guests would see as they entered the Enchanted Forest was the rustic timbered Fort, across the water from the entrance plaza. Here the blueprints for the imposing structure show the final design of the building, which was built in just less than five months from groundbreaking to opening day. (GreatAdventureHistory.com collection.)

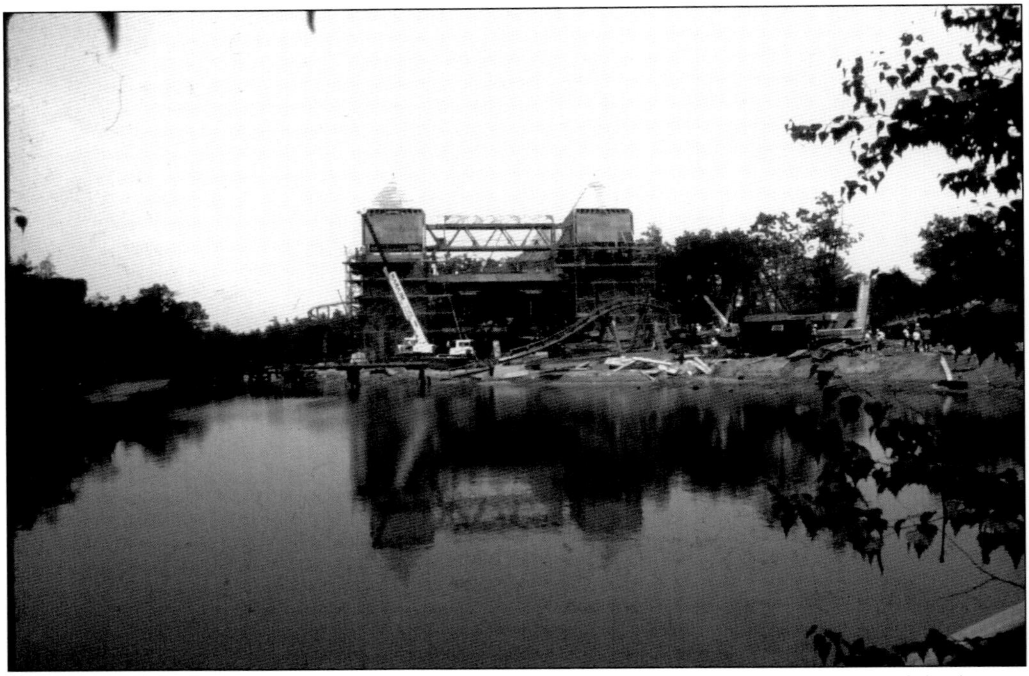

Serving as the station for the Skyride and Runaway Mine Train, the Fort was one of the largest construction projects in the park. Despite the fast pace of the construction crews, the Fort and the rest of the Rootin' Tootin' Rip Roarin' section were not quite ready in time for the park's opening day and opened three days later on July 4. (GreatAdventureHistory.com collection.)

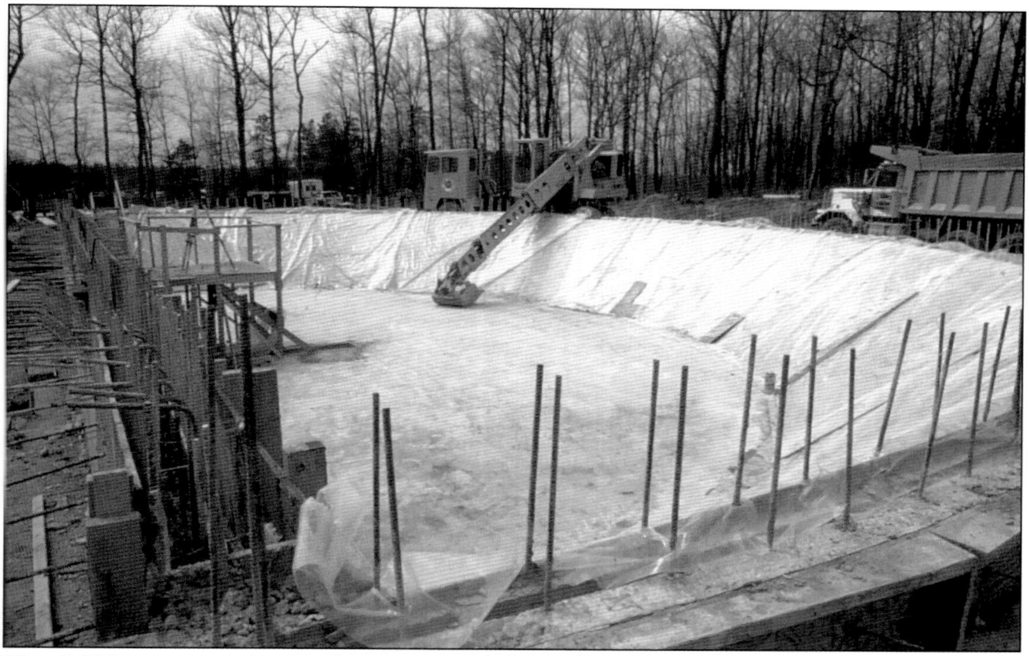

The 3,500-seat Aqua Spectacle was one of the park's more labor-intensive structures. The 430,000-gallon pool, measuring 80 feet in diameter and 16 feet in depth, had just been poured, and the rebar for the pool sides was in place when this picture was taken in April 1974, ready for the next stages of construction. (GreatAdventureHistory.com collection.)

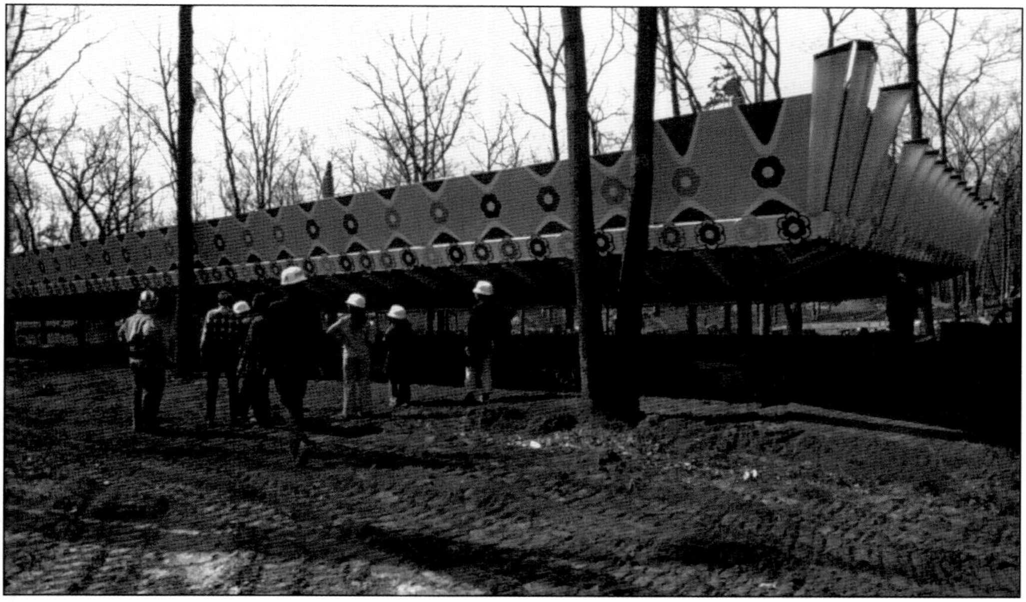

Some of the first structures to be completed in the park were the smaller "flat" rides like the Traffic Jam bumper cars seen here, which was billed as the world's largest ride of its kind. Designed for portability on the European fair circuit, most of the rides were quickly and easily assembled. Here the roof is being raised into position as Warner LeRoy and others look on. (GreatAdventureHistory.com collection.)

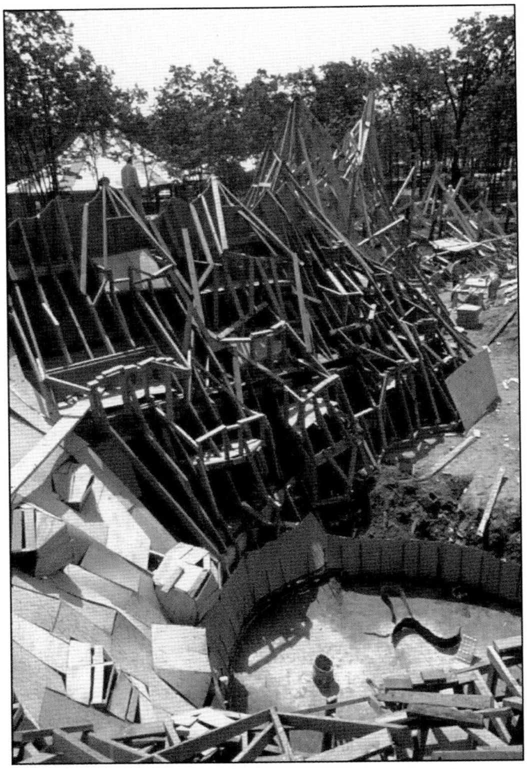

The unique landscape of the Garden of Marvels featured man-made mountains, which served as a dramatic backdrop for the miniature versions of the European landmarks and beautiful gardens. Here the framework for the mountain range takes shape, masking the control room for the motorized boats and trains that ran throughout. (GreatAdventureHistory.com collection.)

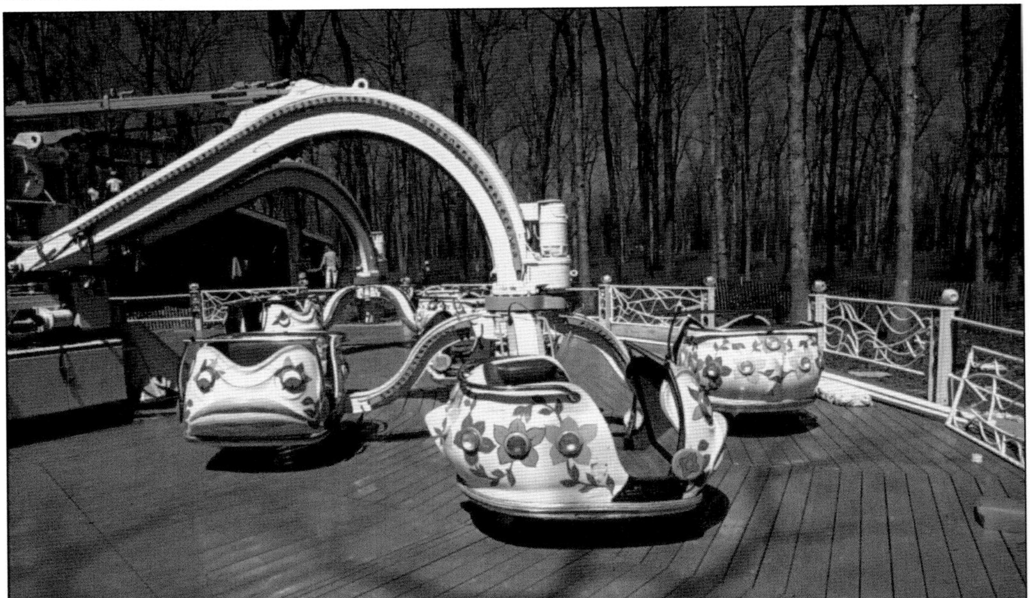

The Pretty Monster ride was fully assembled long before the concrete walkways of Dream Street had been poured, sitting on its wooden platform above the surrounding mud of the construction area. The white ride with its colorful flowers and eyelashes gave it a unique look compared to other monster-style rides of the time.

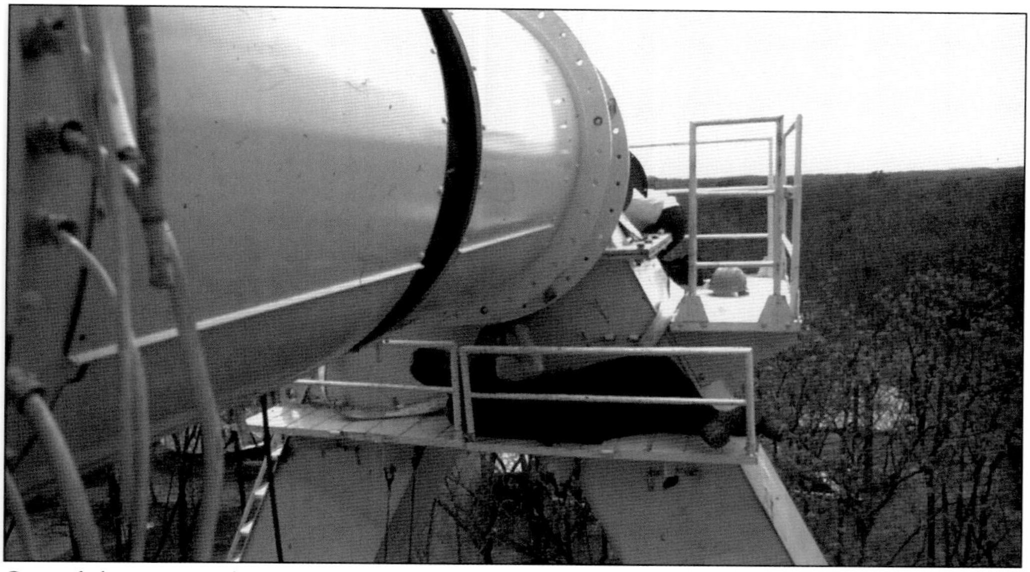

One of the most striking rides in the park was the Giant Wheel, standing at the far end of Dream Street. The ride, billed as the world's tallest Ferris wheel at 150 feet, stood high above the surrounding canopy of trees. Here workers are seen connecting the wires in the hub for the thousands of lights that create the wheel's floral displays.

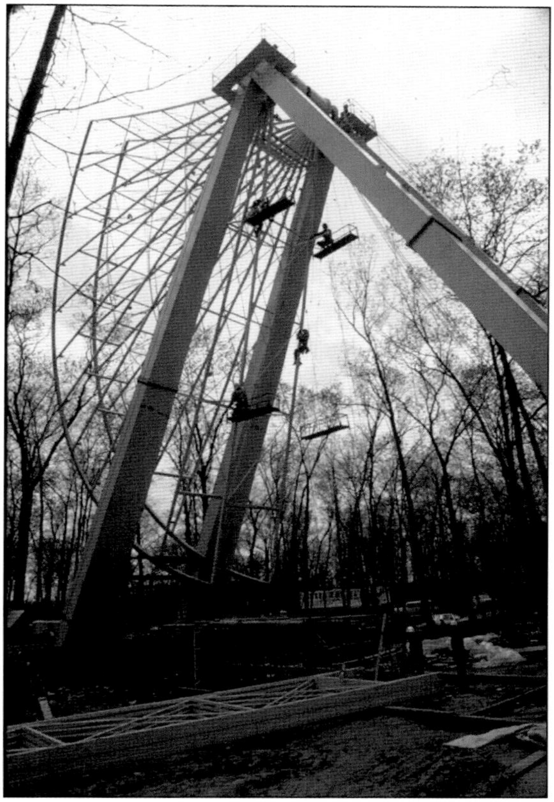

Workers attached the spokes and outer ring to the center hub of the Giant Wheel, assembling the structure from the bottom and rotating it to the next section until it was a full circle. The ride was originally designed to be a portable ride and served as the centerpiece of the Holland Tulip Festival before being purchased by Great Adventure and brought to America.

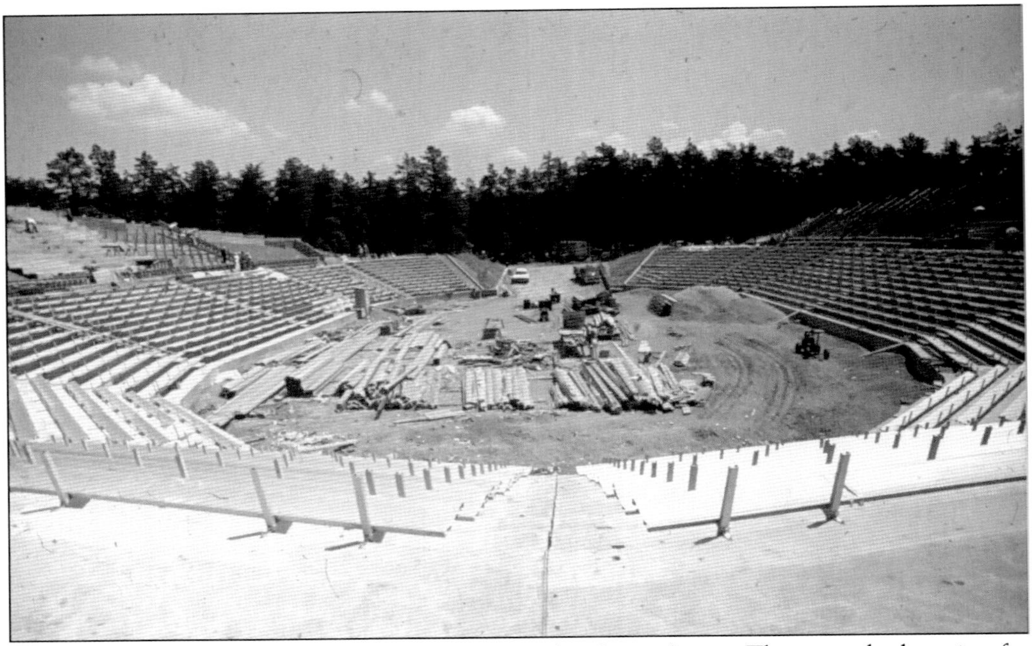

The premier showplace of Great Adventure was the Great Arena. The arena had seating for 6,000 guests to view the spectacular western shows and chariot races. Originally the arena had a dirt floor to accommodate the horses and other livestock. Large wooden gates placed at the far end allowed the performers to enter and exit. (GreatAdventureHistory.com collection.)

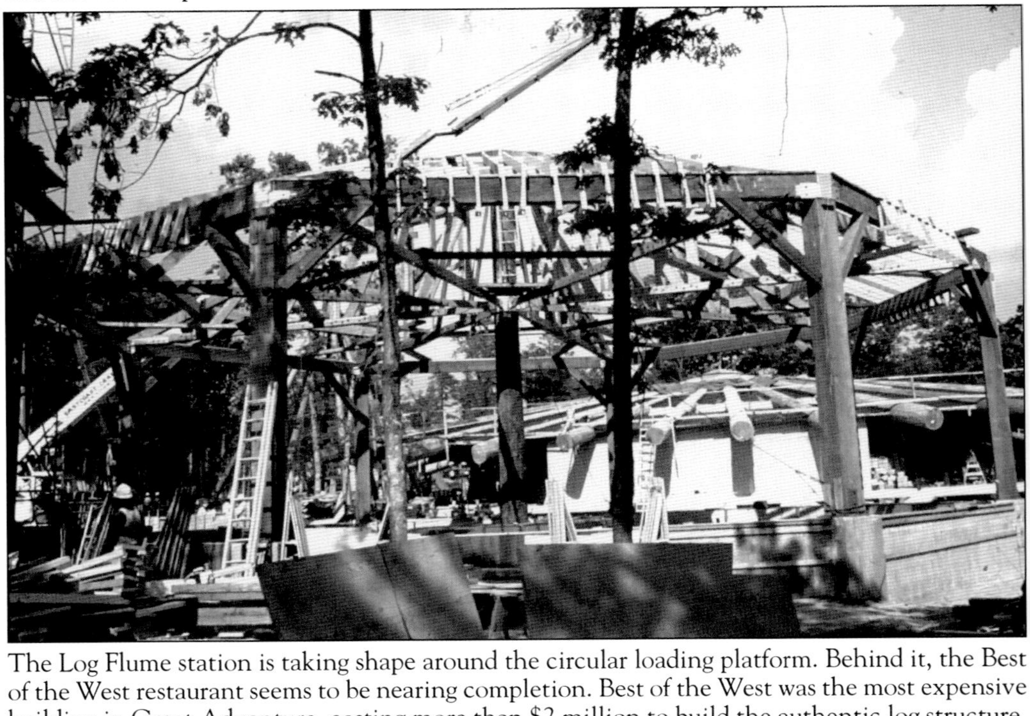

The Log Flume station is taking shape around the circular loading platform. Behind it, the Best of the West restaurant seems to be nearing completion. Best of the West was the most expensive building in Great Adventure, costing more than $2 million to build the authentic log structure. (GreatAdventureHistory.com collection.)

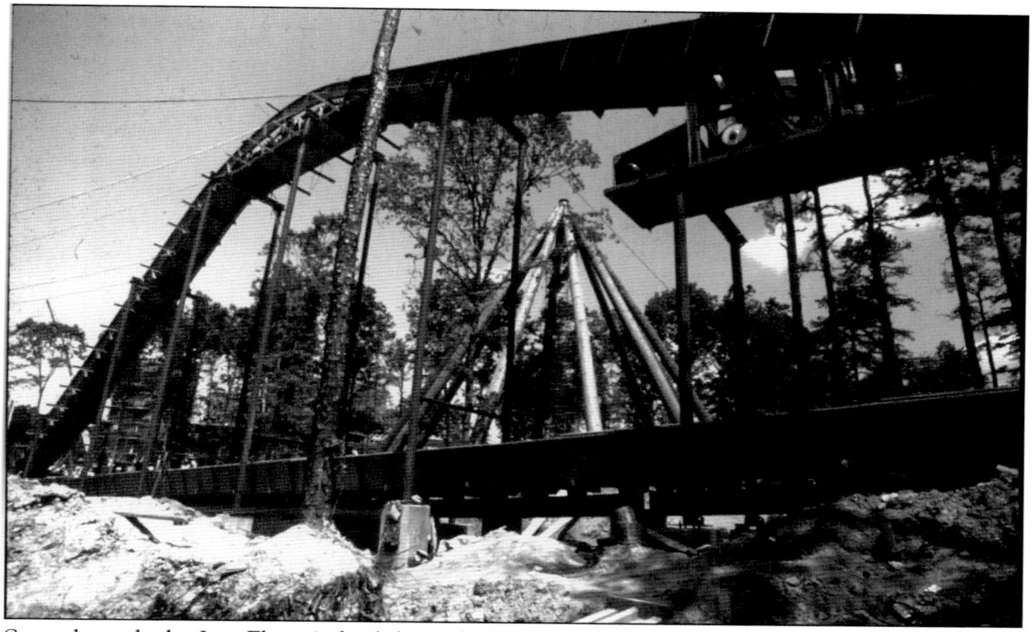

Seen through the Log Flume's final drop, the log structure of the Super Teepee is set and ready for the colorful canvas skin to be attached. The massive logs for the Super Teepee and Best of the West restaurant were trucked in from Canada's Yukon Territory to give the area a very authentic appearance with a larger-than-life feel. (GreatAdventureHistory.com collection.)

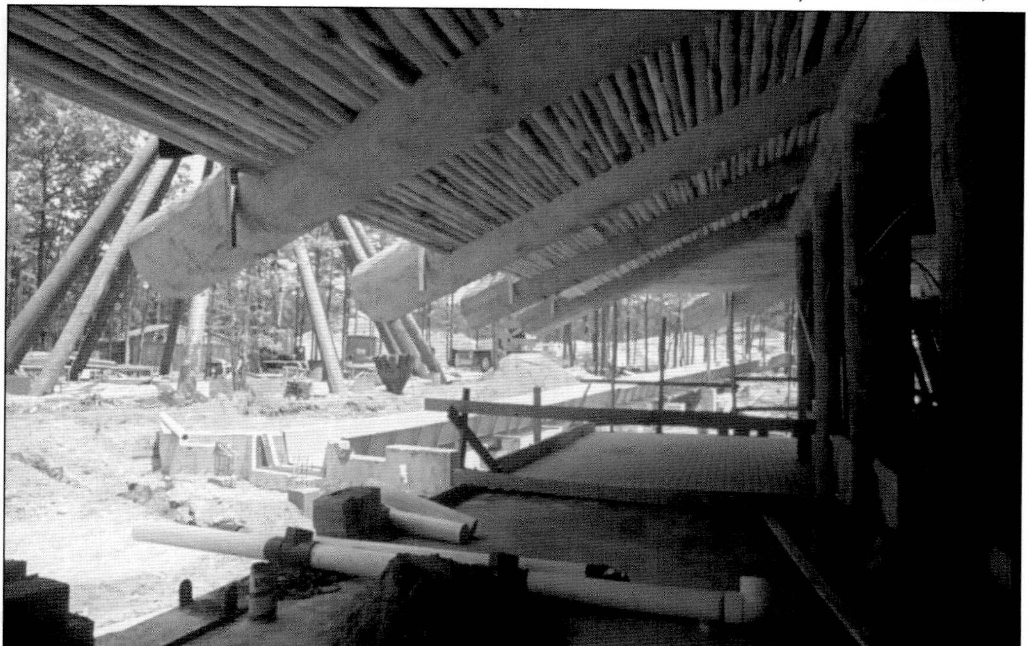

The covered patio of Best of the West would soon offer a shady spot to see the Log Flume and the Super Teepee, which were under construction just beyond. The restaurant stood in the center of the Log Flume, offering views of the riders' treetop journey on one side and splash down on the other. (GreatAdventureHistory.com collection.)

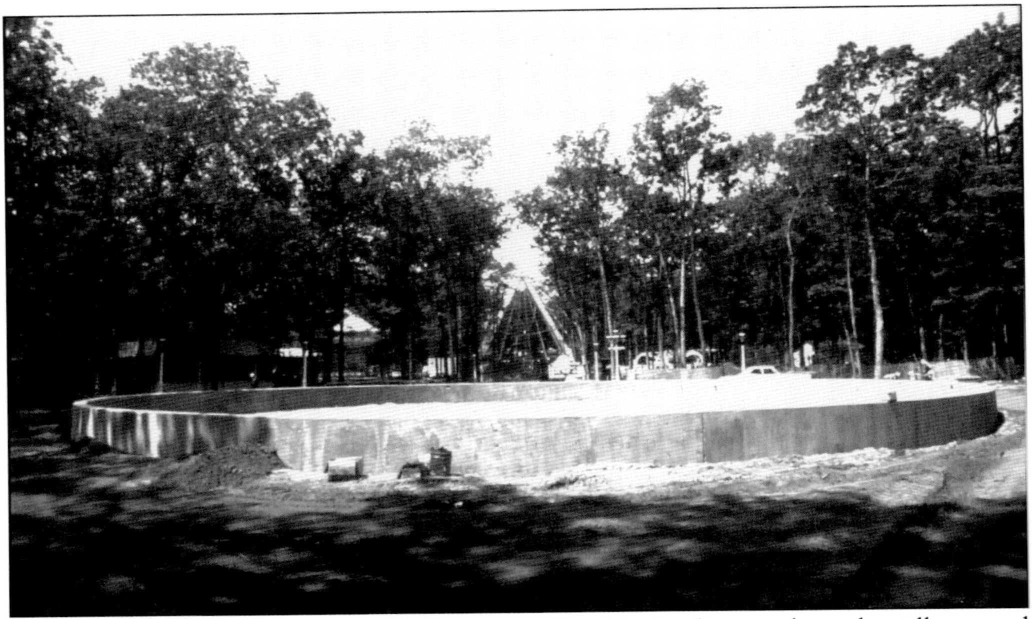

The fountain is in the foreground with the Giant Wheel in the distance down the still unpaved Dream Street. The fountain was the midway point between the carousel and Giant Wheel and was a tranquil hub of dining, entertainment, and attractions. The simple concrete pool walls would have decorative stone facing applied when the park entrance was relocated in 1976. (GreatAdventureHistory.com collection.)

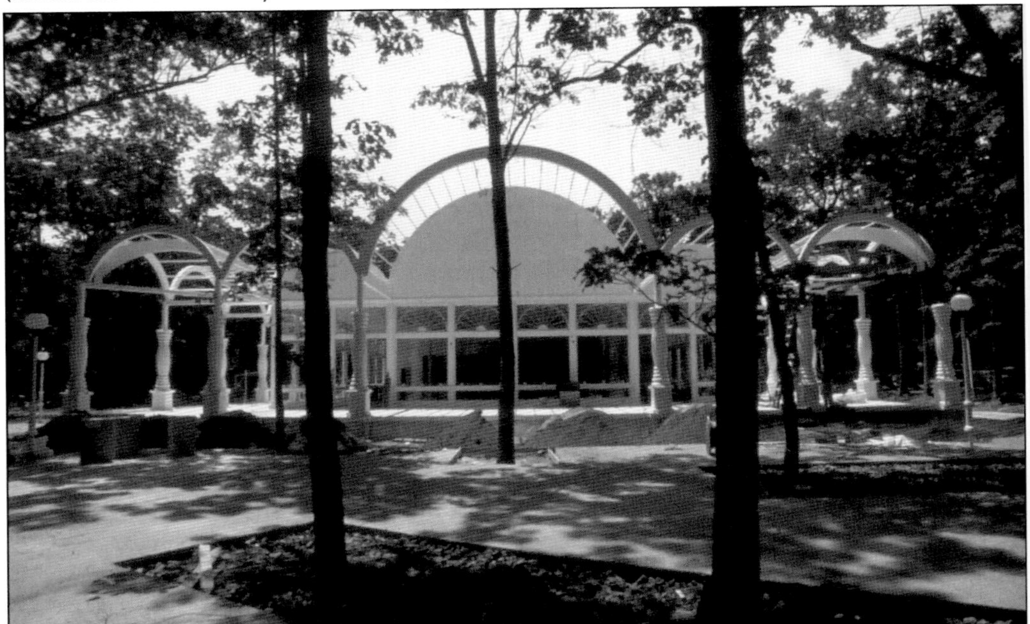

The distinctive arches of the Gingerbread Fancy restaurant are nearing completion. Originally the porch roof was made of colorful canvas printed with red, yellow, and brown leaves on the underside creating a unique ceiling. Yet to be installed are the thousands of lights in Victorian gingerbread-style scrolls. (GreatAdventureHistory.com collection.)

Workers assembled the giant ice-cream cone on the roof of the Yum Yum Palace, the park's premier ice-cream parlor and restaurant. The giant fiberglass creations made the building one of the most unique and picturesque structures in a park full of amazing and larger-than-life creations.

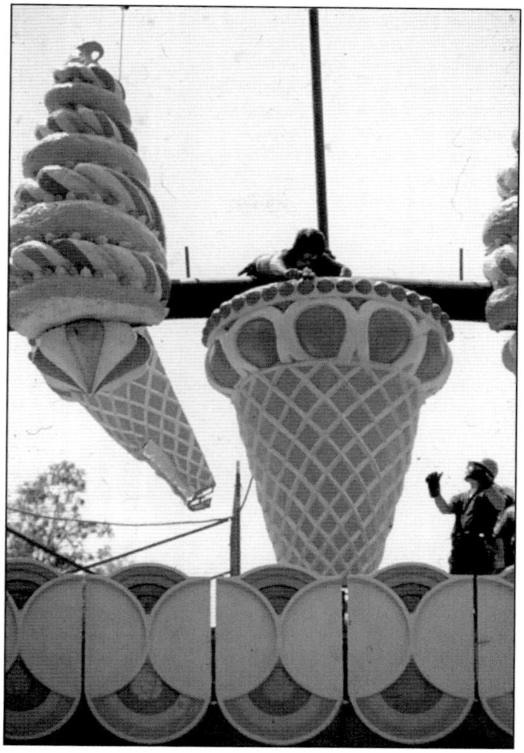

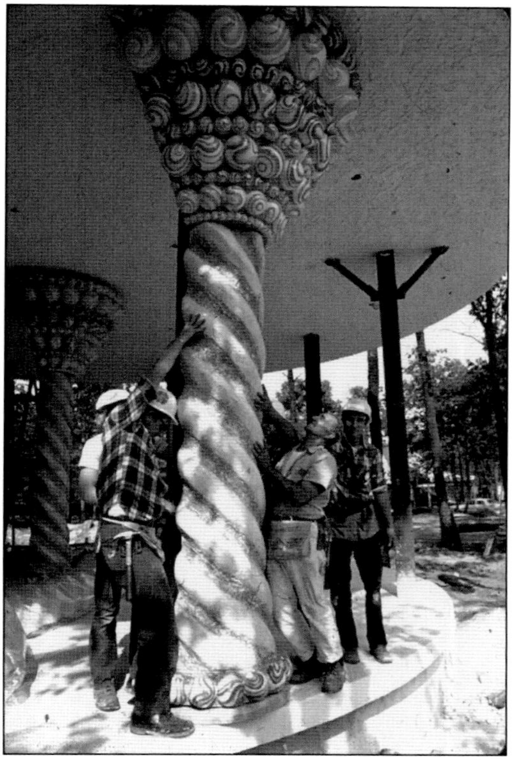

The framework of the Yum Yum Palace was steel and covered with the decorative fiberglass creations resembling scoops of ice cream, puffs of whipped cream, and ice-cream cones. Painted in bright colors, Dream Street's most fanciful eatery stood out against the surrounding trees of the Enchanted Forest.

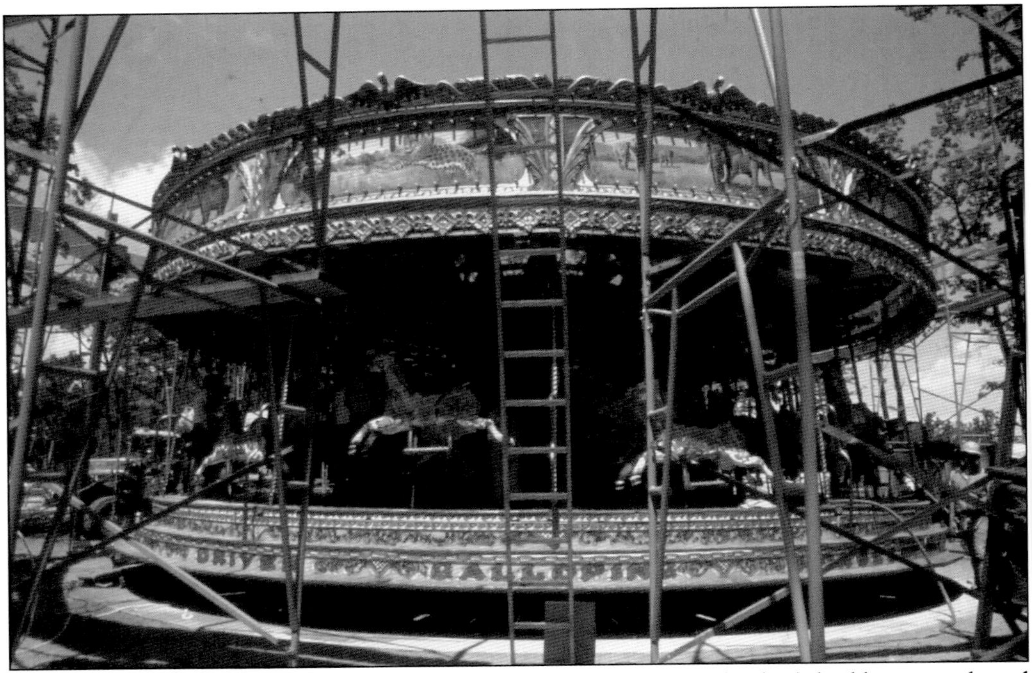

One of the last rides to be assembled was the 19th-century carousel, which had been purchased in England and brought to the park. The brightly colored horses and cockerels along with the jungle-themed rounding boards fit Great Adventure perfectly. An elaborate and colorful roof structure would soon be built around and over the fully assembled carousel.

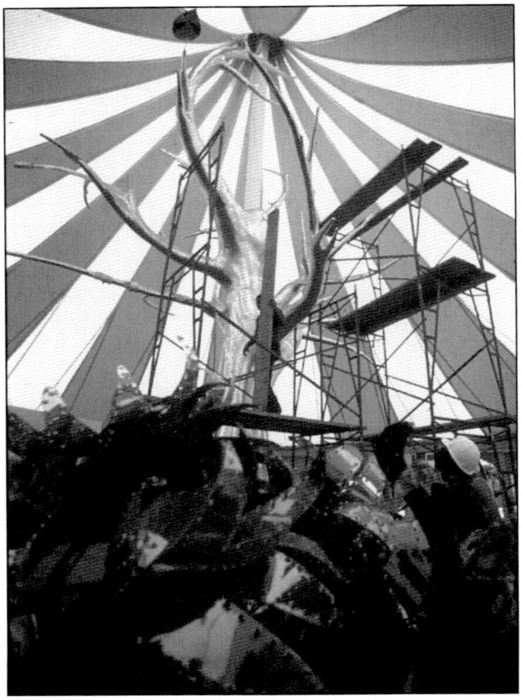

The shops of Great Adventure featured fantastic gifts in fantastic settings. Originally the interiors of the tents were open to the pinnacle, with colorful decorations throughout. Offering a panorama of souvenirs from disguise kits to glassware, Dream Street's Fairy Tales tent featured a giant silver tree in the center, displaying stuffed animals of all shapes and sizes.

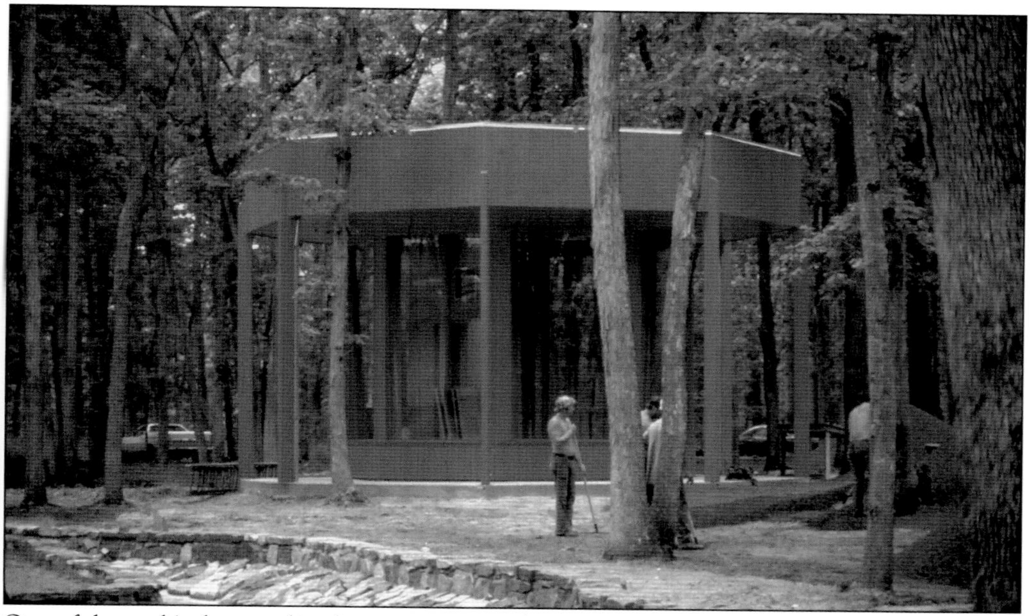

One of the park's shortest-lived attractions was the Happy Feeling area, which was part petting zoo and part animal display. The snake house is seen here under construction and was home to a dozen snakes all displayed behind glass. The building would later be converted into a shop as the park expanded. (GreatAdventureHistory.com collection.)

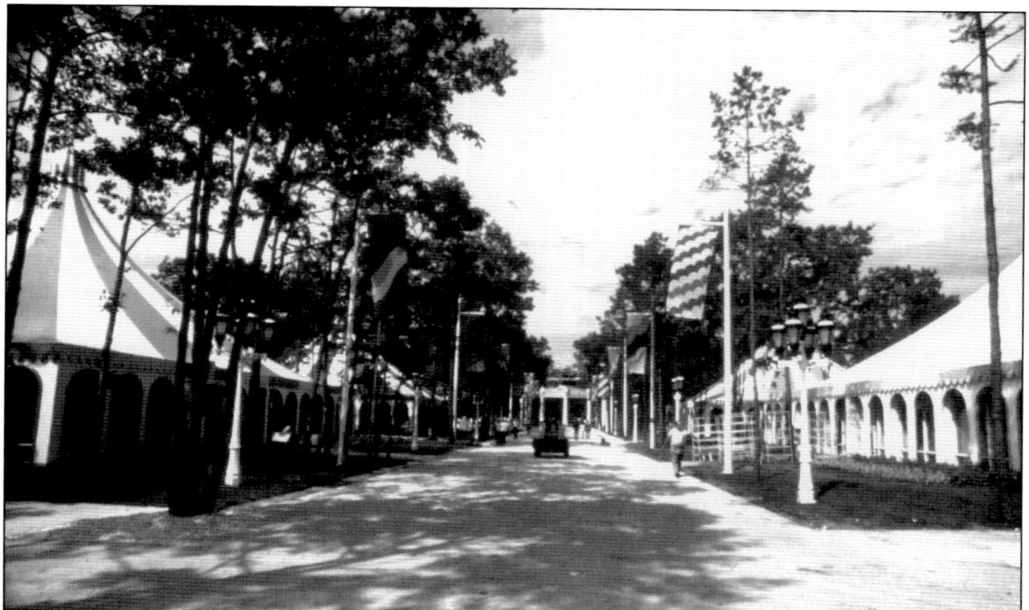

In late June, all the details were falling into place. Looking from the park's entrance down Dream Street, the grass, the flags, and the now-completed carousel can be seen as the July 1 opening day draws near. Dream Street was initially lined with grassy areas and flower beds, which would later give way to expanded walkways as the crowds demanded. (GreatAdventureHistory.com collection.)

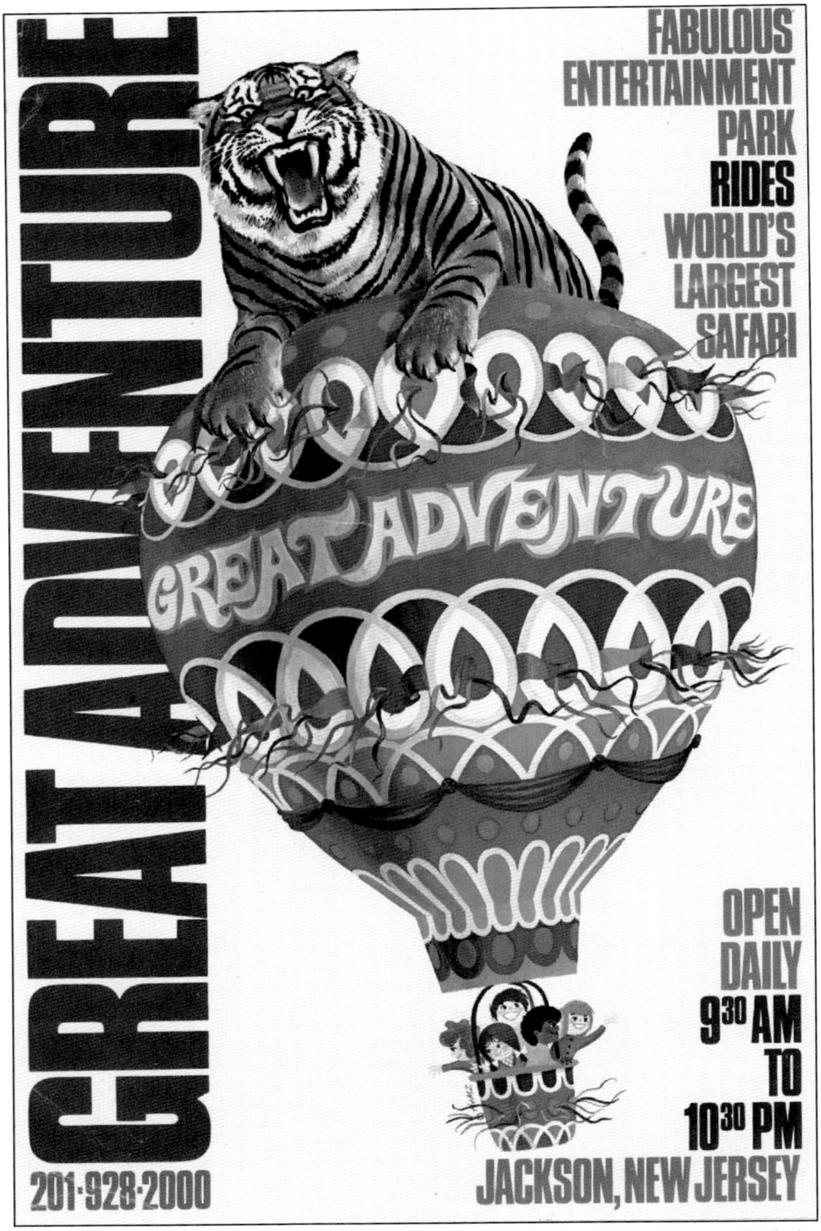

These lobby card–style posters were plastered all around New York City and Philadelphia to announce Great Adventure's grand opening. The colorful balloon and tiger logo gave a preview of the spectacular larger-than-life nature of the park. For the first season, the park was open daily from July 1 through late fall. The park had two hot-air balloons, and the world-record-holding larger of the two did a publicity tour of Central Park to help promote the grand opening. The tiger and balloon image, designed by artists Harry and Marion Zelenko, was used on a multitude of park publications, souvenirs, and trinkets. These included posters, patches, pins, plates, and an elaborate Broadway show–style souvenir program. The image captured the spirit of both the Enchanted Forest and the Safari. (GreatAdventureHistory.com collection.)

Two

The Greatest Day of Your Life

The opening season for the park was a qualified success, drawing large crowds during its inaugural season. However, the rush to get the park open on time for July 1, 1974, meant things were somewhat unfinished. The limited numbers of rides and snack stands meant long waits throughout the park. Even restrooms were inadequate for the numbers of guests, and early reviews of the park were less than glowing.

Plans were made immediately to expand the park for the second season, with a second, larger flume and an entirely new section of attractions being added, bringing the number of rides from 14 in 1974 to 21 in 1975. Also added in 1975 were the new Fortune Festival games area and additional food establishments and restroom facilities throughout the park.

Some other plans made at the time were announced in park promotional materials but never came to pass, although in some cases they were even included on park maps. Among these was the International Food Fair, which was to have been built on the edge of the lake, on the peninsula beneath the Log Flume. Later the same site was scheduled to become the new home to the park's Antique Car ride when it had to be relocated for construction of the park's new front gate.

With each of the earliest seasons lessons were learned from the growing pains of the park, and improvements were made in all areas to create a better guest experience. Consultants who had worked with established theme park companies like Disney and Six Flags helped lend their expertise.

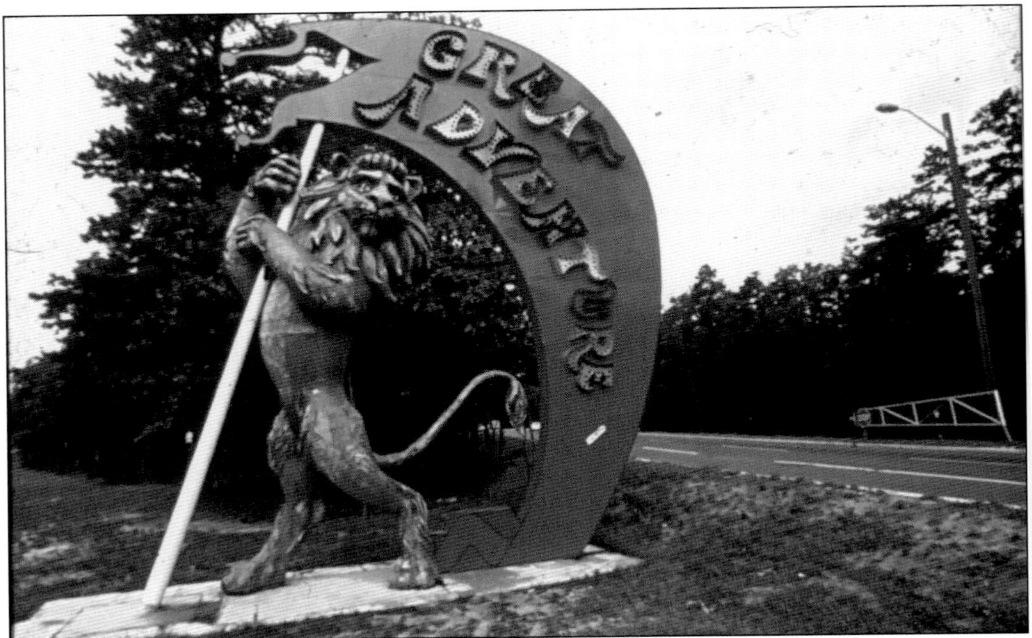

Great Adventure's entrance on Route 537 was marked by a huge stylized fiberglass lion holding a pennant with the park's name in colorful letters. Standing at the foot of the overpass, the lion sign was later moved to the hospitality center at the Safari entrance when it was replaced with a newer marquee. (GreatAdventureHistory.com collection.)

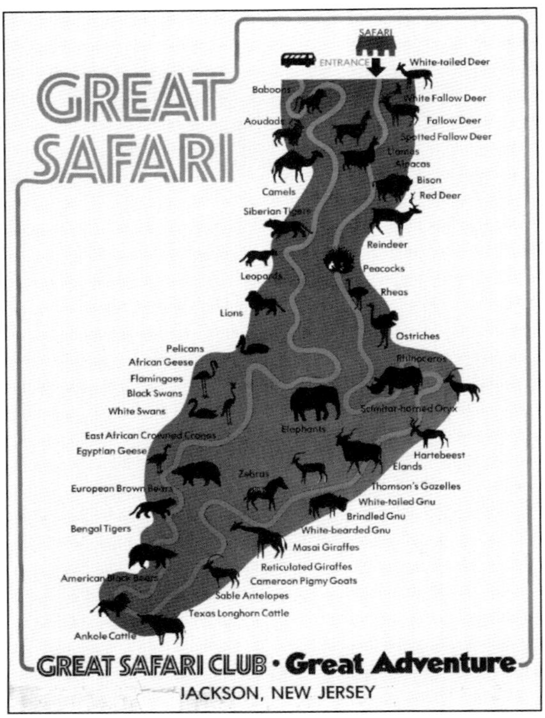

The Safari was a very popular part of the Great Adventure experience, offering a unique animal adventure unlike the zoos of the time. For many guests, a full day at the park began with a tour of the thousands of animals along the four-and-a-half-mile-long winding roadway, which included species from around the globe. (GreatAdventureHistory.com collection.)

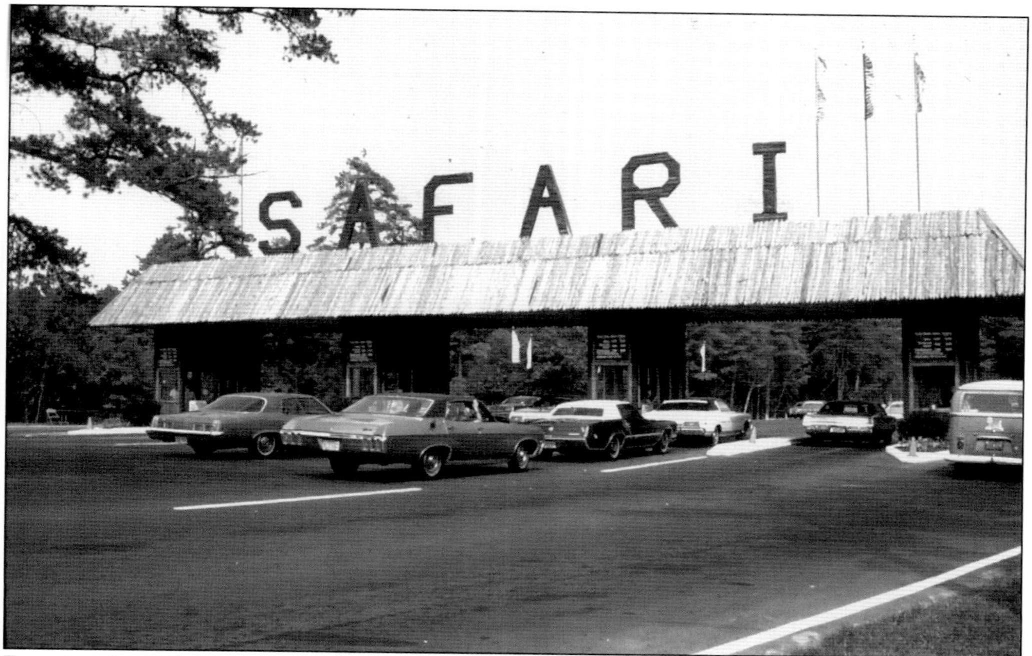

Entering the Safari gates was like entering another world, with the giant Safari sign hinting at the scale of the park beyond. Paying $2.50 for each adult ticket ($2 for kids), carloads of families went on safari without having to leave the comfort of their vehicles, complete with narration through crackling AM car radios.

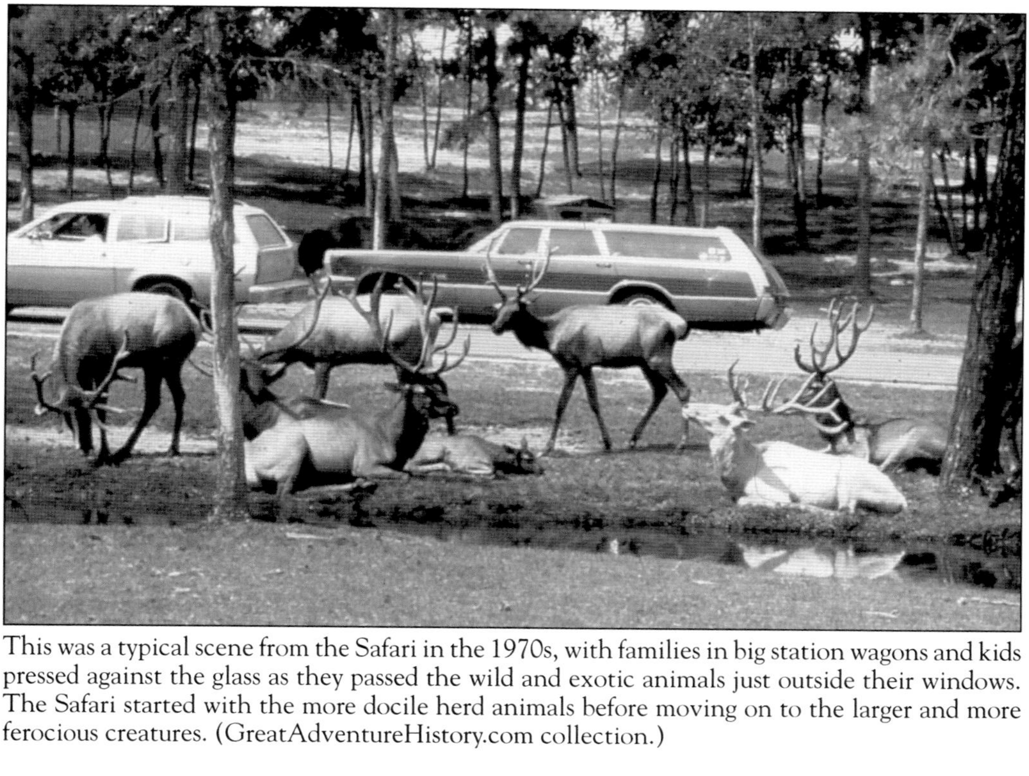

This was a typical scene from the Safari in the 1970s, with families in big station wagons and kids pressed against the glass as they passed the wild and exotic animals just outside their windows. The Safari started with the more docile herd animals before moving on to the larger and more ferocious creatures. (GreatAdventureHistory.com collection.)

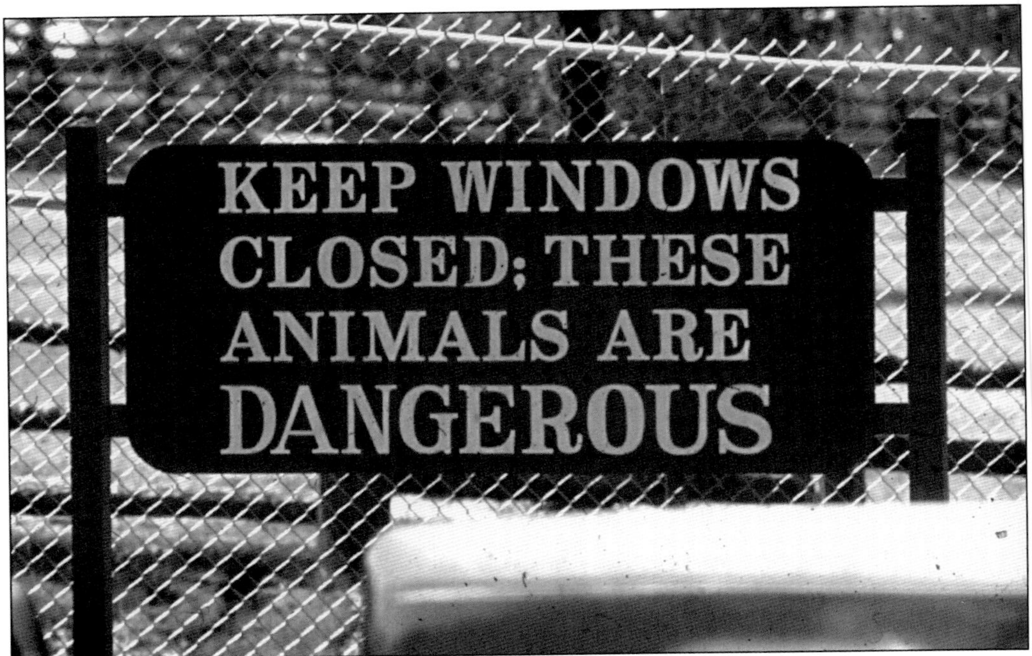

Warning signs like the one seen here were found throughout the Safari, as all the animals, including some of the most dangerous ones, ran free, walking between (and sometimes on top of) the cars. This rule was enforced by roaming wardens as well as gamekeepers stationed at the gates between animal sections. (GreatAdventureHistory.com collection.)

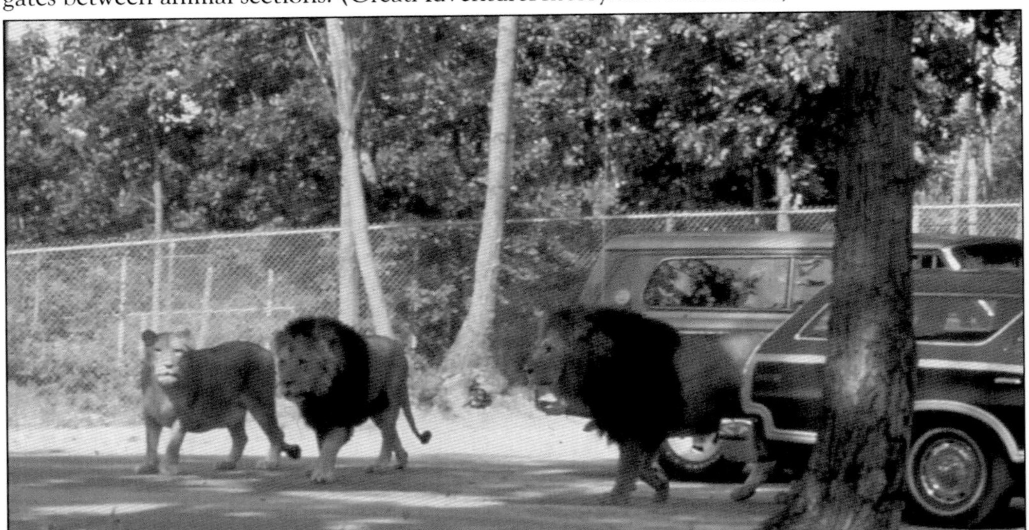

The lions would often wander across the roads, stopping traffic as they passed. Seeing these giant cats so close was one of the most unforgettable experiences the Safari offered. The Safari had a large pride of lions that dined on specially prepared meals, curbing their appetite and lessening the temptation of passing meals. (GreatAdventureHistory.com collection.)

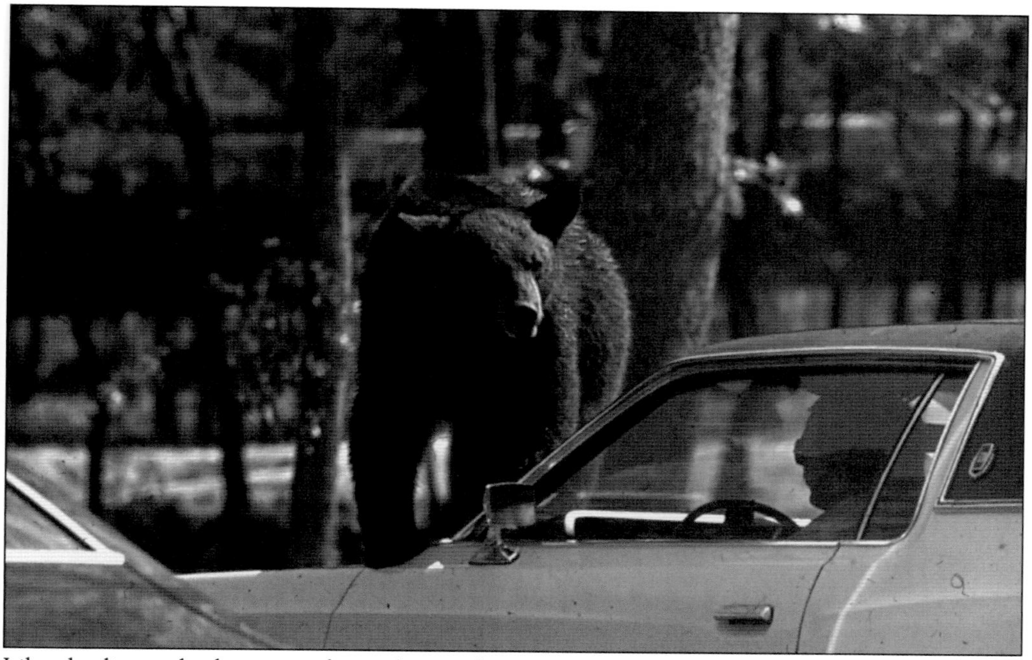

Like the lions, the bears ran free, often walking right up to the cars to see the people inside. In some cases the huge animals would choose to climb onto the cars, not moving until one of the park's roving wardens came along to shoo them off. Occasionally a bear would fall asleep on the warm car hood, making removal more difficult and snarling the flow of traffic. (GreatAdventureHistory.com collection.)

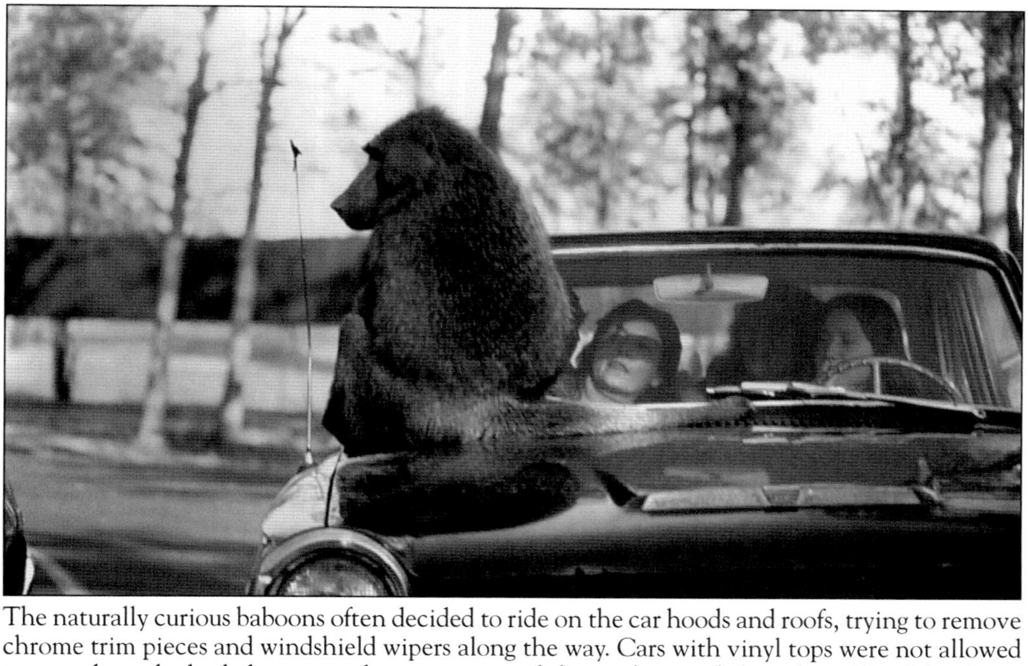

The naturally curious baboons often decided to ride on the car hoods and roofs, trying to remove chrome trim pieces and windshield wipers along the way. Cars with vinyl tops were not allowed to pass through the baboon area but were instead directed around the other side of the fence through the "Baboon By-Pass."

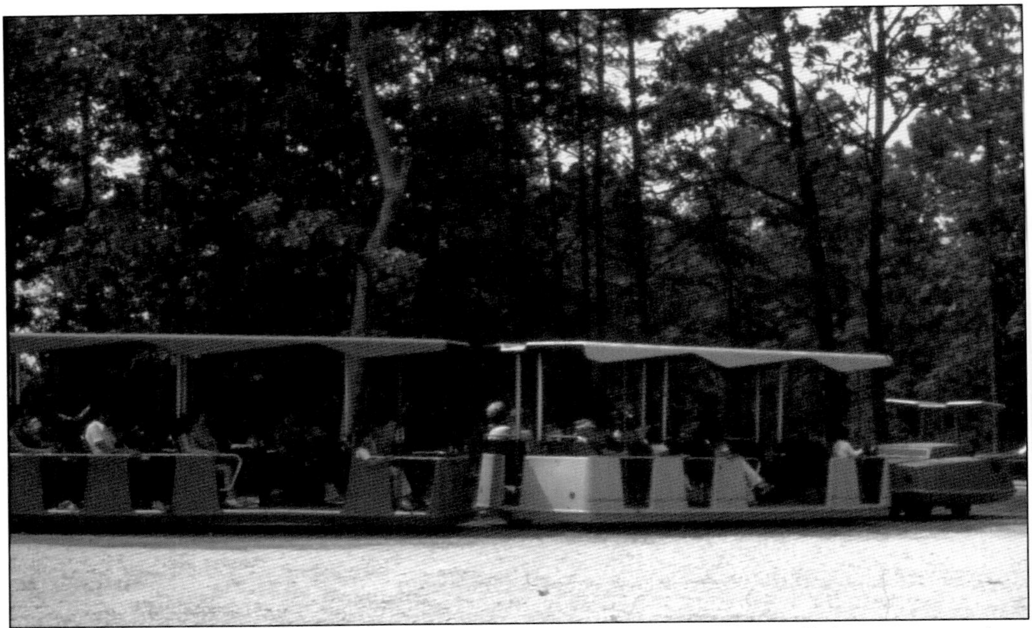

Designs for the property included having the parking area set apart from all the attractions by a large buffer of trees, maintaining the feel of the Enchanted Forest. Colorful trams shuttled the guests from the huge parking lot to the front gate, which was originally quite a distance away. (GreatAdventureHistory.com collection.)

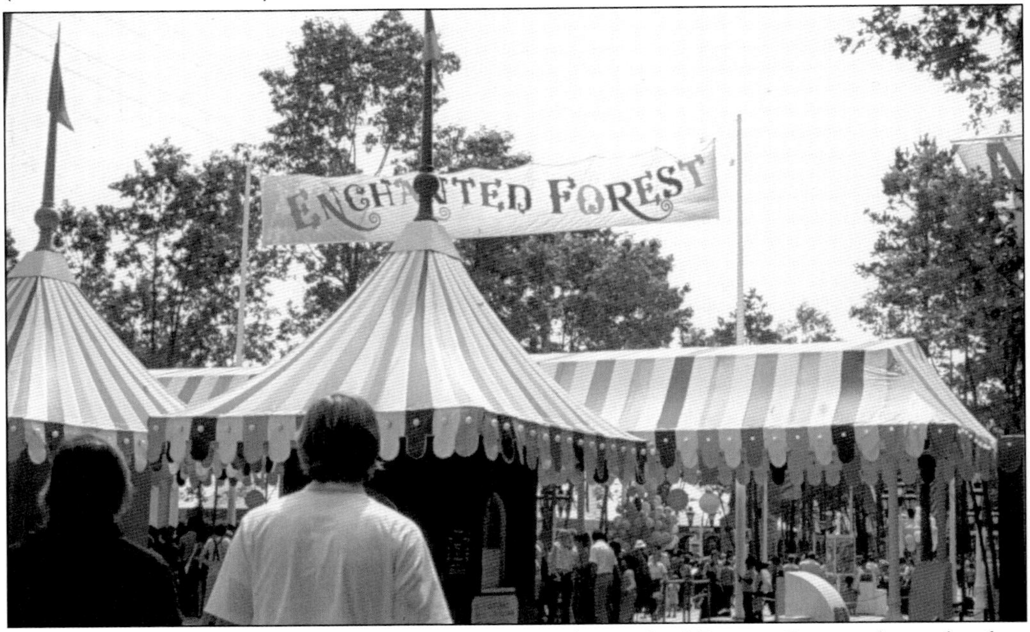

The original park entrance plaza was located at the end of Dream Street where the four tents stand. The structure was a simple canvas-roofed set of turnstiles with matching ticket booths, all adorned with brightly colored stripes. This gate was short-lived as the park grew and traffic patterns changed, giving way to a relocated entrance near the fountain in 1976. (GreatAdventureHistory.com collection.)

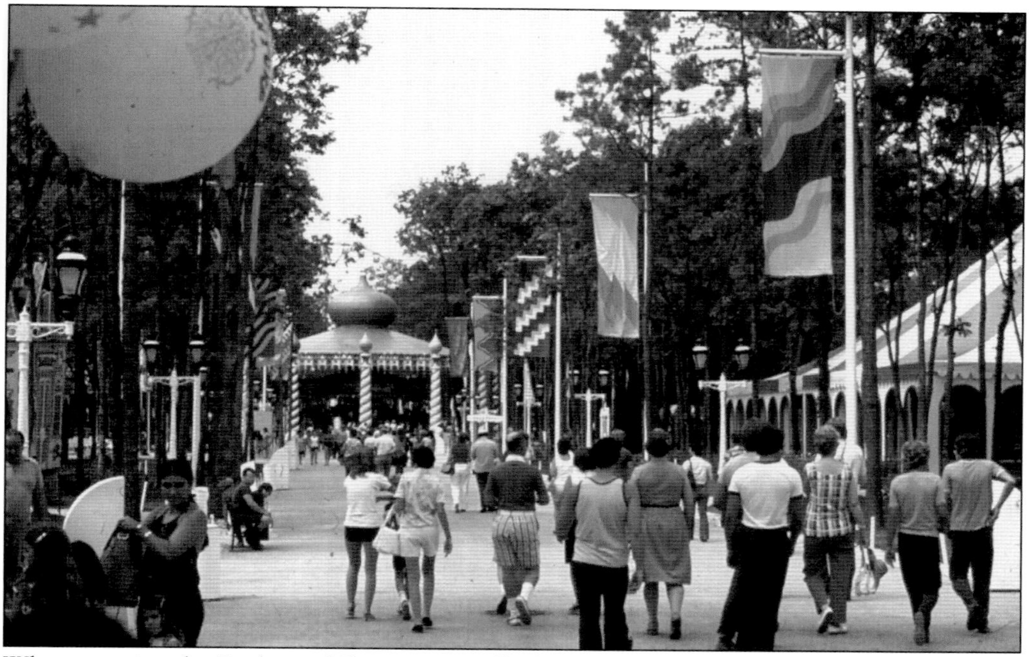

When entering the Enchanted Forest, one walked into a world of vibrant colors set against the canopy of foliage. The buildings, banners, balloons, rides, and flowers all added up to a rainbow of kaleidoscopic wonder. The sensory experience was completed with the smells of delicious food and the sounds of music filling the air. (GreatAdventureHistory.com collection.)

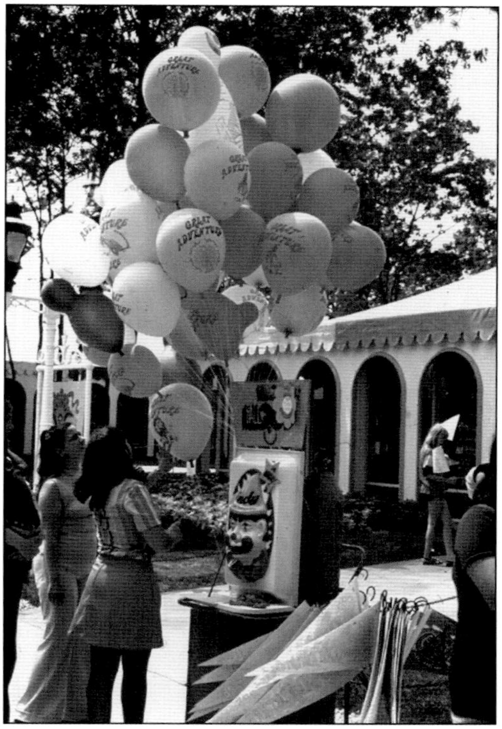

Balloon sellers were found throughout the park, selling colorful balloons in a variety of shapes and sizes. These balloons featured park icons, including the Giant Wheel, Rootin' Tootin' Rip Roarin, and the lion. Besides the sidewalk sellers like this, balloon girls also strolled through the park with huge bunches of balloons for sale. (GreatAdventureHistory.com collection.)

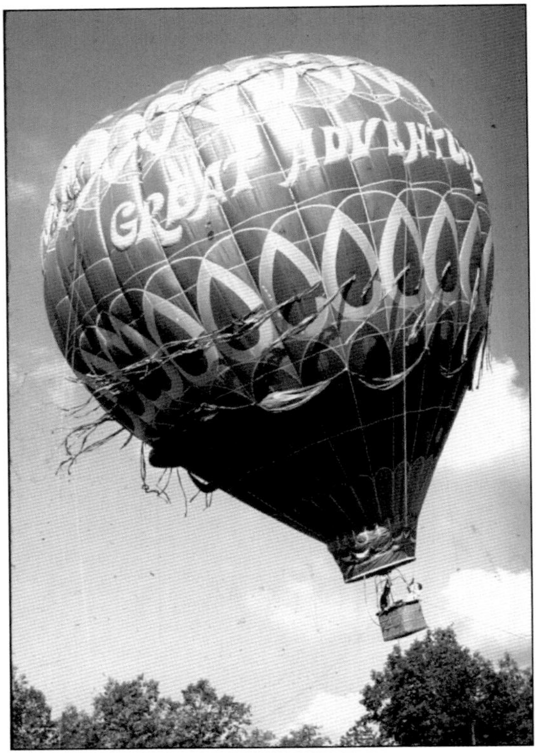

Visible from the parking lot, the Big Balloon was one of the first things guests saw. There were actually two hot-air balloons, one of regular size (seen here), and the big one, which was the largest free-flight hot-air balloon in the world at 110 feet high, 95 feet wide, and holding over 400,000 cubic feet of air with the ability to carry a crew of five.

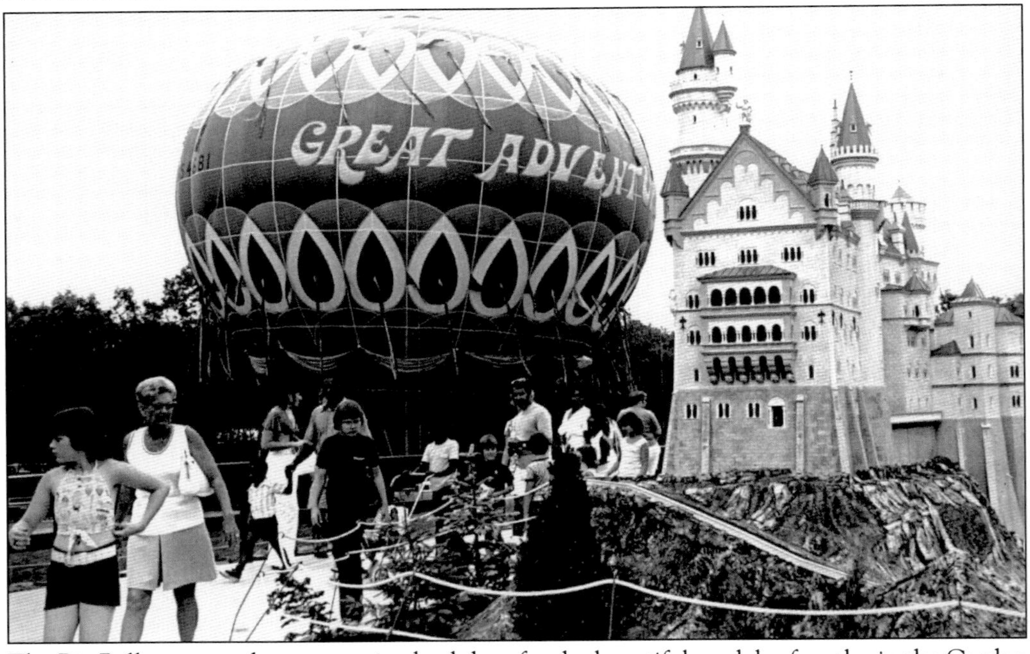

The Big Balloon served as an amazing backdrop for the beautiful models of castles in the Garden of Marvels. The Big Balloon tethered to the ground and floating among the huge trees of Great Adventure was a quiet but spectacular reminder to visitors that Great Adventure was a world of fantasy—bigger than life.

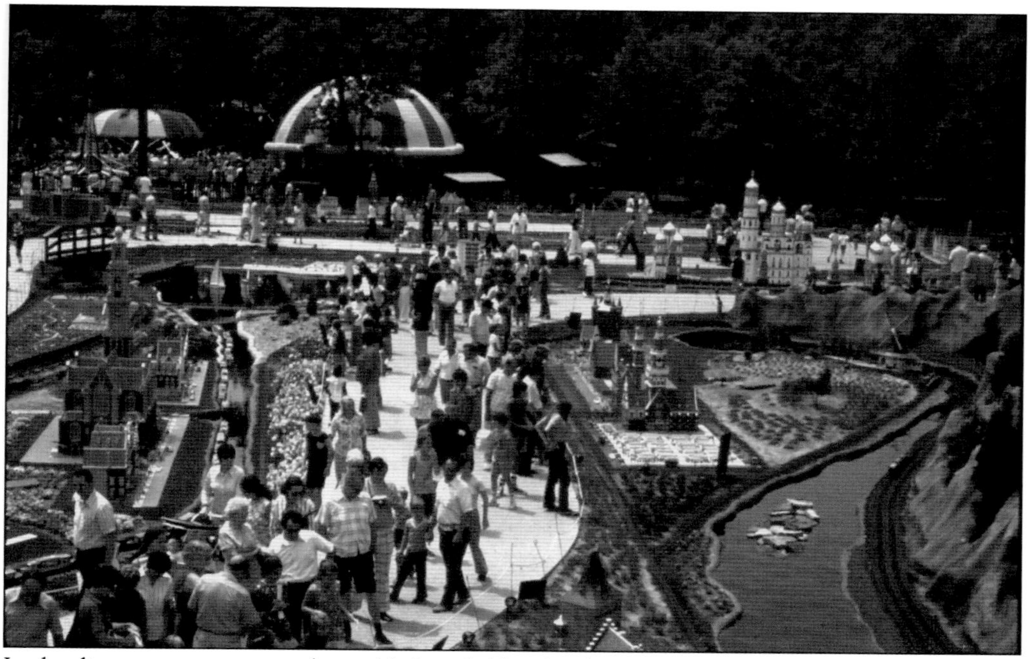

In the distance, one can see the park's first children's ride section, Ride-A-Rama, and the striped hat on the Clown Bounce. In the foreground is the Garden of Marvels, a bustling, highly detailed miniature world built in a scale of 1/25 life-size, making visitors feel like Gulliver on his travels. (GreatAdventureHistory.com collection.)

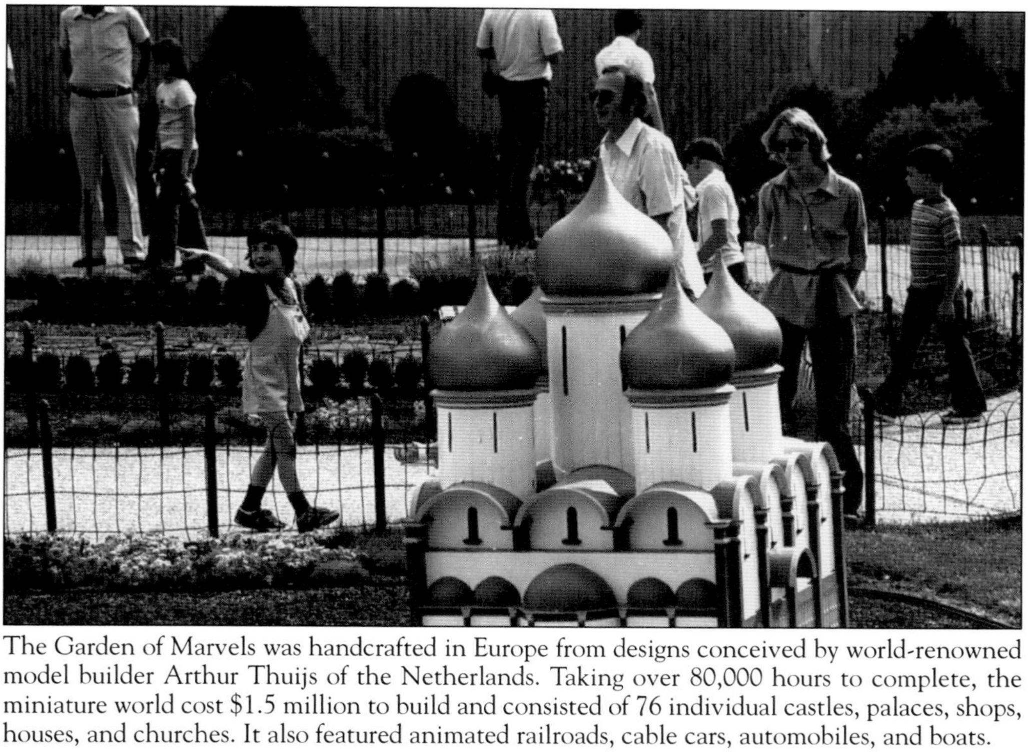

The Garden of Marvels was handcrafted in Europe from designs conceived by world-renowned model builder Arthur Thuijs of the Netherlands. Taking over 80,000 hours to complete, the miniature world cost $1.5 million to build and consisted of 76 individual castles, palaces, shops, houses, and churches. It also featured animated railroads, cable cars, automobiles, and boats.

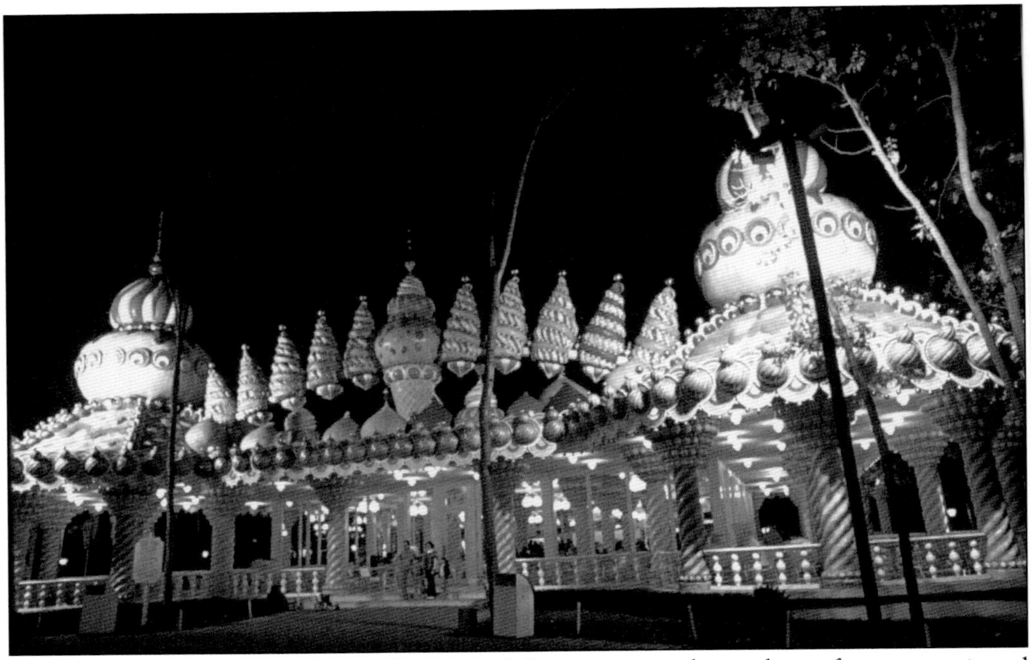

The incredible Yum Yum Palace with its gracefully curving porch was the perfect spot to sit and enjoy an ice-cream sundae or root beer float on a summer evening. The treats available inside were as extravagant as the exterior of the building, and the interior resembled an old-fashioned ice-cream parlor, evoking the charm of days gone by.

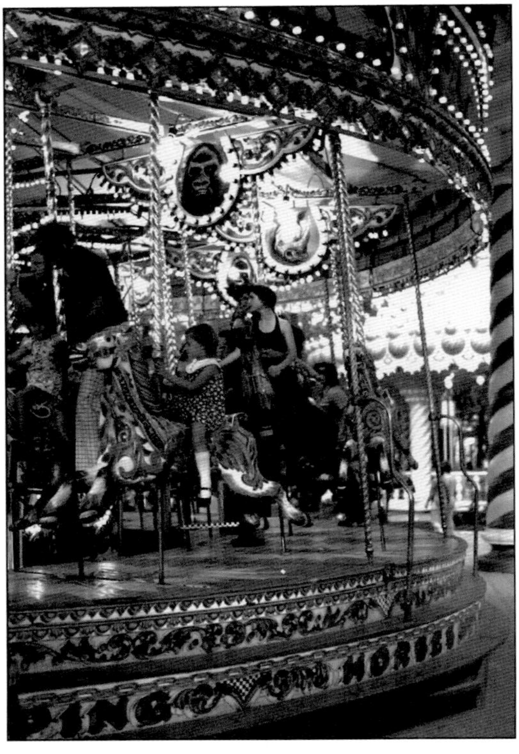

The beautifully restored Patrina Williams Carousel originally featured a full-sized band organ and large lightbulbs that hung down to illuminate the overhead animal plaques. The entire ride was painted with elaborate designs on the floor and the steps, as well as the other woodwork surrounding the animal paintings on the rounding boards.

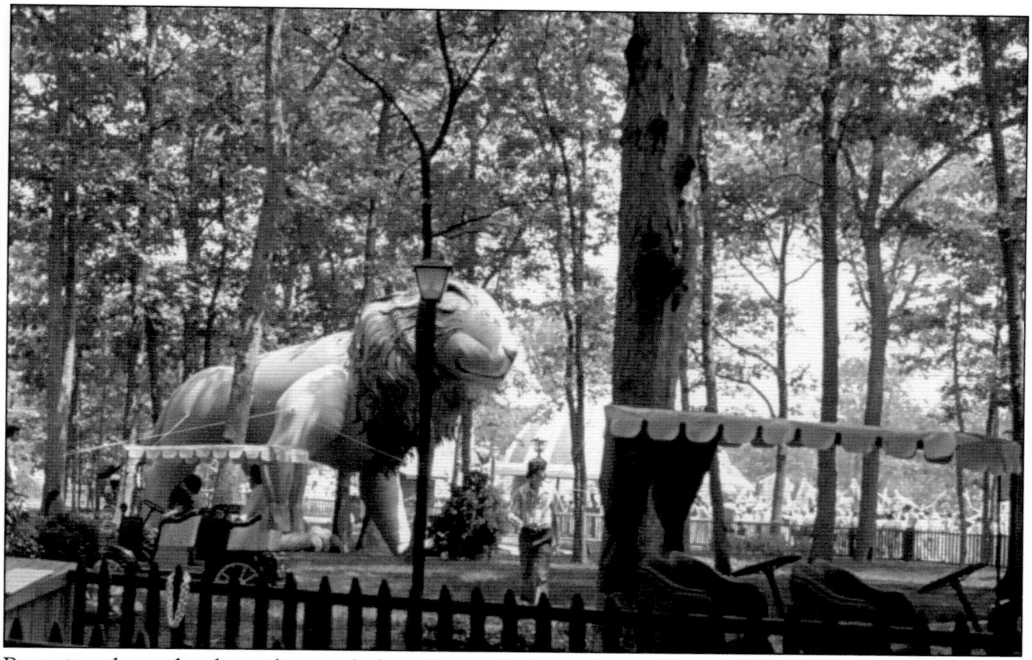

Running through a heavily wooded and beautifully landscaped area, the Antique Cars followed a winding path with some unique scenic elements such as the inflatable lion shown here. The electric-powered cars quietly followed a guide rail and carried up to four guests each. After just two seasons, the ride was removed to make way for the relocated park entrance. (GreatAdventureHistory.com collection.)

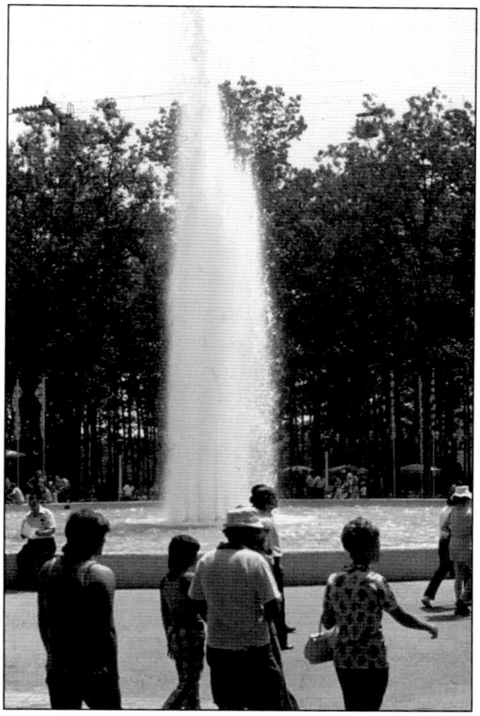

At the center of Dream Street was the fountain with its single water jet. The fountain was another of the park's record holders, billed as the world's tallest water jet spraying more than 100 feet into the air. This original fountain would be replaced in the coming years with a second incarnation, featuring a center jet and surrounding sprayers. (GreatAdventureHistory.com collection.)

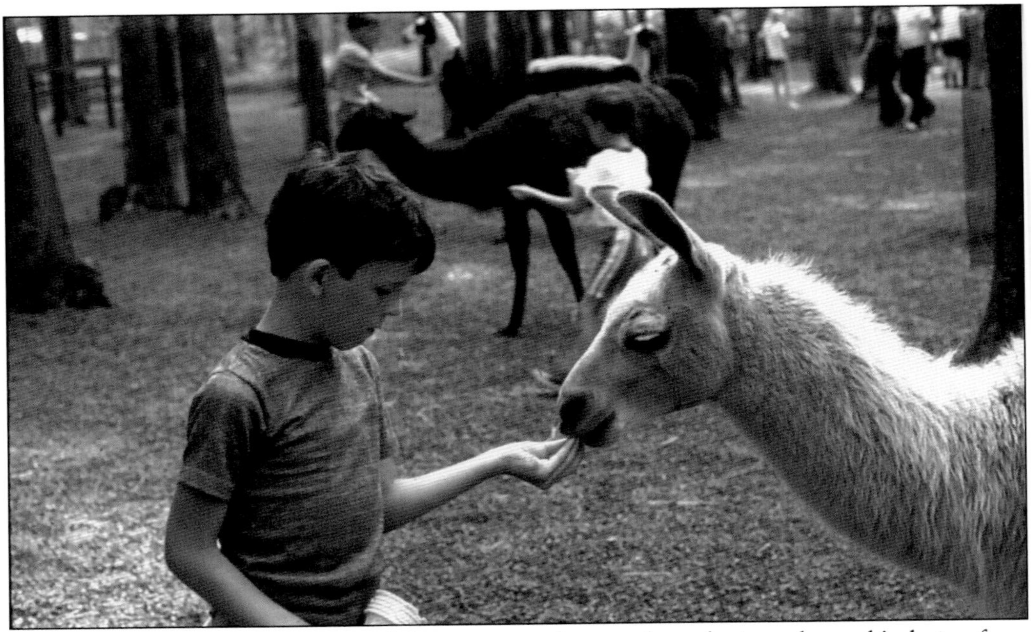

The Happy Feeling area was one of the concepts that was brought into the park's design from the Over the Rainbow plans. The idea was a land of tame animals, including llamas, goats, and deer, that could be petted and fed, as well as an island of colorful and exotic birds and a snake exhibit. (GreatAdventureHistory.com collection.)

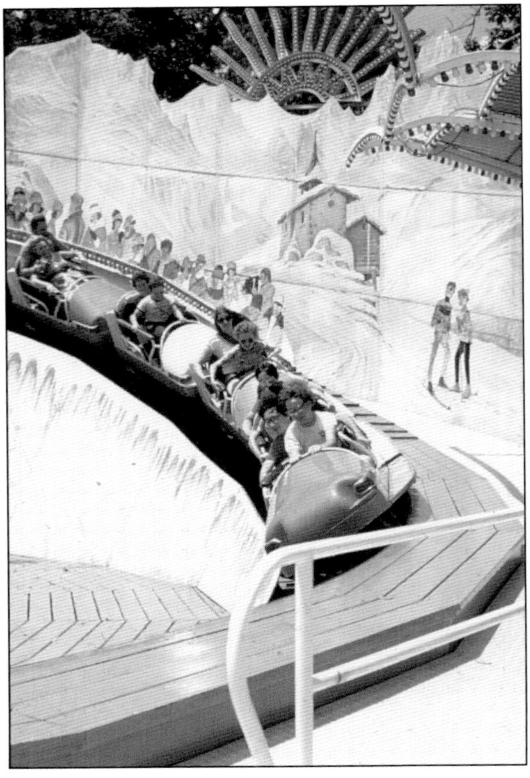

A favorite flat ride in the park for many years was the Swiss Bob, a small bobsled ride that featured a train of realistic bobsled vehicles that spun around the track's banked curves. The ride was originally located next to the Gingerbread Fancy restaurant in the Strawberry Fair section at the end of Dream Street and featured an elaborate backdrop.

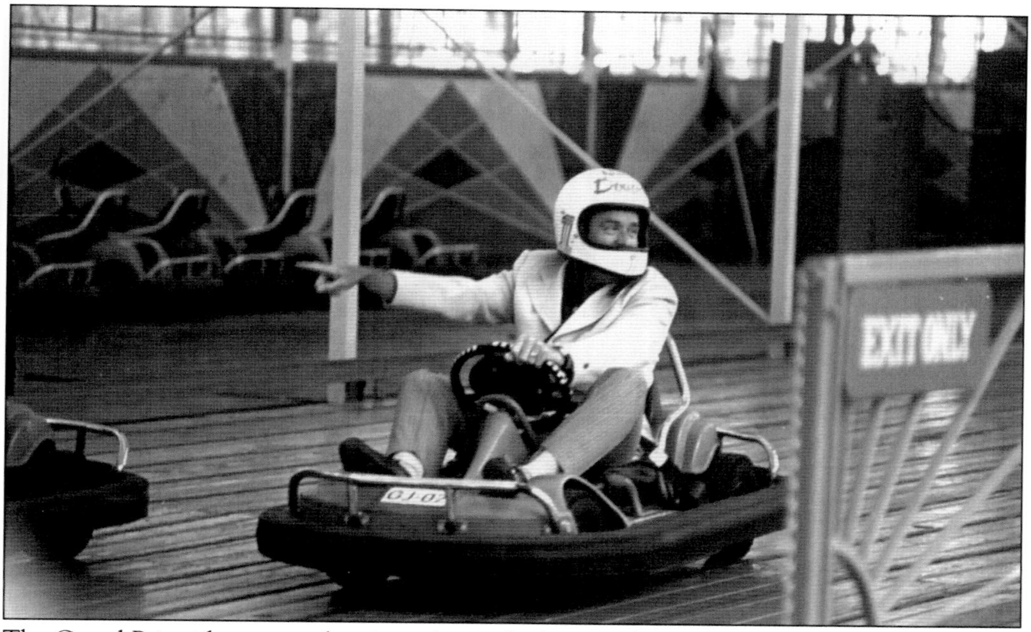

The Grand Prix ride was an electric go-kart ride that was located on what is now the location of the Studio 28 Arcade. Here television host Mike Douglas takes one of the karts for a spin as part of a week of filming his popular talk show at Great Adventure in 1974.

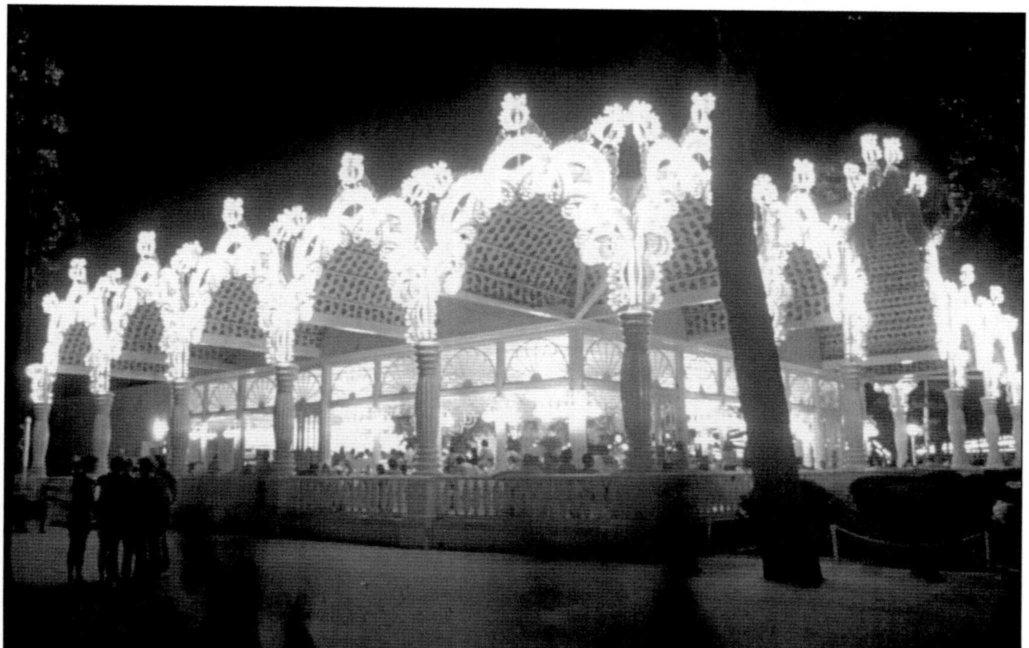

One of the park's three major restaurants was the Gingerbread Fancy, located in the Strawberry Fair section of the park. Its standout feature was the arched porch, which was covered with Victorian scrolls featuring hundreds of multicolor lightbulbs. Inside were equally elaborate columns of curlicues hung with live ferns, which created an elegant atmosphere.

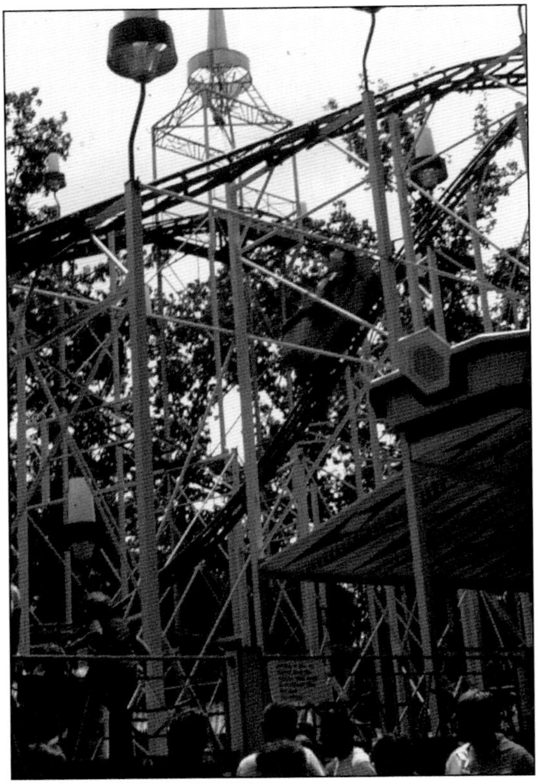

In addition to the Runaway Mine Train, the Big Fury was one of only two roller coasters that opened with the park in 1974. The coaster was set off Dream Street in the Strawberry Fair section, near the Giant Wheel, in an area that was left heavily wooded, keeping it hidden from view from most of the park.

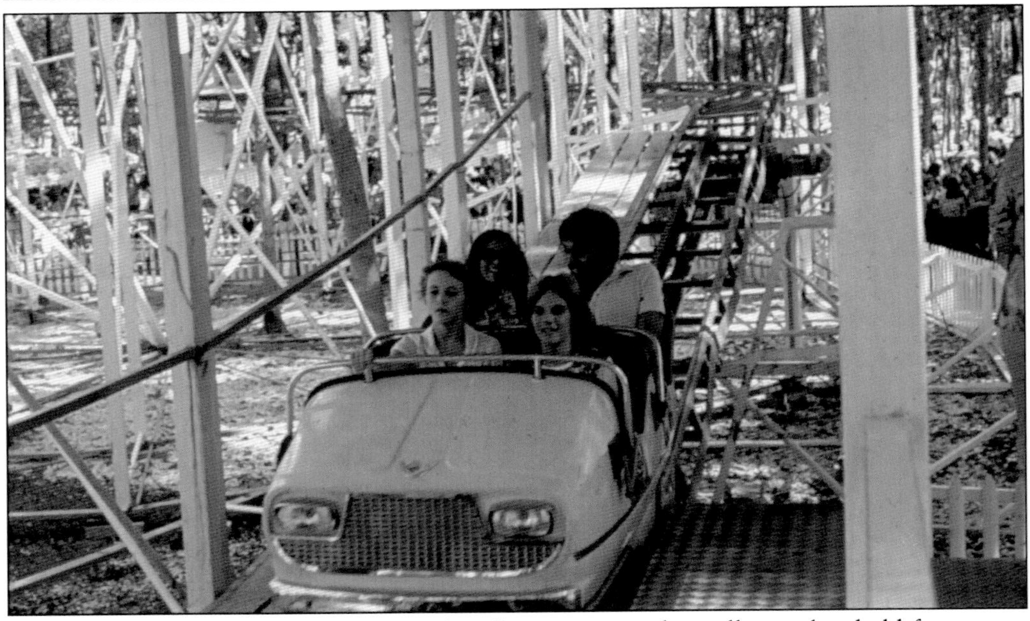

Big Fury was a portable wild mouse–style roller coaster, with small cars that held four guests each, navigating a very compact track of tight turns and dips. Everything about the ride looked very temporary, including the ride's station, which was assembled with fiberglass panels on an aluminum framework.

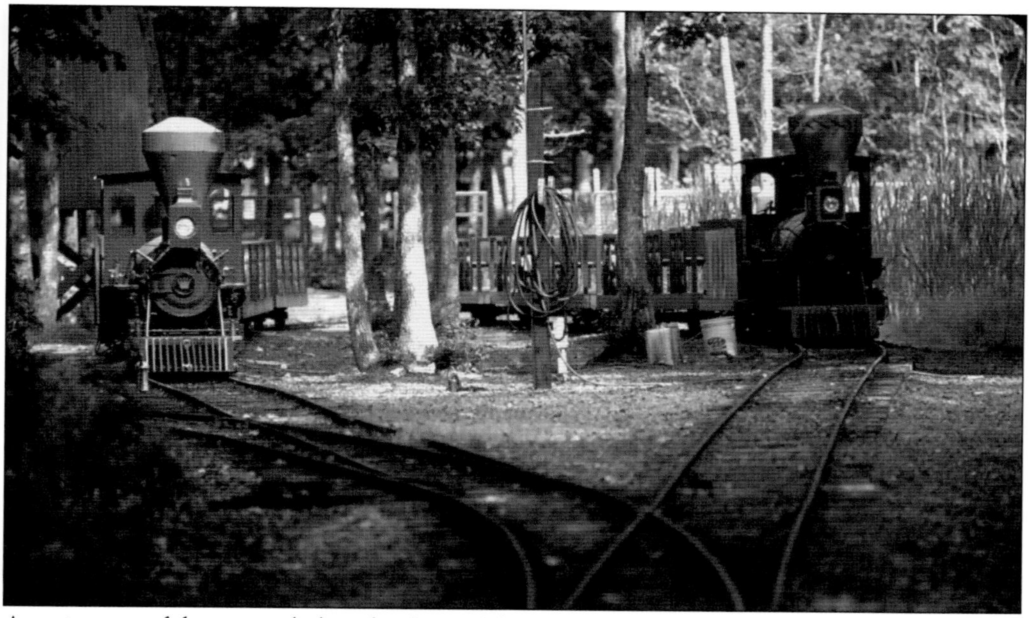

A major part of the original plans for Great Adventure was the park's network of transportation systems, which were to have included an elaborate railroad. The Great Train Ride was a live steam railroad that opened with two trains in 1974 and added an additional two trains for 1975 in anticipation of eventually becoming part of the park-wide transportation system.

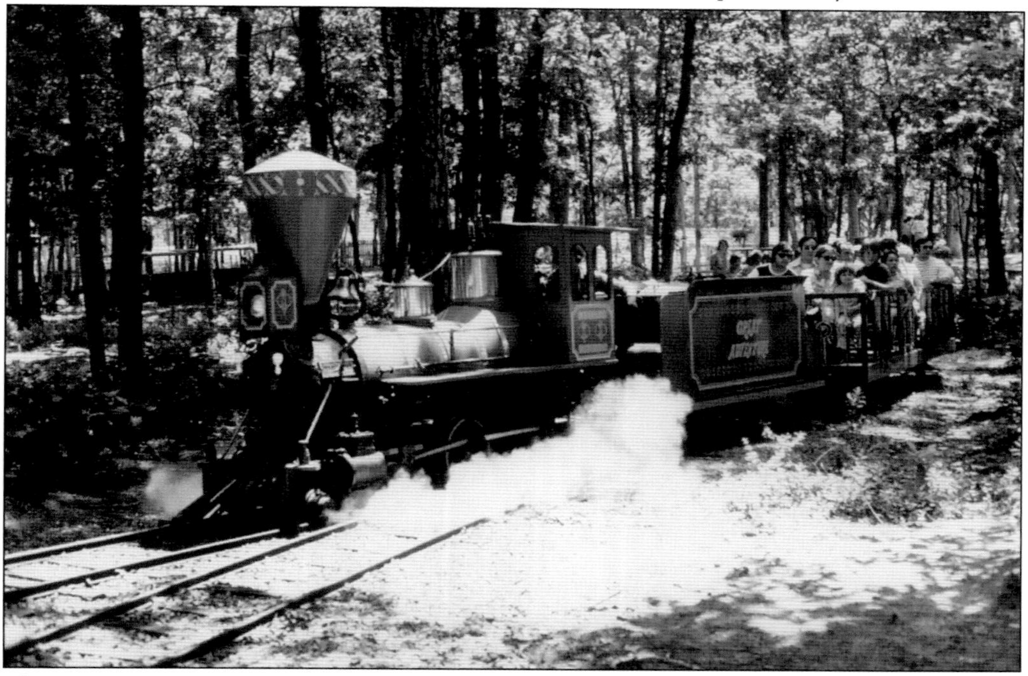

The Crown Metal Products 24-inch-gauge trains traveled through the unspoiled woods along the edge of Prospertown Lake. The park's second flume ride was added over and around the tracks for the 1975 season. The heavily wooded atmosphere of the trains even extended to the ride's loading platform, which featured a tree growing right through the station roof.

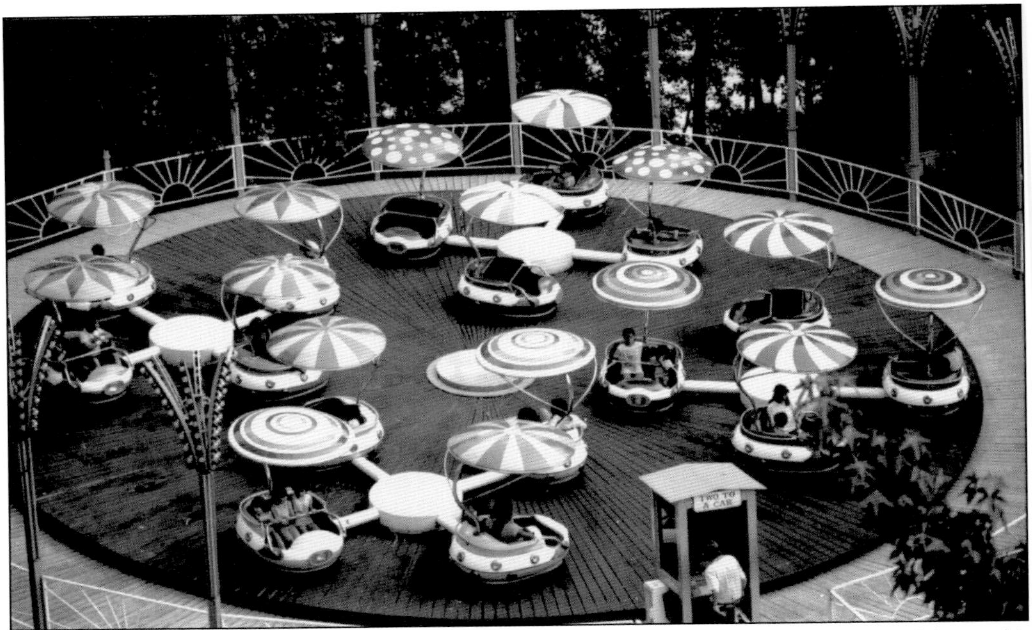

Another of the flat rides that was built in the Strawberry Fair section and was part of the park's opening season was the Calypso, a brightly colored spinning ride mounted to a slanted platform. The cars each had small round roofs, which had polka dots, stripes, and swirls in vibrant color combinations.

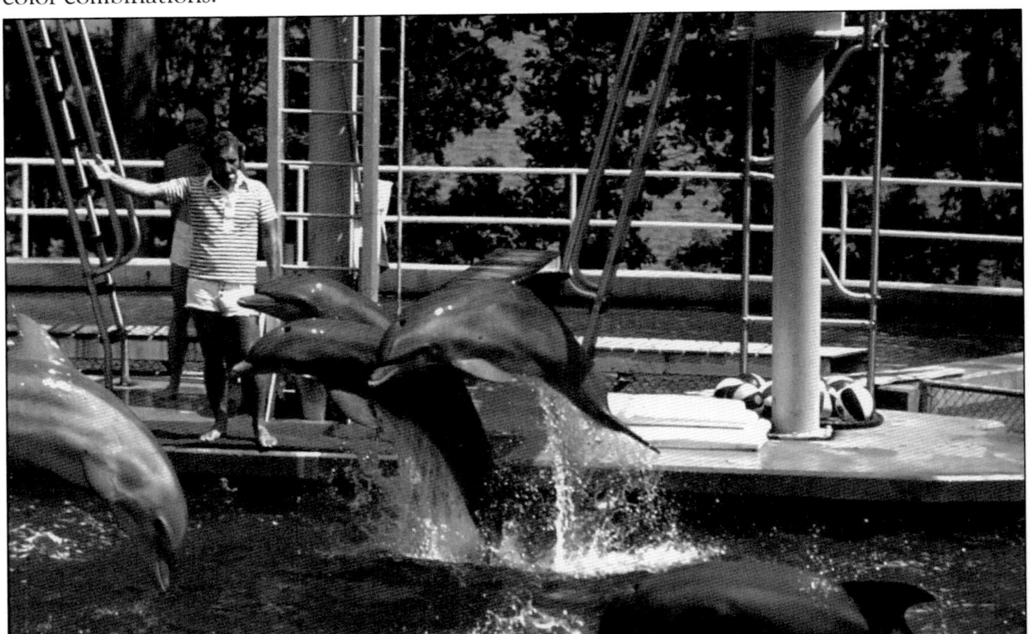

The most popular attraction at the park for many years was the Aqua Spectacle and its dolphin show. Originally the show featured 10 dolphins performing at one time, claiming to be the world's biggest dolphin show. The dolphins alternated shows with the Acapulco Cliff Divers throughout the day. (GreatAdventureHistory.com collection.)

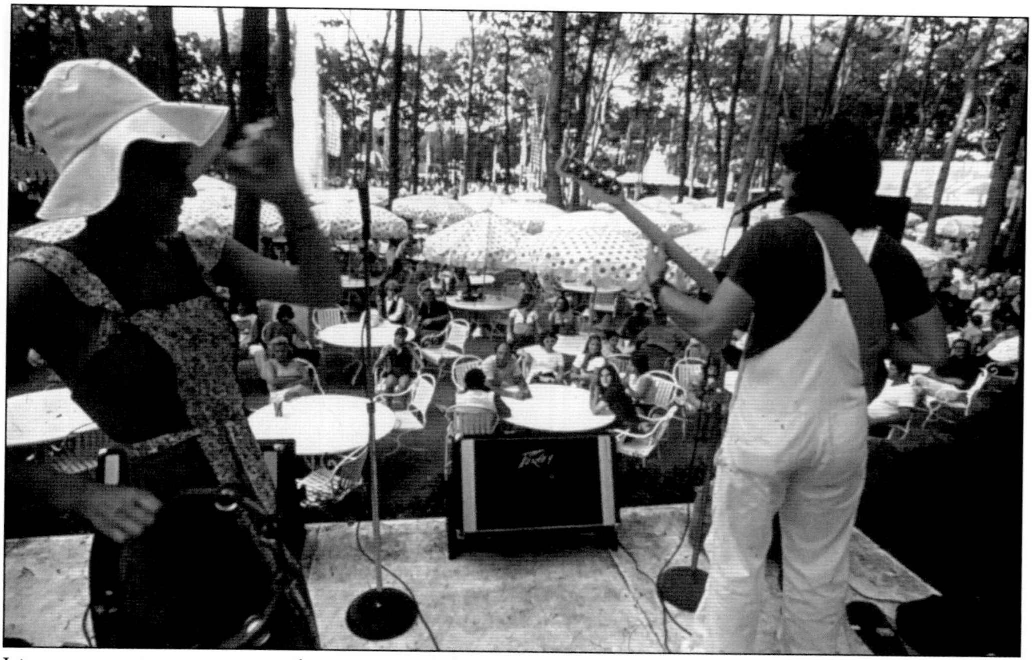

Live entertainment was a huge part of the park's attraction lineup. Bands played on stages and even on the streets of the park, along with the clowns and characters. Here a band is playing at the gazebo beside the fountain for the crowds of diners at Fountain Café. (GreatAdventureHistory.com collection.)

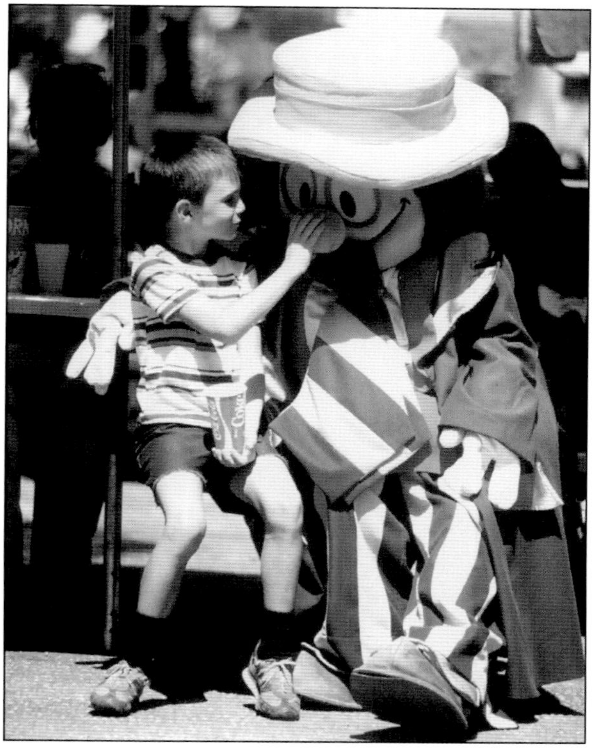

The park originally had its own unique lineup of characters that inhabited the streets. Here is Hock N. Swippet, the "Mayor of Great Adventure," meeting one of the park's young guests along Dream Street. Other characters included Wilden Wooly the Safari ambassador, Keystone Cops, a clown fire brigade, and even a giant chicken.

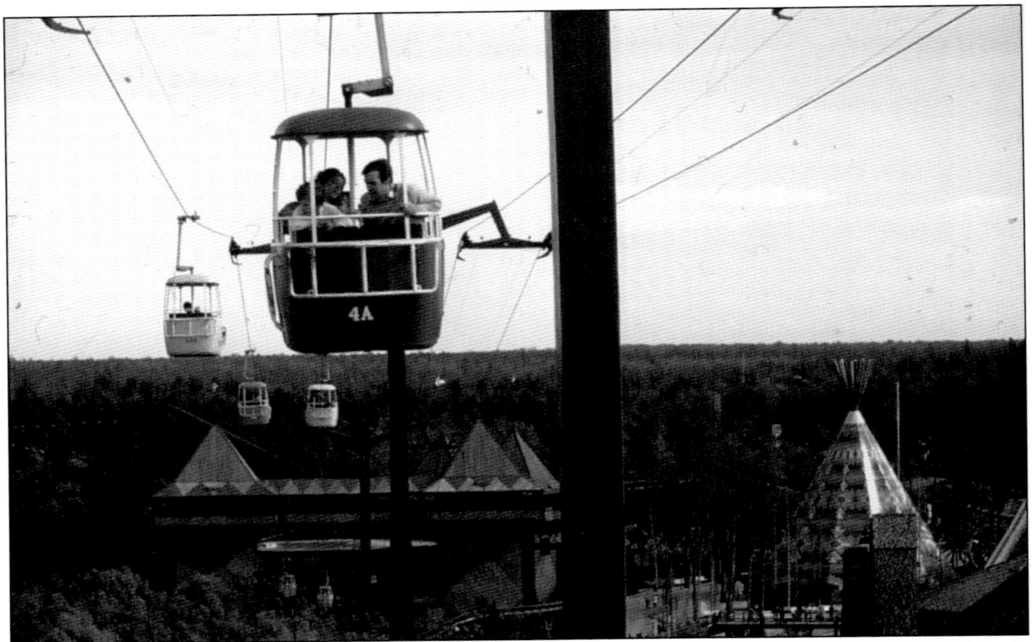

The best way to get from one side of the park to the other was to take the Skyride. The Skyride structure was originally located at the 1964–1965 New York World's Fair and was moved to Great Adventure where it still operates today. The trip across the park brought guests from the end of Dream Street in the Strawberry Fair section into the Fort at the heart of Rootin' Tootin' Rip Roarin'.

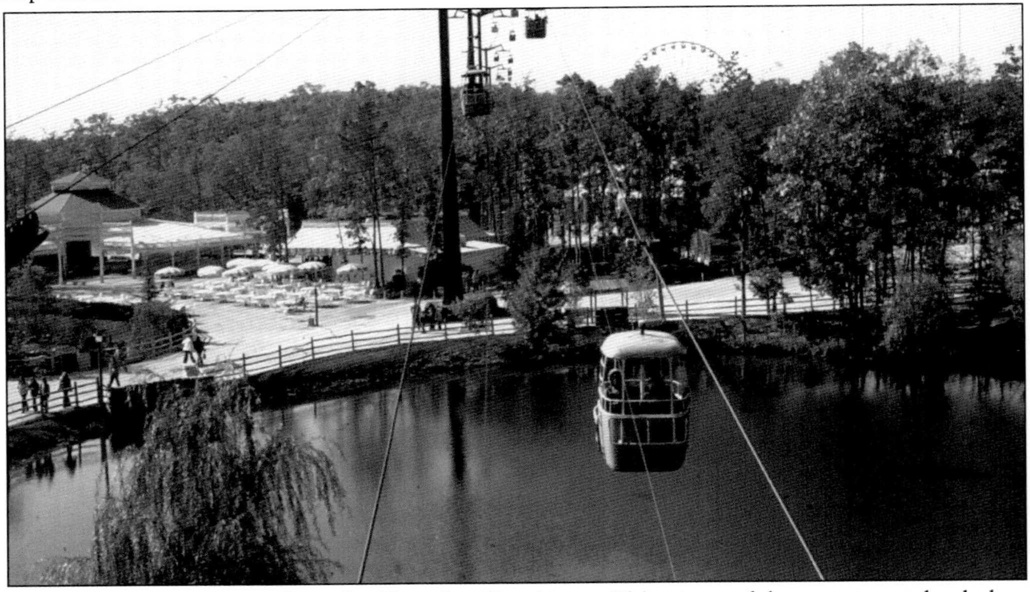

Flying high above the park on the Skyride offered incredible views of the amazing sights below the treetops. This is the view from the catwalk between the Fort's towers, looking toward the Bandstand on the Lake with the Giant Wheel in the distance. Original plans called for the Fort's towers and connecting walkways to be open to the public, but due to safety concerns, they never were.

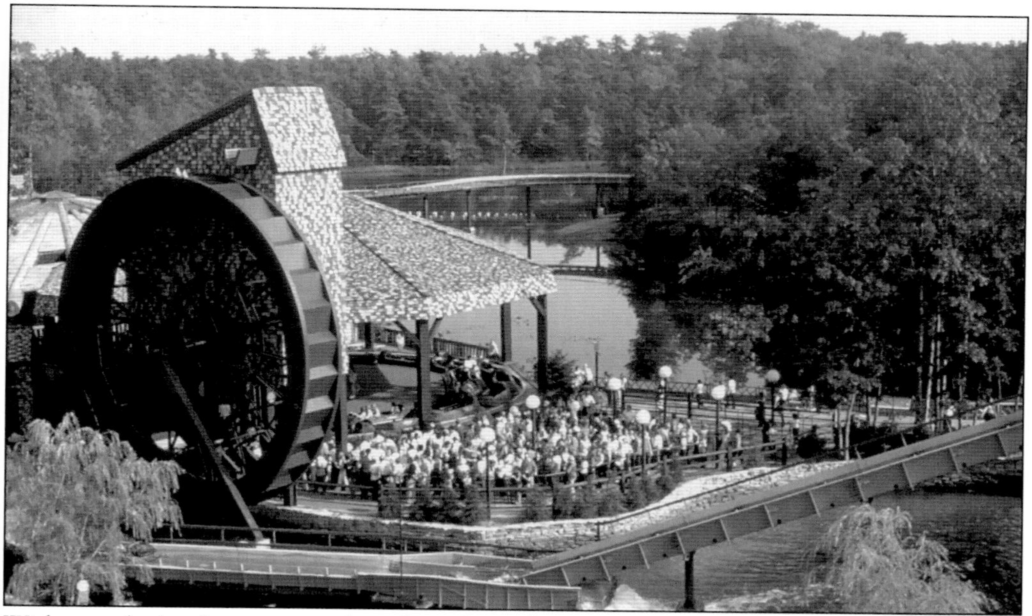

Without a doubt, the most popular ride in the park was the Log Flume, a favorite for guests of all ages. Even with the high capacity of the ride, guests waited in line for hours for the spectacular flume, originally standing in the hot sun until a queue house was added, which offered shade. (GreatAdventureHistory.com collection.)

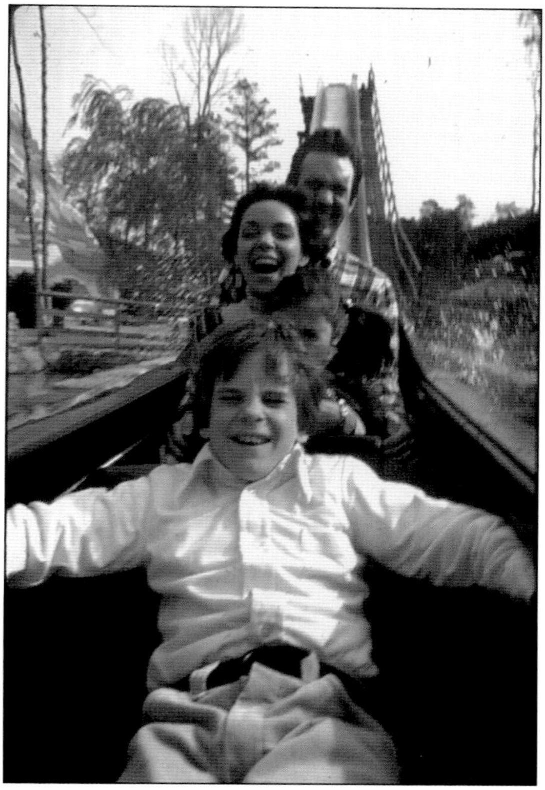

A park original, the Log Flume has been a favorite since the park's first season, allowing entire families to ride together. Another of the park's record holders, the Log Flume was the world's longest flume ride. There was no better way to cool off on a hot summer day than to splash down on this classic.

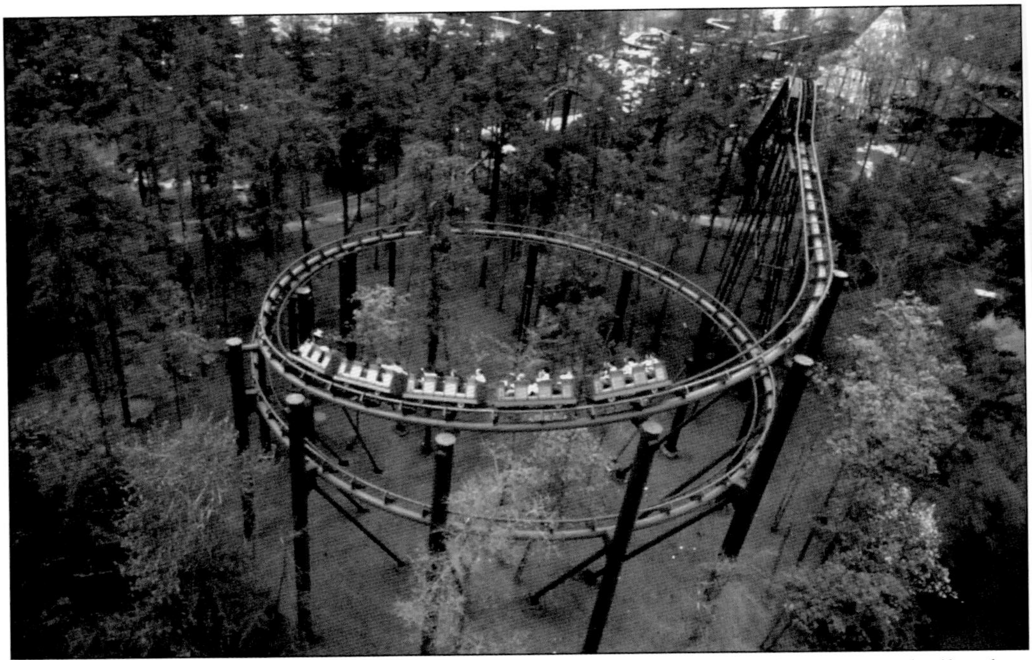

The Runaway Mine Train was the park's largest roller coaster for several seasons and offered an out-of-control ride through the woods and out over the lake. The coaster was part of the initial proposal for the Enchanted Forest, which was incorporated into the final design of the park.

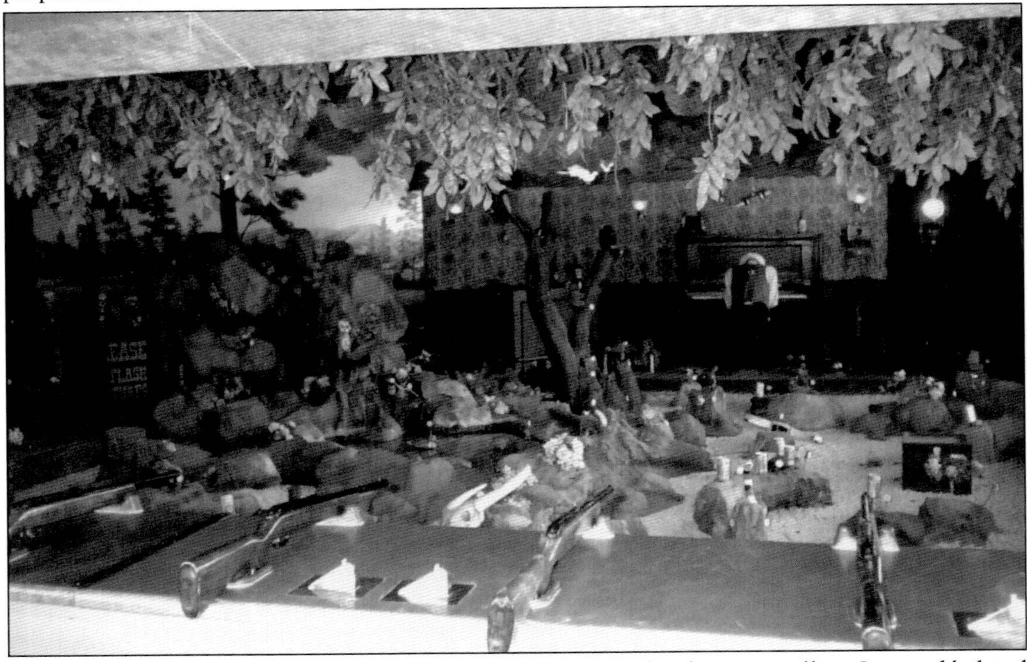

One popular attraction in the park that is long forgotten is the shooting gallery. Located behind Best of the West and under the Log Flume, the shooting gallery was so popular that for the 1976 season the park added the Safari Shooting Gallery as part of the Fun Fair expansion and the Chicago Shootout after that. (GreatAdventureHistory.com collection.)

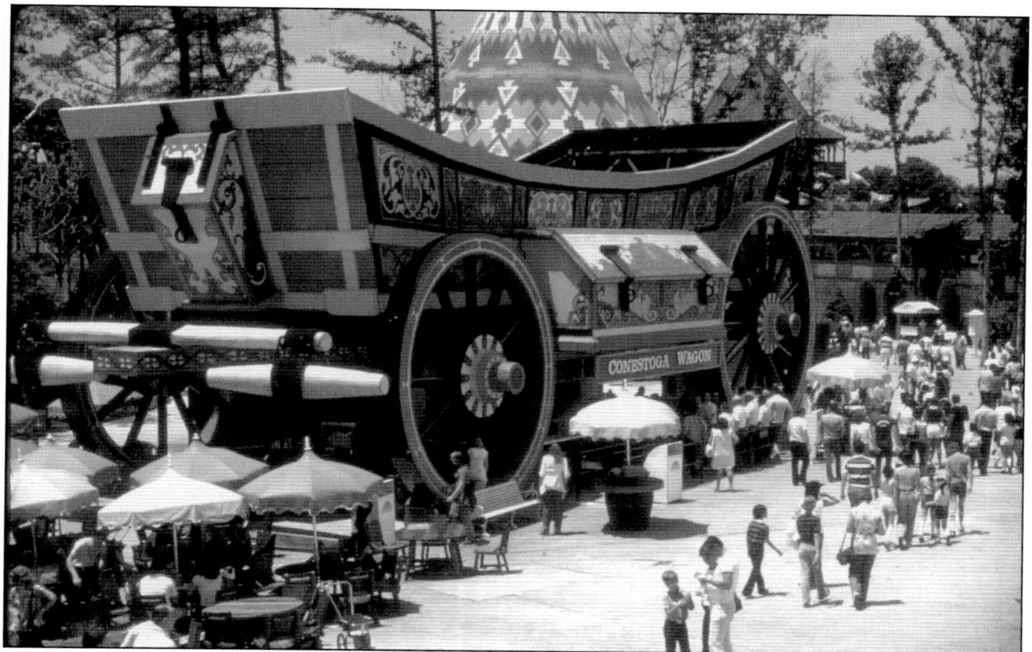

The larger-than-life Conestoga Wagon was a very unique structure in a park full of the spectacular. The restaurant was painted in a very bright and elaborate color scheme and originally included giant hitches for an animal team on the front side and small barrel-shaped tables around it.

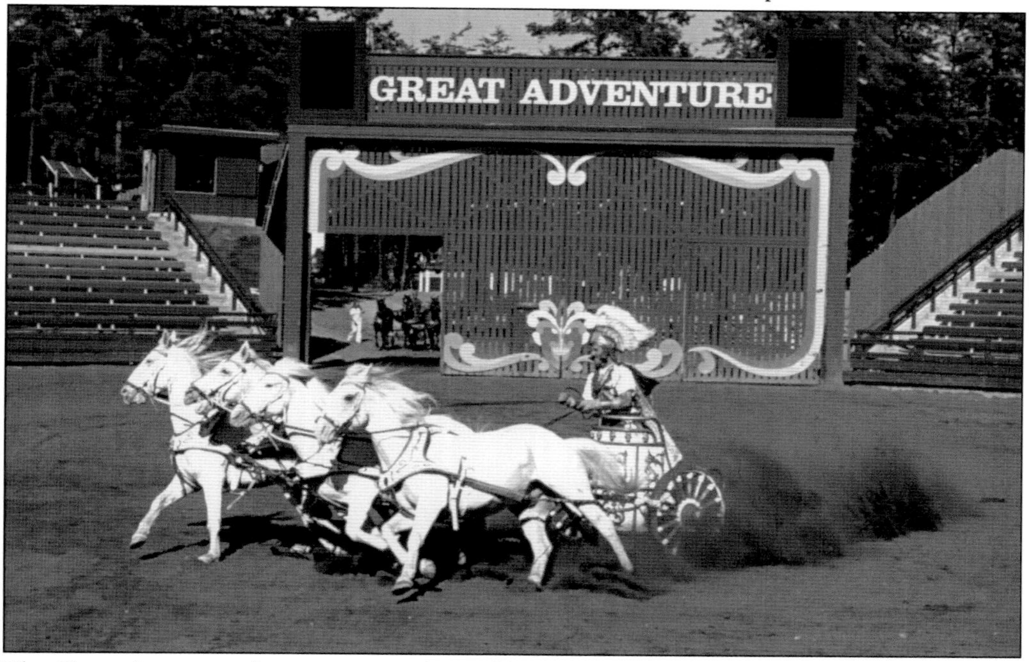

The Great Arena was home to some the park's most unique shows. The first shows included a western rodeo, jousting, chariot racing (seen here), and the Fearless Bauers, a team of aerial daredevils who balanced precariously from the tops of huge sway poles high above the amazed audiences. (GreatAdventureHistory.com collection.)

For the 1975 season, the park made huge expansions to increase ride capacity by 50 percent. The big attraction was a second flume ride called the Moon Flume, which featured even bigger drops. The park's footprint was expanded with an entirely new section of rides called Fun Fair, which would add a group of flat rides including a second Ferris wheel. Also added was the

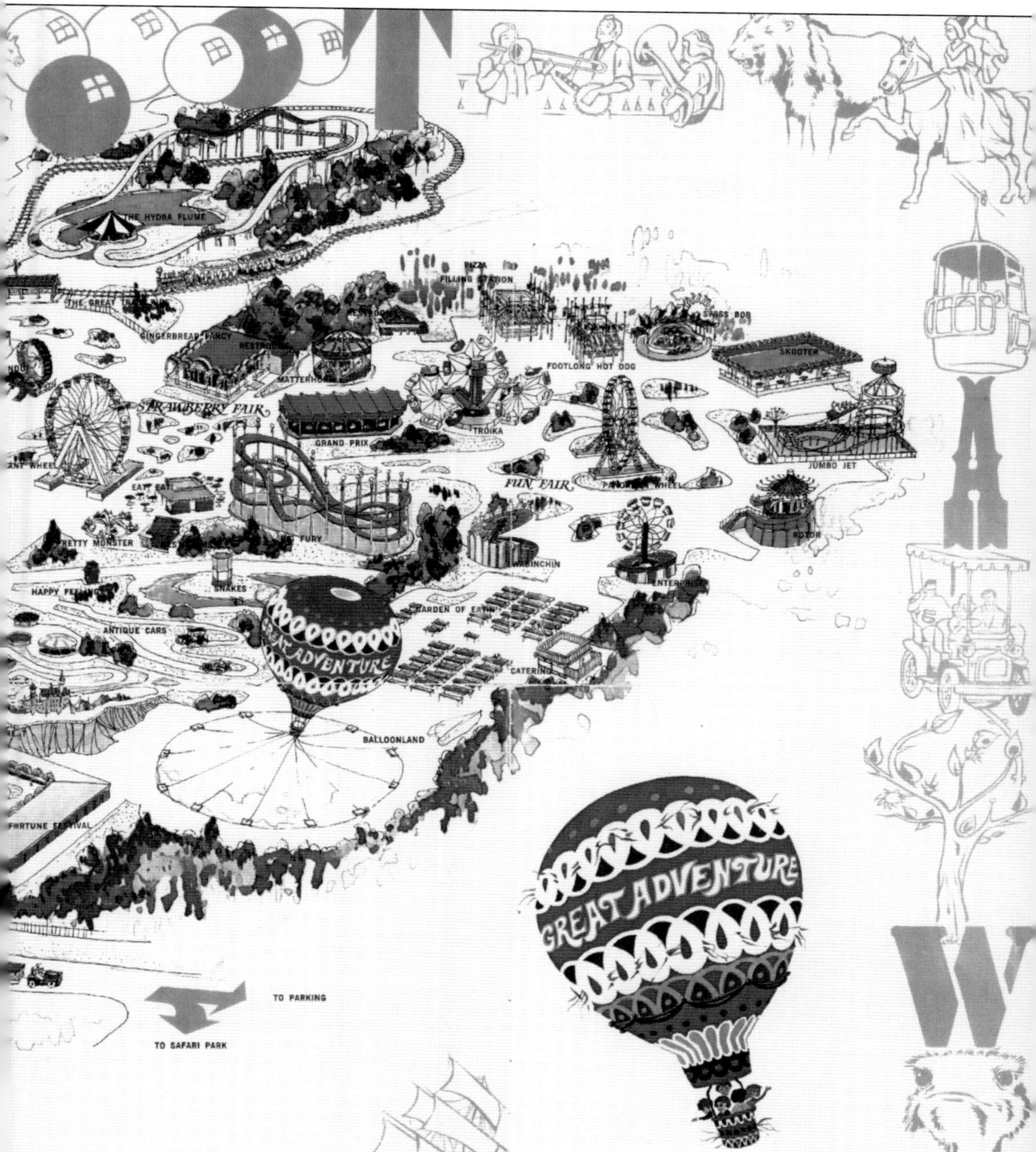

Fortune Festival games area, which had games of skill, including a High Striker bell ringer game that claimed to be the biggest in the world. Other improvements throughout the park included additional restroom facilities, food outlets, and wider and more direct walkways to better accommodate the crowds. (GreatAdventureHistory.com collection.)

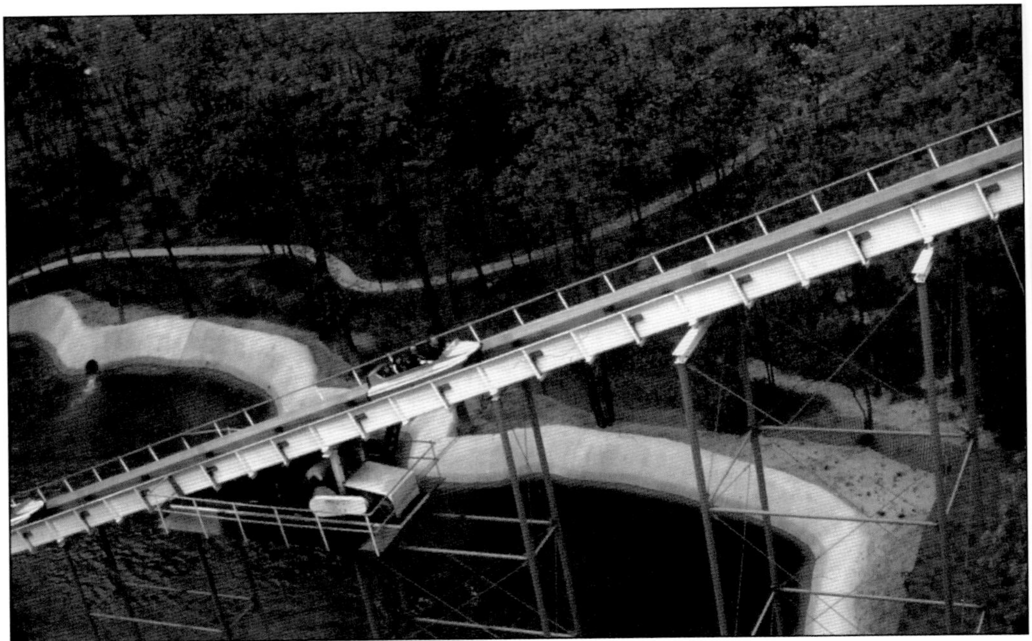

With the unqualified success of the Log Flume, a second, larger flume was added to the other side of the park. The Moon Flume differed from the Log Flume with its sleek boats and dual drop, which featured a bunny hop splashdown. The Moon Flume was built in an area left heavily wooded that it shared with the Great Train Ride.

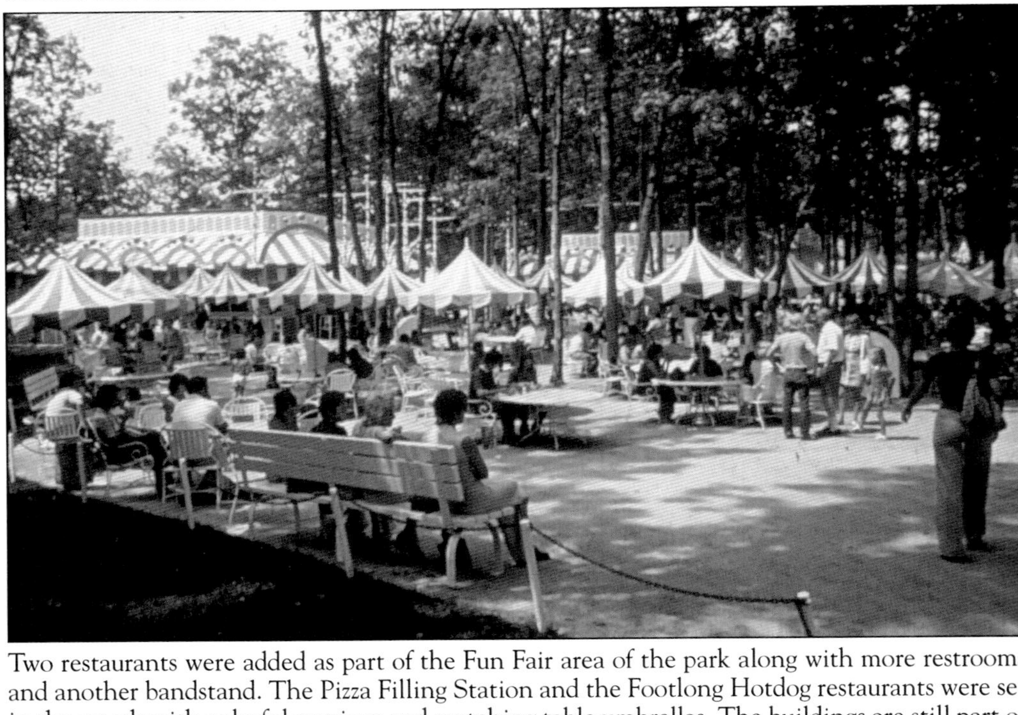

Two restaurants were added as part of the Fun Fair area of the park along with more restrooms and another bandstand. The Pizza Filling Station and the Footlong Hotdog restaurants were set in the woods with colorful awnings and matching table umbrellas. The buildings are still part of the Movietown section today. (GreatAdventureHistory.com collection.)

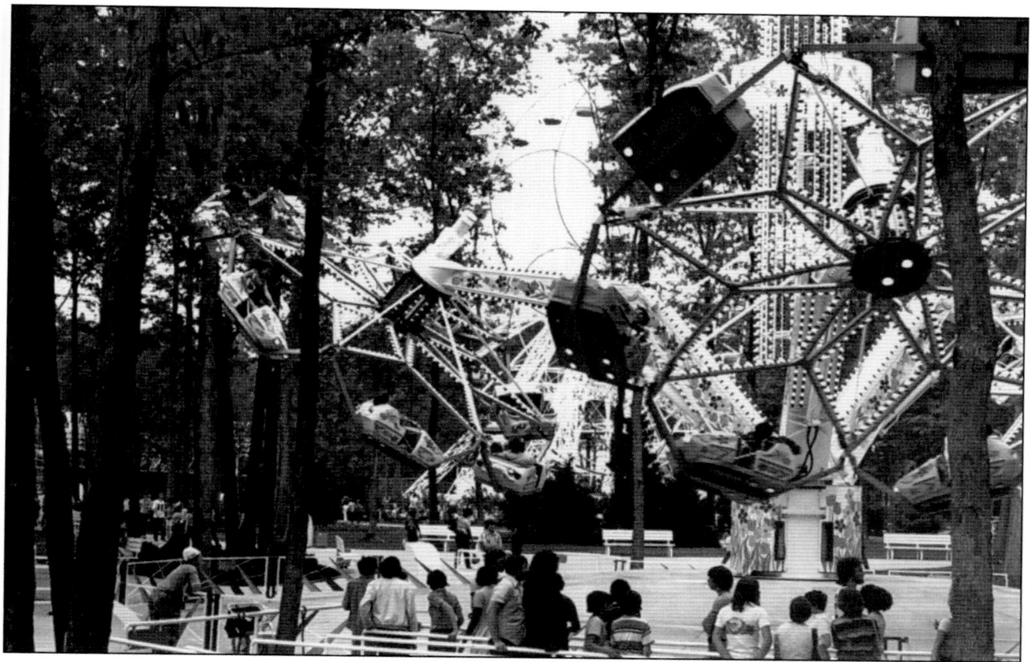

Many of the rides added to the Fun Fair section were leased and were not at the park for very long. One of those rides was the Wild Rider, a troika ride that only stayed for a few seasons. The Wild Rider name was later given to a roller coaster after the troika had been removed in 1978.

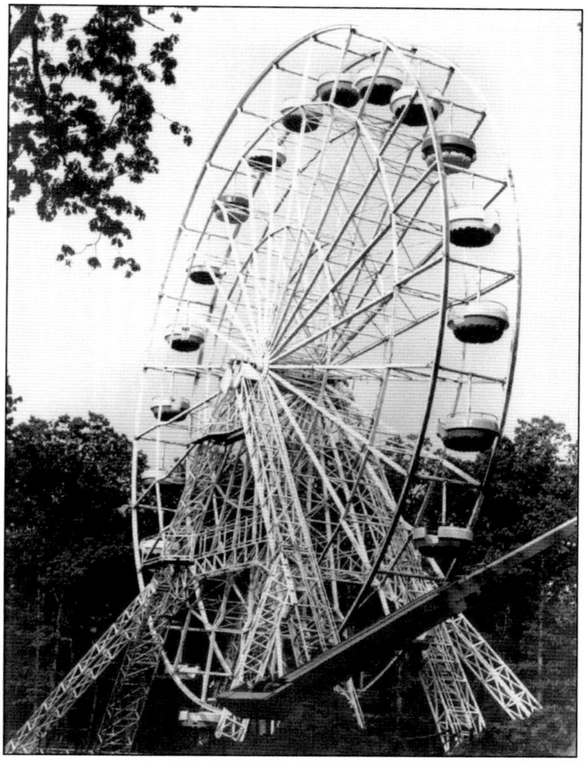

The Panorama Wheel (also known as the Little Wheel) was unique with its delicate canvas roofs and spinning round cars that looked like flowers. The wheel was fitted with lighting in a floral pattern to match the Giant Wheel for a short time. The Panorama Wheel added to the park's ride capacity and helped reduce lines for the Giant Wheel.

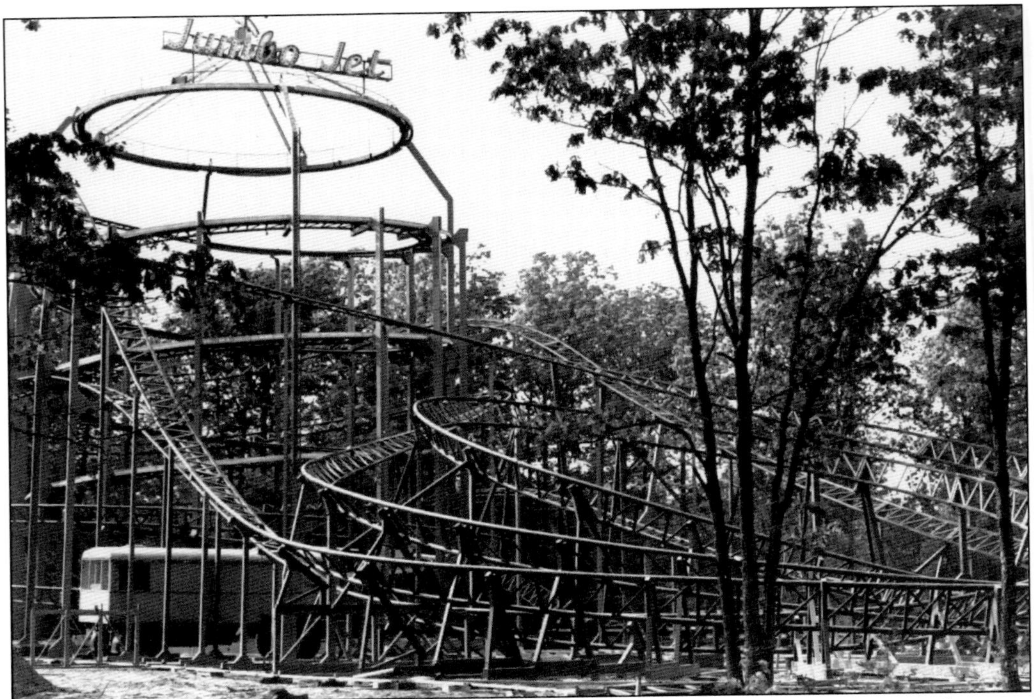

A third roller coaster was added to the park as part of the Fun Fair section in order to offer more coaster thrills. The Jumbo Jet was a portable roller coaster that was fully assembled but never went into operation in the few months it was at the park.

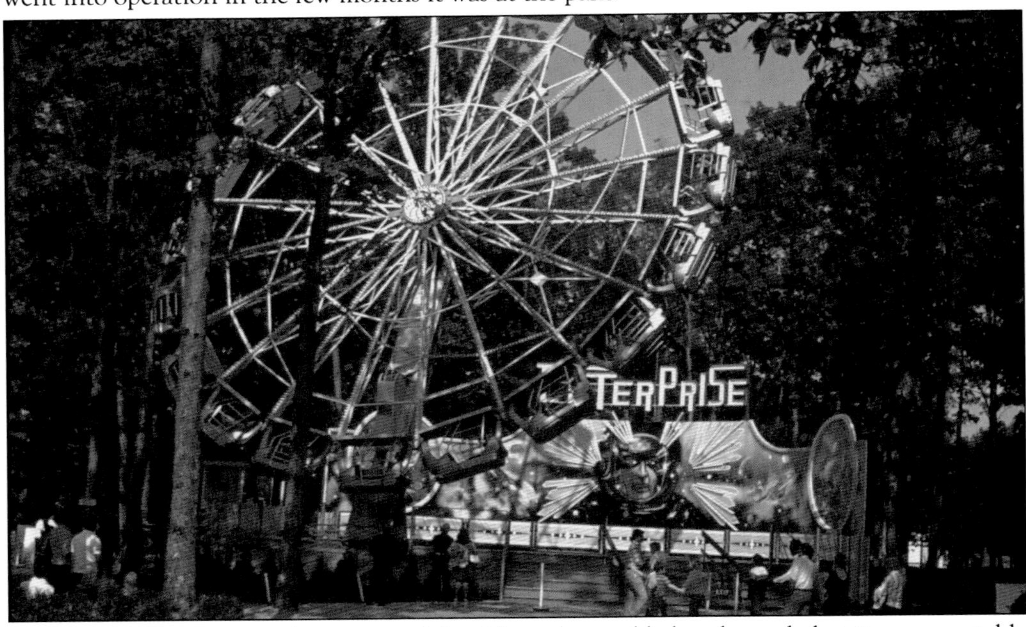

For 1975, an Enterprise ride was part of the ride package added to the park, but it was a portable model (complete with space-age backdrop) that was removed after only two seasons. The Enterprise was popular and led to the park adding a more permanent park-model version of the ride in 1979. (GreatAdventureHistory.com collection.)

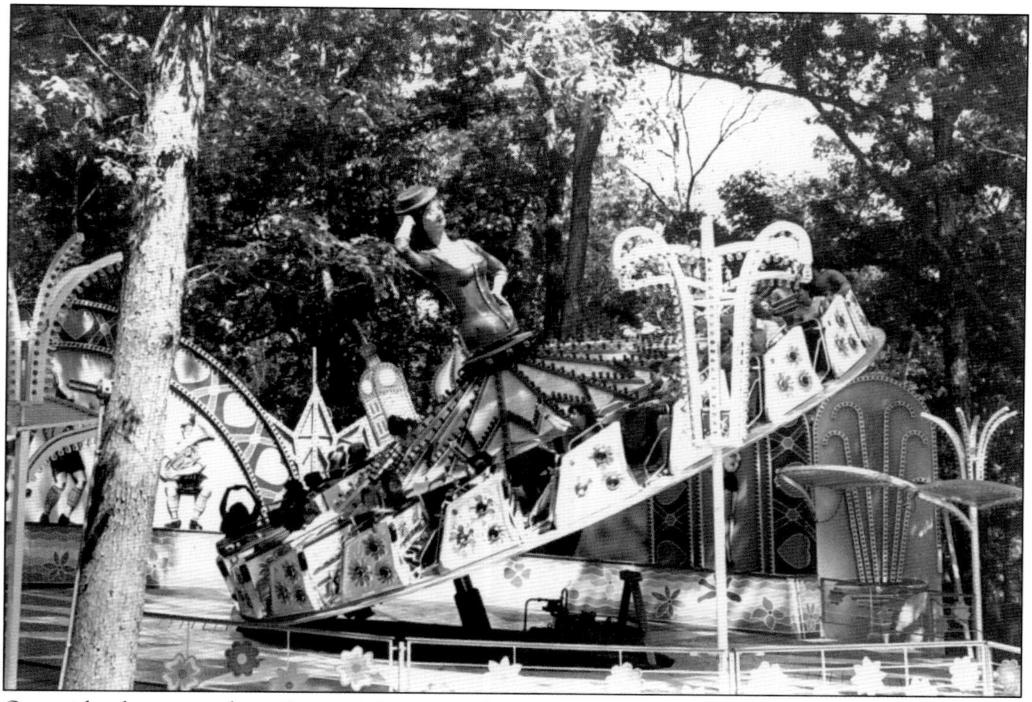

One ride that stayed at Great Adventure for many years was the Schwabinchen ride. The German Hully-Gully model ride featured an elaborate Oktoberfest-style backdrop, featuring famous landmarks of Munich and an elaborate light display. The ride itself was designed to resemble a dancer with her twirling skirt.

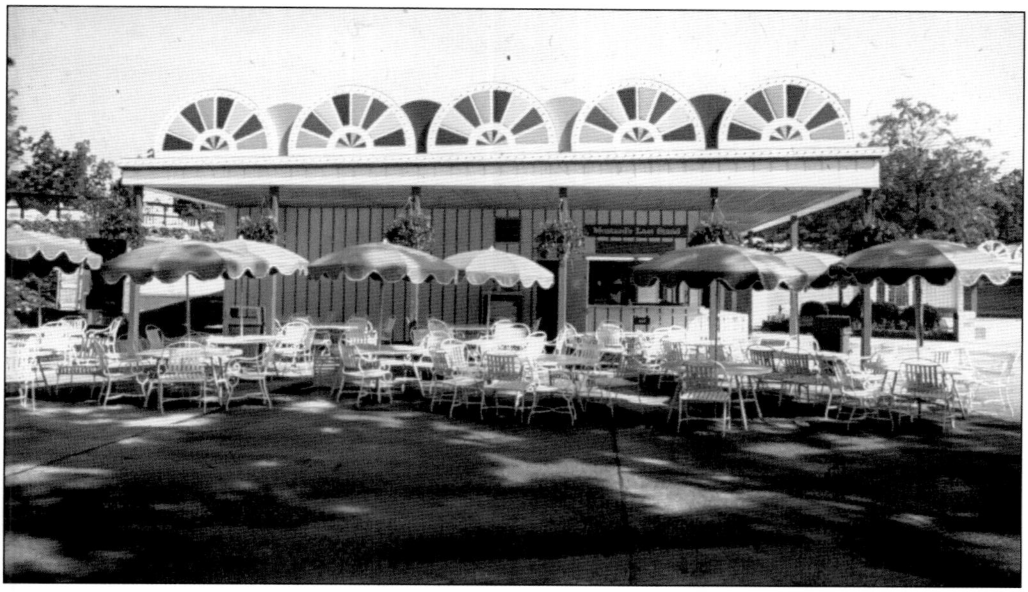

The original Fortune Festival games area was located just off Dream Street, next to the four tent buildings. The U-shaped structure featured games of skill and two additional restaurants, all painted in bright colors with flashing lights along the soffits. Both arcade games and games of skill were part of Fortune Festival and located both indoors and outdoors.

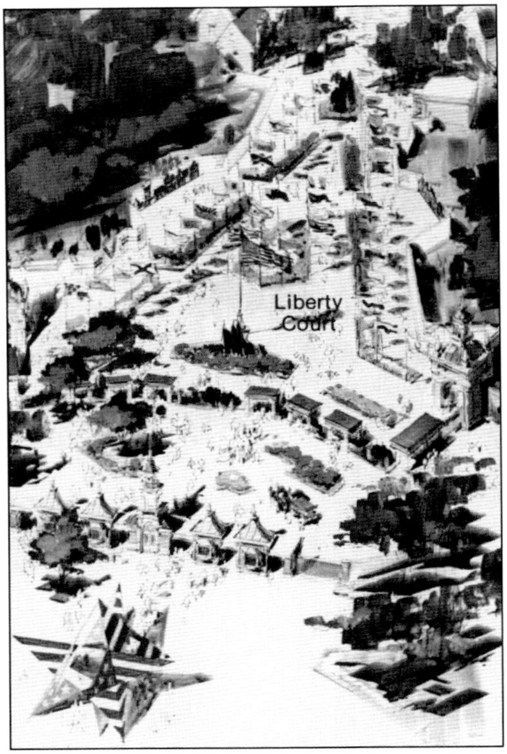

For 1976, the park was reconfigured in a big way, with the entrance moving from the end of Dream Street to the middle of the park near the fountain. Liberty Court was built in the spirit of America's bicentennial, with the new entry buildings designed to look very patriotic. (GreatAdventureHistory.com collection.)

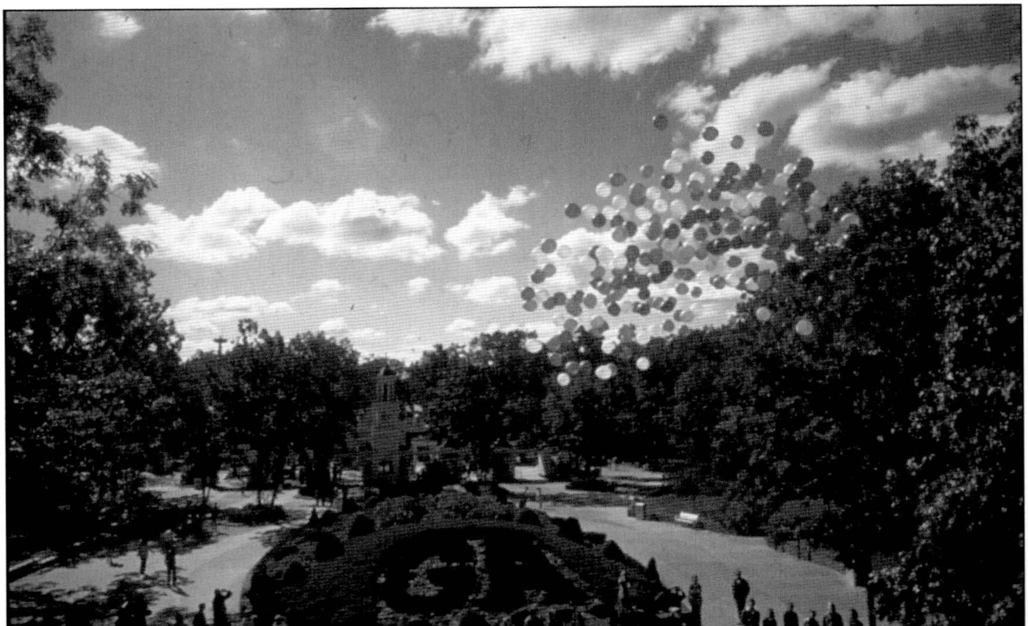

The new entrance area featured a huge topiary "GA" planter in the outer mall area acting as a visual buffer between the park and the parking lot. The expanded entry was 10 times larger than the original and was built at a cost of $500,000. The ticket booths were more substantial, and the permanent gate structures still serve as the park's entrance today.

Inside the gates was the Avenue of the States, which featured flags of all the states lining the walkways. Beautiful landscaping lined the street along with new gift shops, including Red White and Balloon, Declaration of Gifts, Bicentennial Photos, the Jewelry Box, and the GAF Photo Fair.

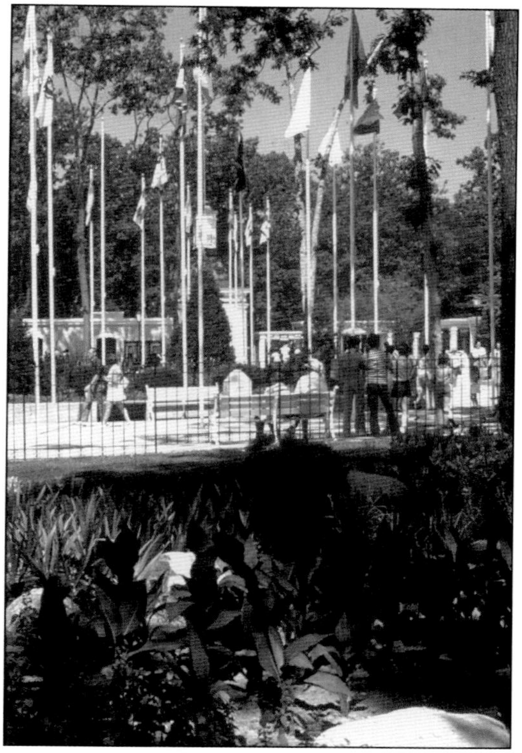

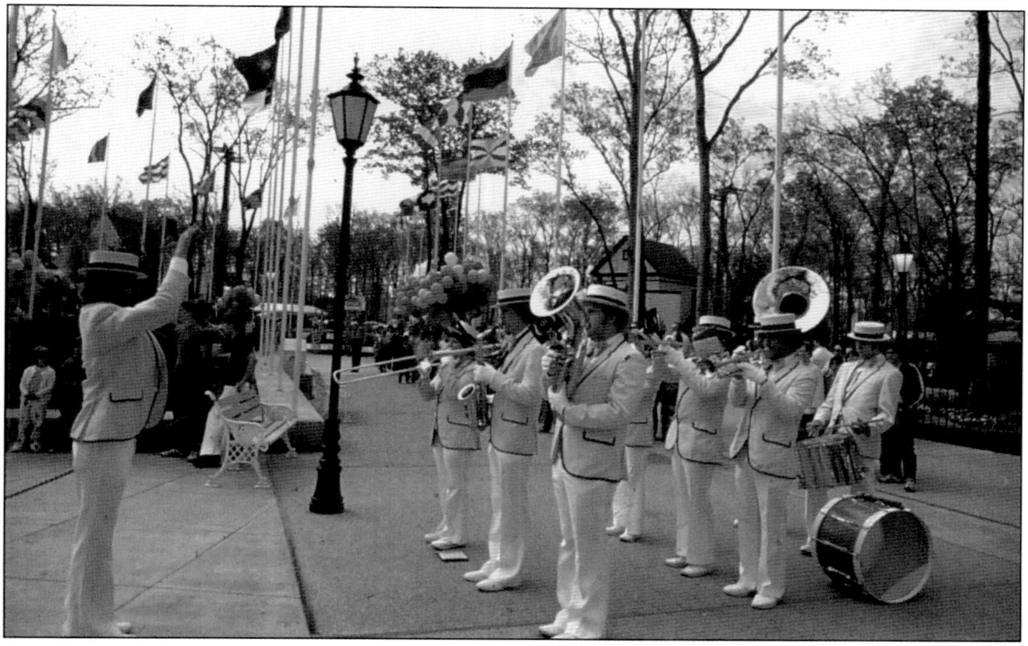

Marching bands have appeared throughout the park and were a regular feature of the Avenue of the States, providing patriotic music to fit the bicentennial-themed section. The Avenue of the States and Liberty Court took over the area that had been home to the Antique Cars for the first two seasons.

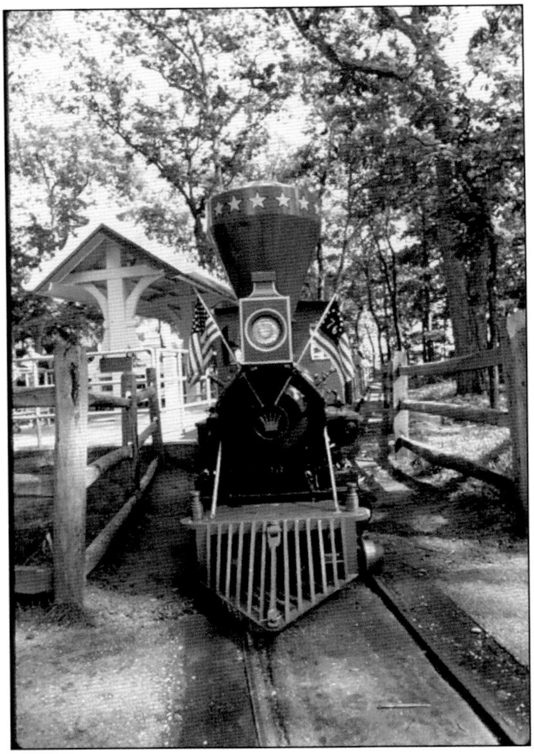

Bicentennial fever was sweeping the nation, and even the Great Train Ride, also known as the Woodland Express, got in on the act with the trains decked out in red, white, and blue and sporting American flags for the 1976 season. This view of the train is from the pedestrian crossing at the Moon Flume entrance with the train waiting for passengers to board at the station.

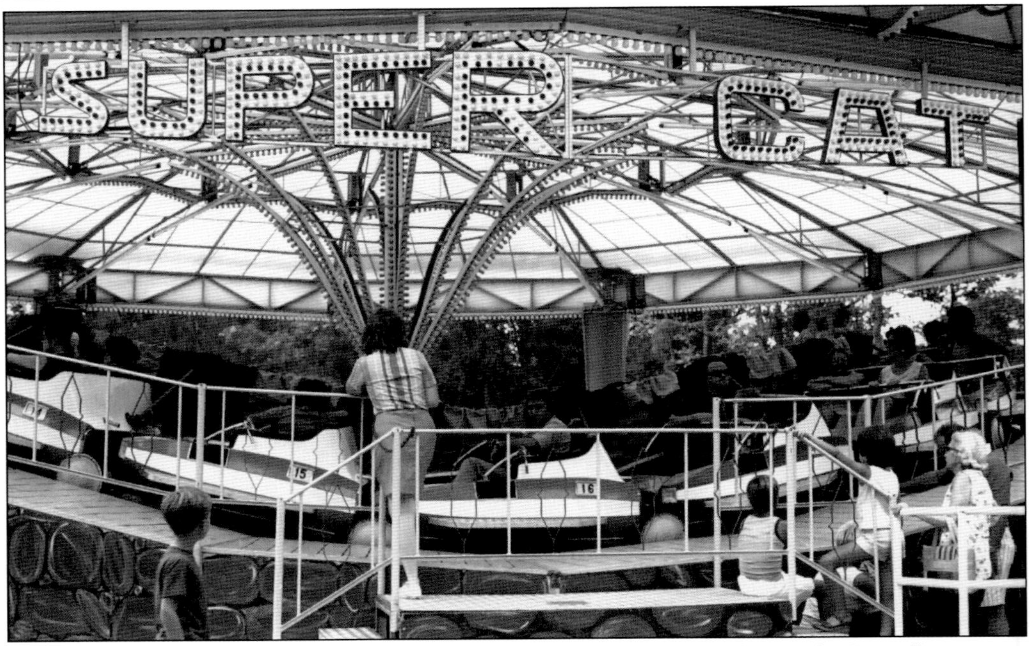

The Super Cat ride came to the park for 1976, taking the place of the Jumbo Jet roller coaster that was added the season before. The ride was unique with its canopy that closed over the cars as they sped around the undulating track. The ride was removed prior to the 1979 season and was replaced with a Tilt-A-Whirl ride.

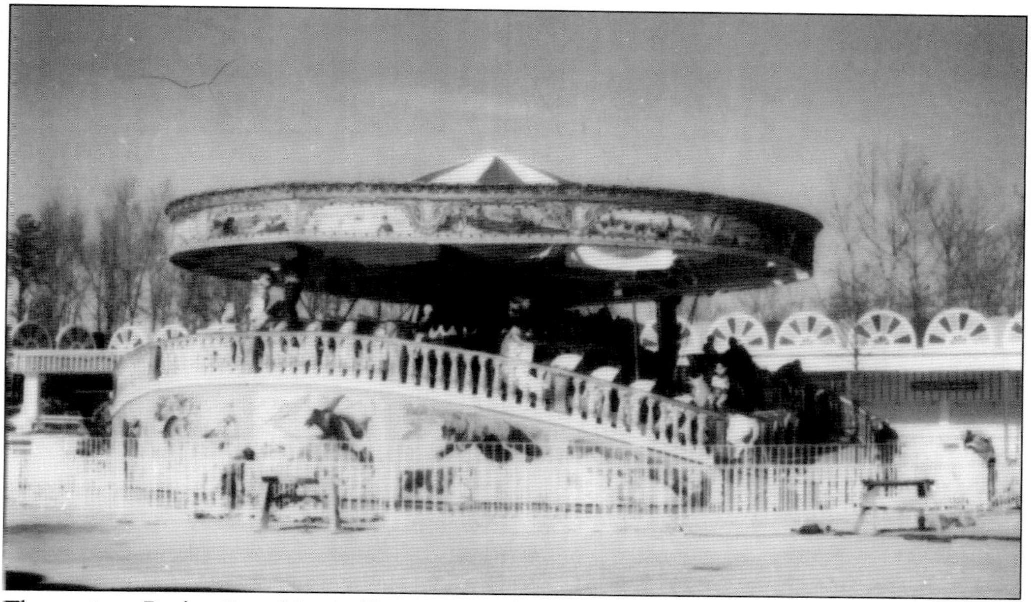

The antique Rodeo Switchback (Spinning Top) Gondola ride was added to the middle of the Fortune Festival games area for 1977. The ride was a sister to the carousel and was restored by the park's maintenance personnel who updated the drive mechanisms from steam to electric. The ride was in the park for a single season before returning to England, where it now operates in a museum.

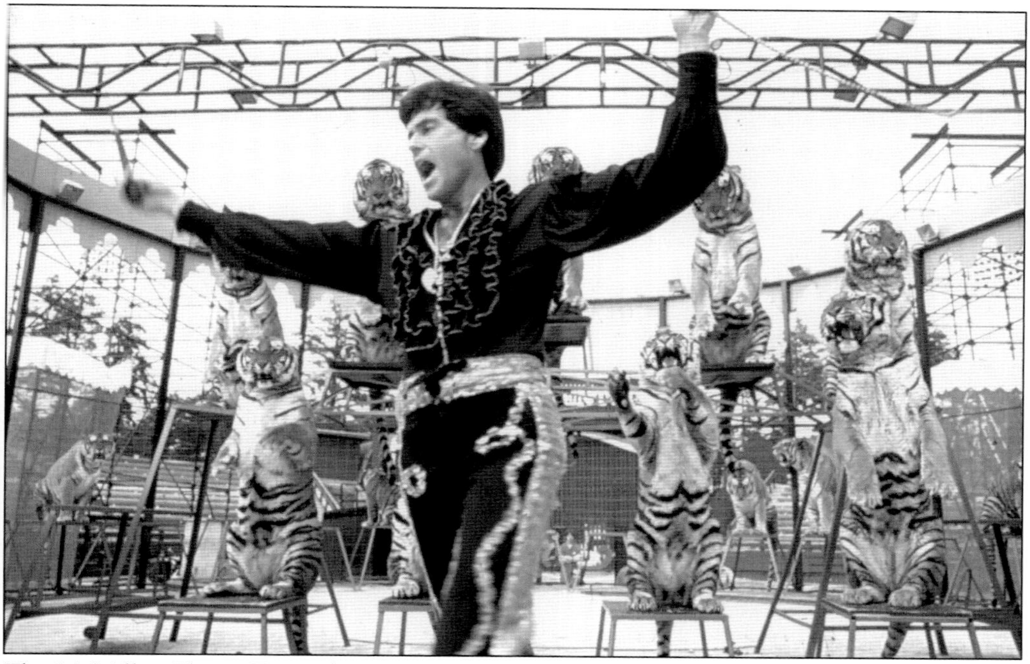

The McMillan Flying Tiger Show was part of the park's entertainment lineup in 1976–1977 and featured a traditional circus-style performing tiger show complete with flashy costumes and death-defying feats. The show was held in the Great Arena, alternating showtimes with a country music revue show that ran throughout the day.

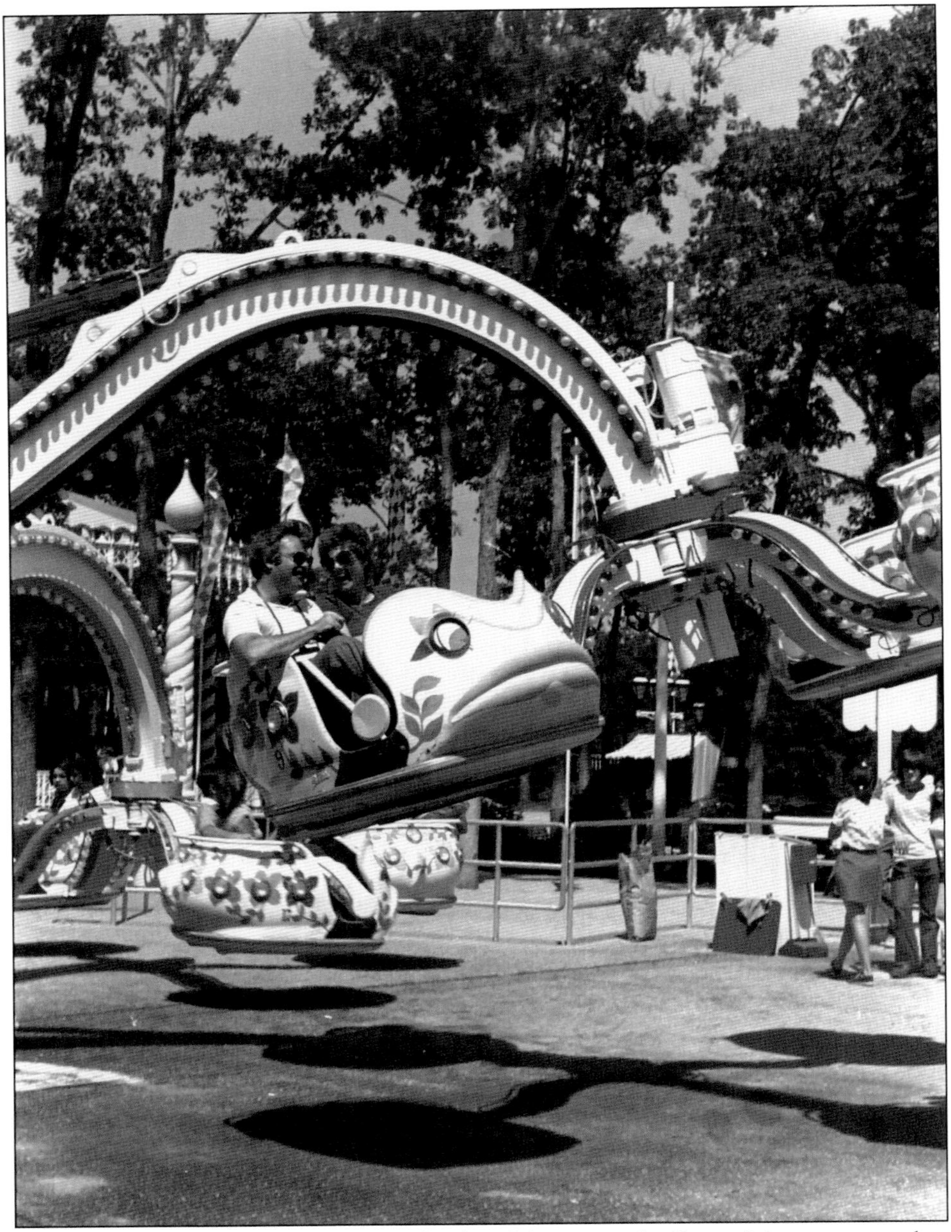

Originally situated between the Giant Wheel and fountain, the Pretty Monster was relocated to a spot next to the Yum Yum Palace, which had originally been home to the Happening, a short-lived show featuring acrobats on trampolines. The ride was renamed the Dream Street Dazzler, and it operated there until 1977 when it was replaced by the more sophisticated Monster Spin ride. When the ride was moved to the new location, the original platform it sat on was removed, and the ride mechanism was sunk below the surrounding pavement, eliminating the need for steps. The Dream Street Dazzler's new location complemented the vibrant colors and fanciful lines of the Yum Yum Palace and nearby carousel. The ride was relocated as part of construction of the neighboring new centrally located front gate and expansion of the Dream Street walkways for the 1976 season.

Three

IT'S A WHOLE NEW ADVENTURE

After successfully building and operating three brand-new theme parks in the 1960s and early 1970s, Six Flags Corporation began expanding by purchasing parks across the country. One of the first of these acquisitions was Great Adventure, which was purchased during the 1977 season. Six Flags brought its expertise in blending family fun and entertainment with state-of-the-art thrill rides to make the park a success.

Now officially known as Six Flags Great Adventure, the expansion of the park accelerated with new attractions coming each season, including new rides, new shows, and of course, bigger and faster roller coasters. Each season the park added something unique and exciting that was state of the art at the time. In keeping with the original spirit of the park, some of the additions were record holders, including the tallest, fastest looping roller coaster and the tallest amusement ride in the United States.

Since the first Six Flags park opened in 1961, the company has worked with ride manufacturers to create exciting new attractions for all its parks, including the first log flume ride, the first river rapids ride, and many innovations in roller coaster technology. Six Flags Great Adventure benefitted from these innovations, receiving many of the first-of-their-kind rides. Some of the rides were incredible successes that still thrill riders to this day, while others lost their appeal as the novelty wore off and were removed and replaced with bigger and better attractions.

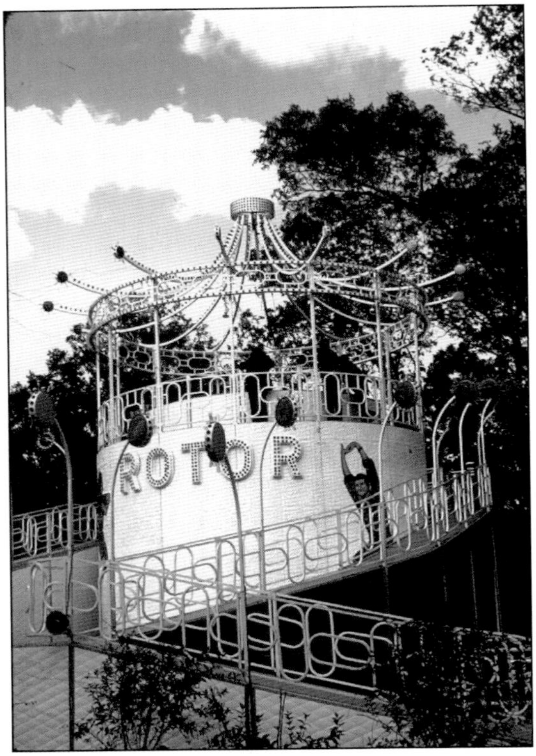

A longtime favorite ride was the Rotor, which was relocated several times in the decades it was in the park. Designed as a portable ride, it was originally located next to the Americana Music Hall before being moved to the lakefront in order to make way for Freefall in 1983.

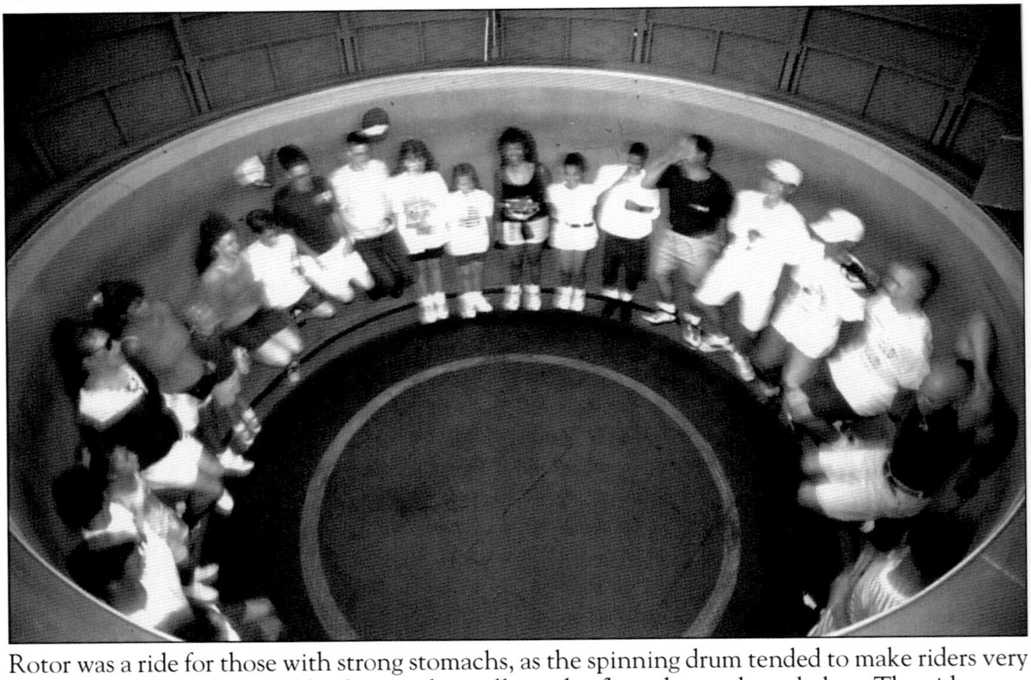

Rotor was a ride for those with strong stomachs, as the spinning drum tended to make riders very dizzy. Centrifugal force held riders to the walls as the floor dropped out below. The ride even offered a viewing platform so non-riders could watch their brave friends and family members from above.

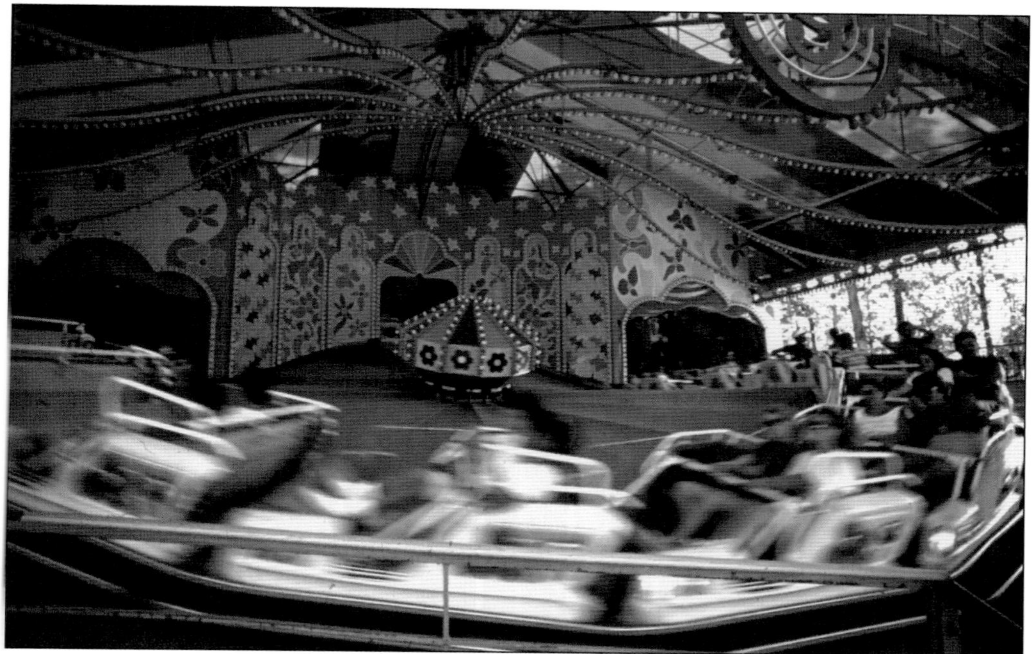

Another carnival-style ride introduced to the park in 1976 was the Musik Express, which was added as part of an expansion into what had been the Happy Feeling petting zoo. The ride usually featured the hit music of the day, generally chosen by the park's teenage ride operators.

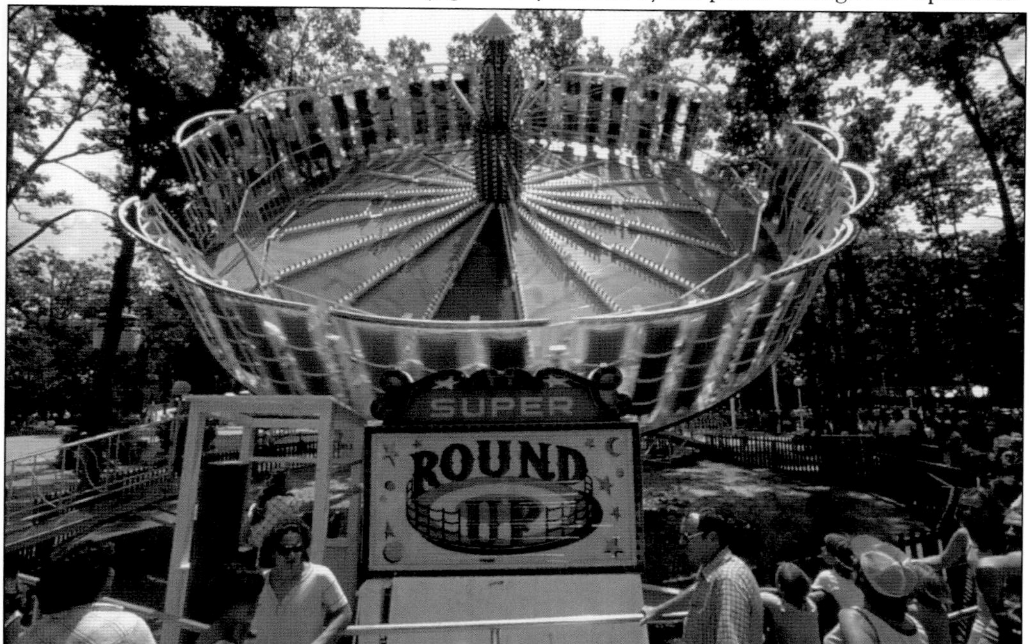

One of the park's original rides (and always a popular one) was the Super Round Up. It was one of the many spinning rides that tested riders' courage and stomachs. The ride stood for many years in the same location between the Gingerbread Fancy restaurant and the Dream Street Skyride station.

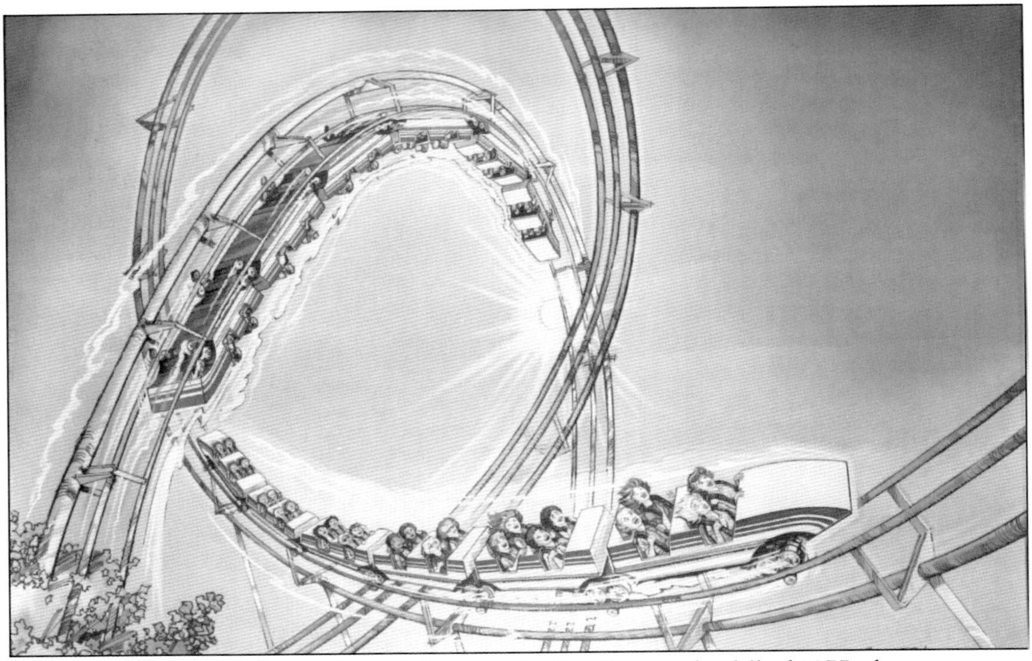

Soon after the acquisition of Great Adventure by Six Flags in the fall of 1977, the new parent company began adding thrills with the addition of Lightnin' Loops, which were the world's first twin interlocking loop roller coasters. The concept art shown here is an artist's fanciful vision of the ride prior to construction. The ride was designed by the Arrow Dynamics Company of Mountain View, California.

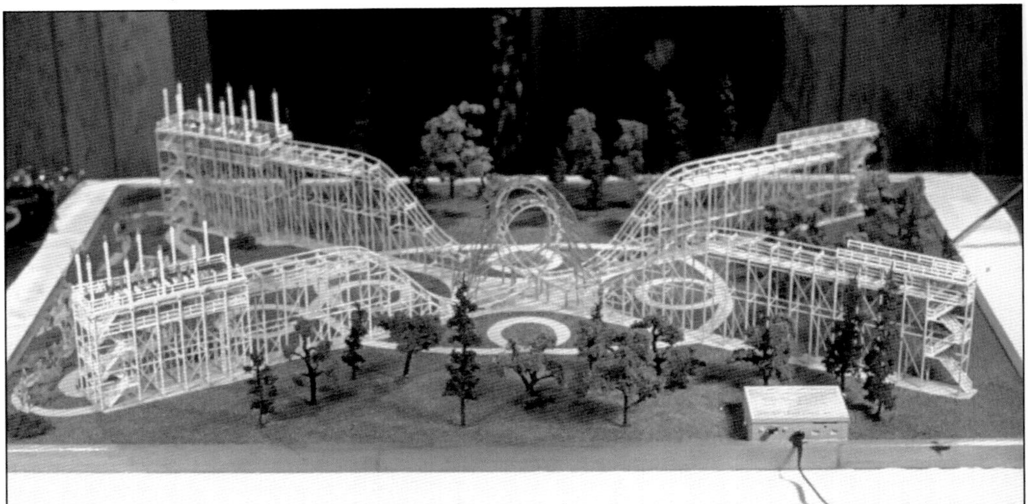

An elaborate model of Lightnin' Loops was constructed, giving a more accurate view of what the finished ride would look like. The interlocking loops were such a unique feature, and since most people had never been on a looping roller coaster at the time, it doubled the excitement and anticipation.

The steel Lightnin' Loops coasters became Six Flags Great Adventure's signature ride for many seasons until bigger and better full circuit roller coasters overshadowed it. For most teenagers in the New York/New Jersey/Philadelphia metropolitan area, getting up the courage to conquer Lightnin' Loops was both a rite of passage and a badge of honor.

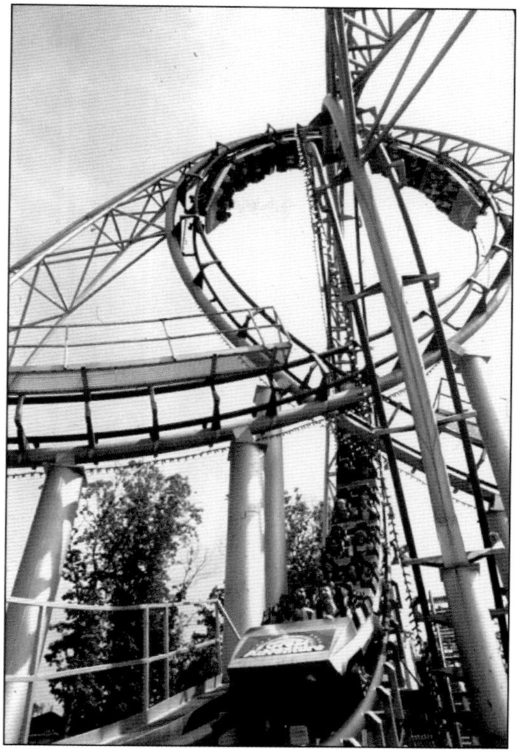

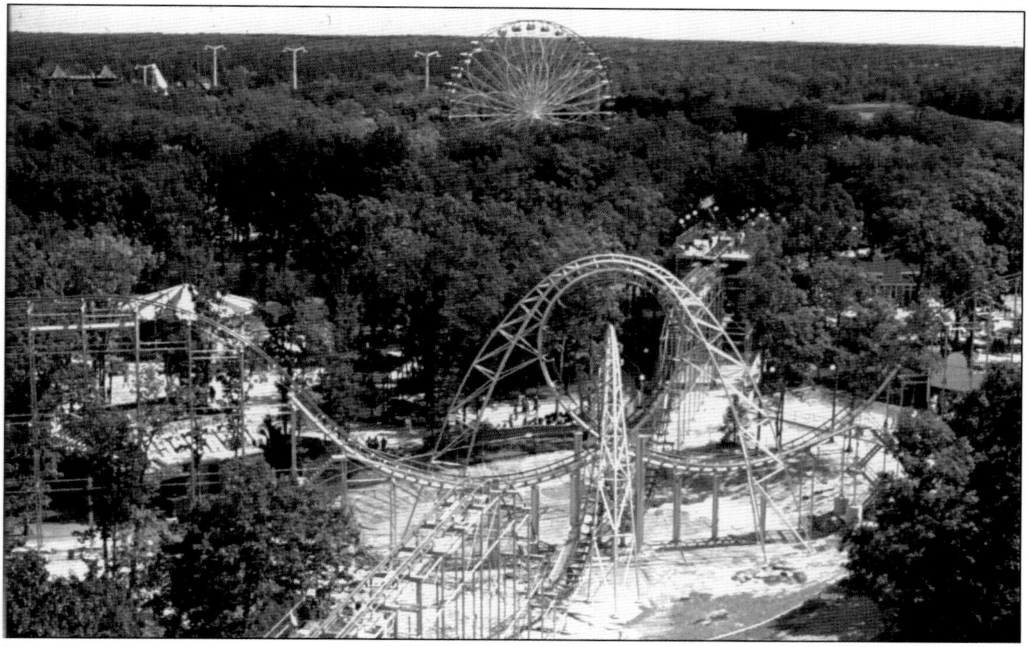

The unique Lightnin' Loops ride was actually two separate and independent "shuttle loop" roller coasters, launching from raised platforms, diving into the loops, and then launching backward through the loop and back to where it started. The launch of the trains shook the towers and the stairs up to the station platform, further testing the nerves of riders.

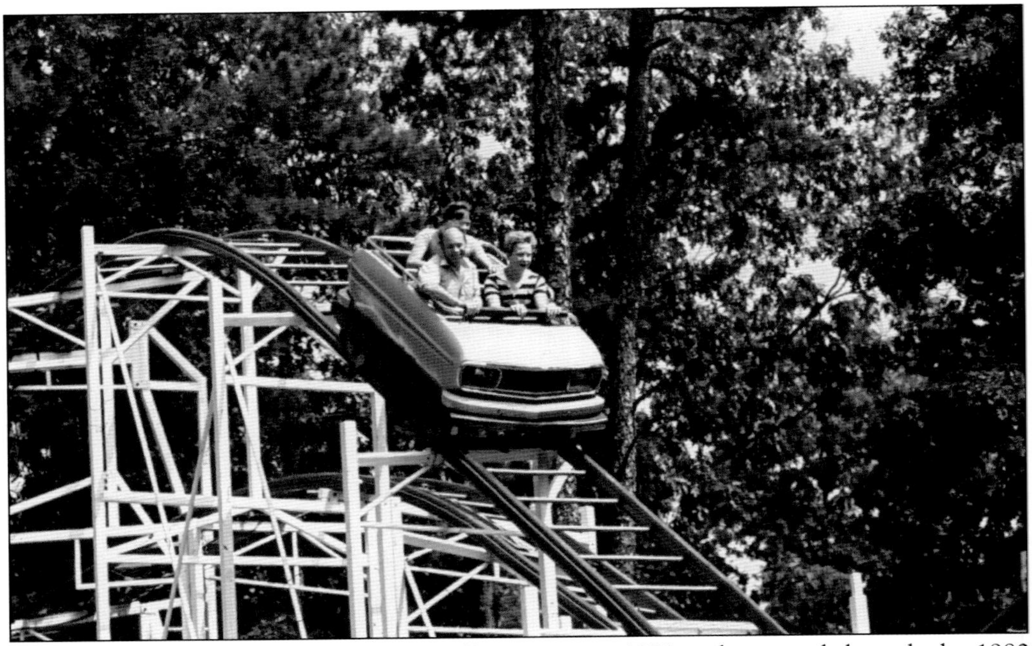

The Wild Rider replaced the Big Fury roller coaster in 1978 and operated through the 1980 season, being closed for the 1981 season and removed before 1982. Wild Rider was very similar to the Big Fury it replaced, with single cars on a wild mouse–type roller coaster track.

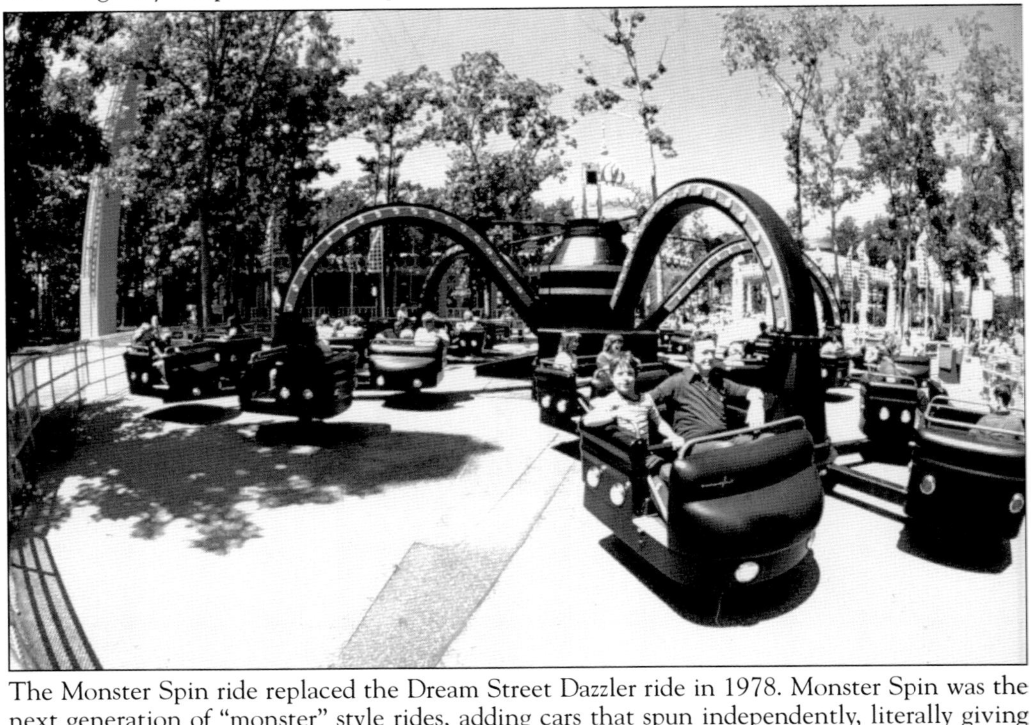

The Monster Spin ride replaced the Dream Street Dazzler ride in 1978. Monster Spin was the next generation of "monster" style rides, adding cars that spun independently, literally giving the ride experience a new spin. The stark, black and gold ride was a sharp contrast to the white and bright Dream Street Dazzler.

For 1979, a new Haunted Castle walk-through attraction and an Enterprise ride were added to the park between the fountain and the Musik Express. The Enterprise was a favorite for many young couples with its seating arrangement of one rider sitting between the legs of the other, offering a chance to get close. The ride was considered state of the art in thrills when it was added.

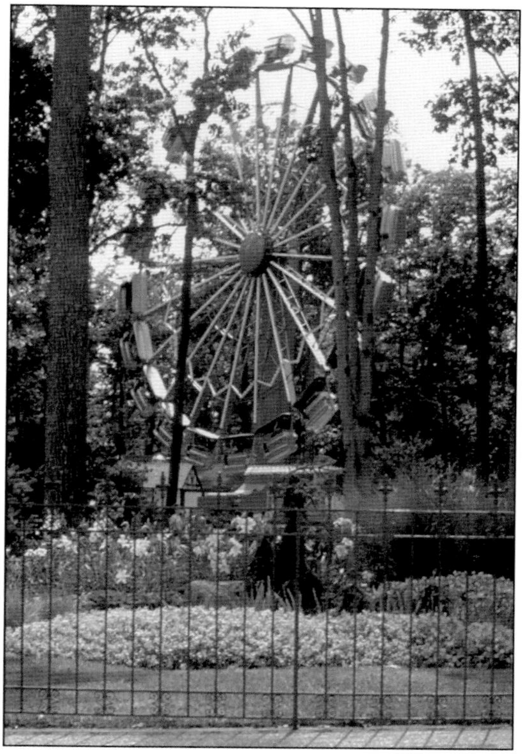

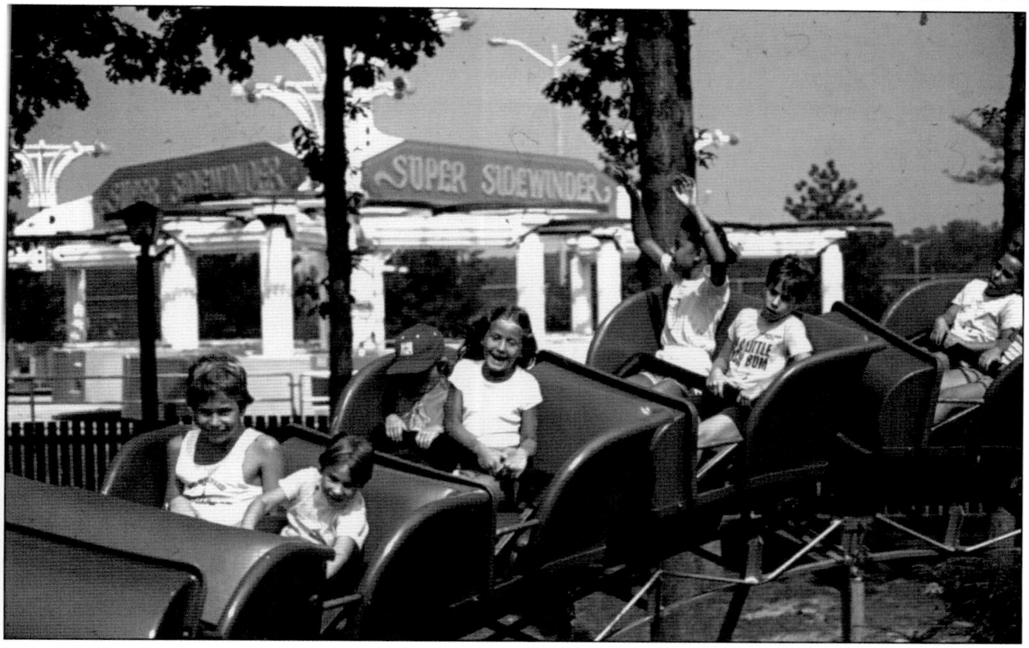

The Kiddie Kingdom section of the park featured this small roller coaster, originally known as the Screamer and later called Lil' Thunder. Just behind it was one of the most unique rides the park ever had, a prototype spinning ride called the Super Sidewinder, which was a huge Scrambler-type ride that twirled 144 riders at a time.

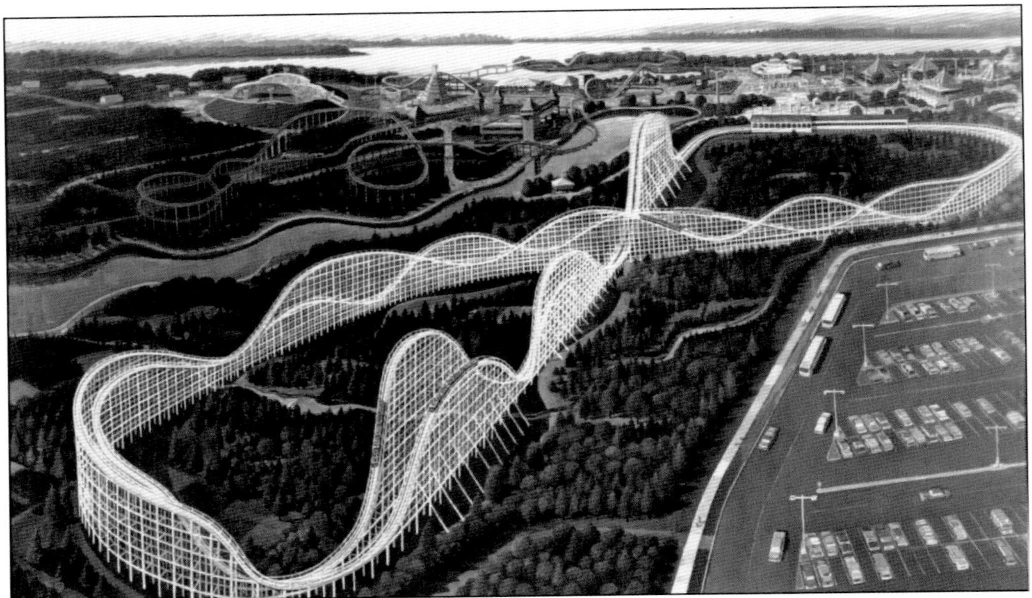

The park's 1979 season saw the addition of what was considered a huge coaster at the time, Rolling Thunder. The 96-foot-tall ride with a top speed of 56 miles per hour was constructed of 850,000 board feet of Douglas fir. Added as part of the entirely new Hernando's Hideaway southwestern-themed section, Rolling Thunder would be the biggest coaster in the park for 10 years.

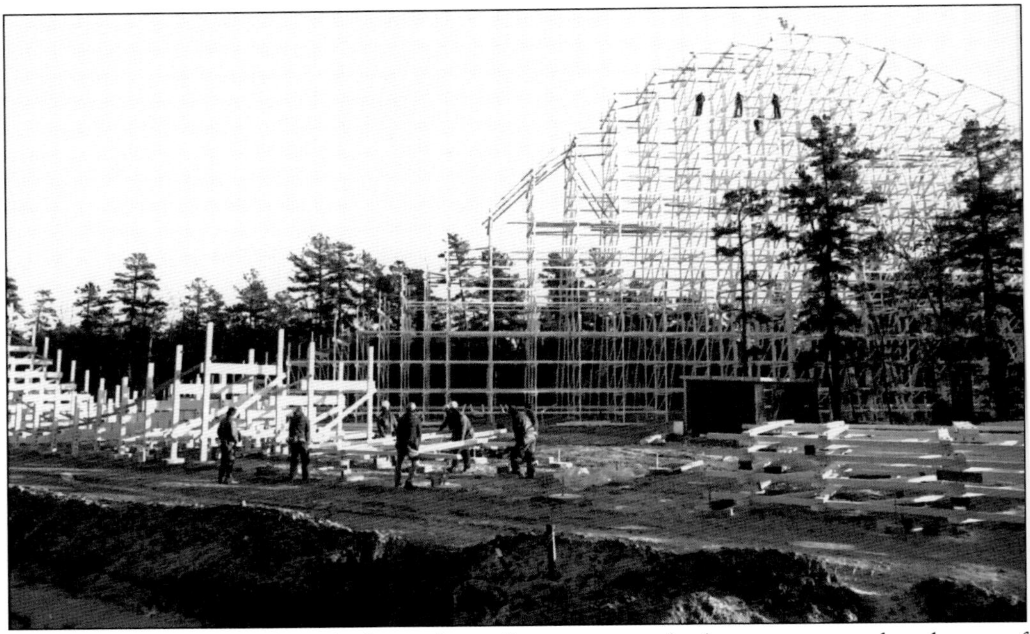

Construction of the dual-tracked, wooden roller coaster took almost a year and took part of the park's original entrance plaza and parking lot. The huge wooden structure was built over the 1978–1979 off-season and required dozens of carpenters building everything by hand with a total ride cost of more than $5 million.

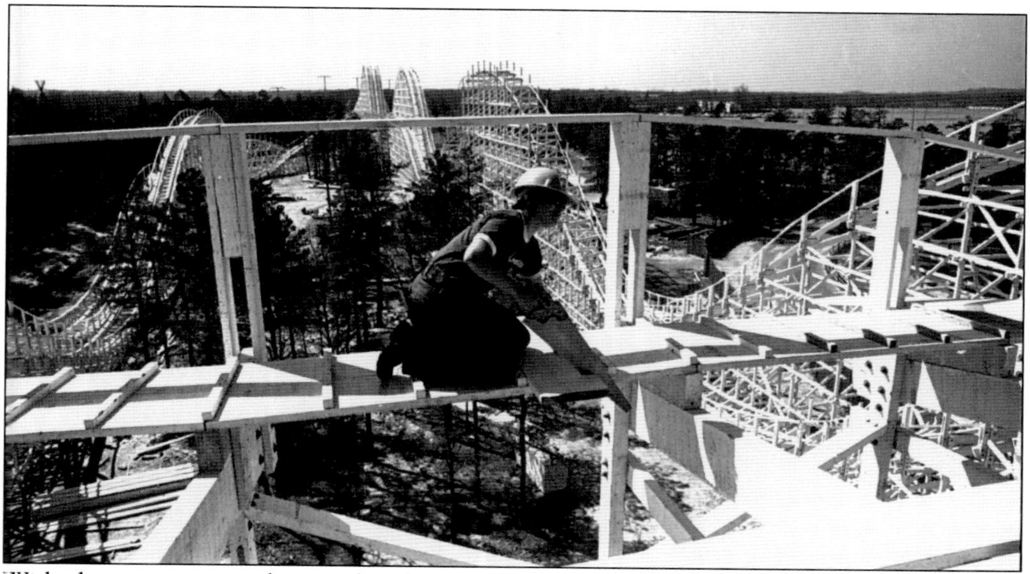

With the structure nearly complete behind him, this worker cuts a board for installation in the turnaround section of the 3,200-foot-long coaster. Cordless power tools were not available at the time, so it took a lot of work with handsaws and hammers to build a wooden structure like this.

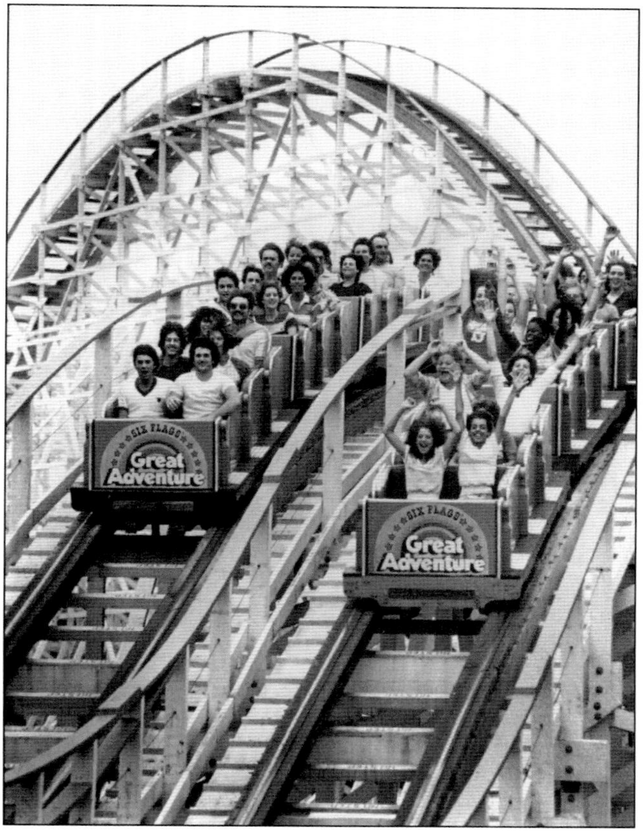

The claim to fame of Rolling Thunder was the fact that the trains raced one another throughout the course of the ride. The unique tracks meant the trains would pass each other several times before racing side-by-side back into the station. For 1984, one side of Rolling Thunder had the trains run backward to celebrate 100 years of roller coasters.

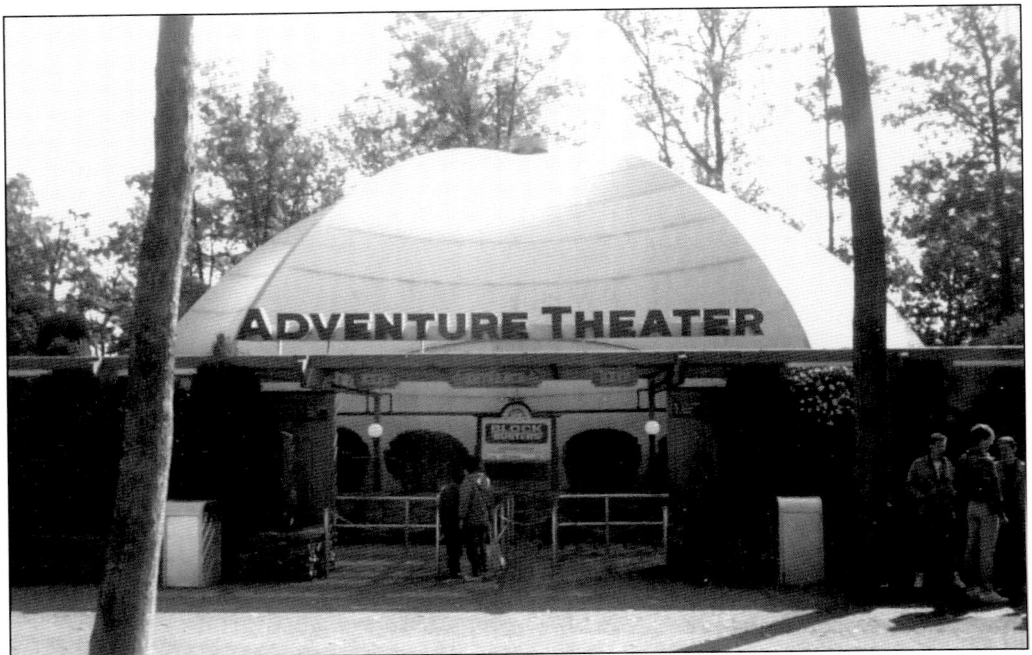

For the 1980 season, a new show venue was added with the Adventure Theater and its 70-millimeter action films were projected onto a 180-degree dome. The theater along with the adjoining Buccaneer ride took the place of the Grand Prix go-karts, which had occupied the site from 1976 until 1979. (GreatAdventureHistory.com collection.)

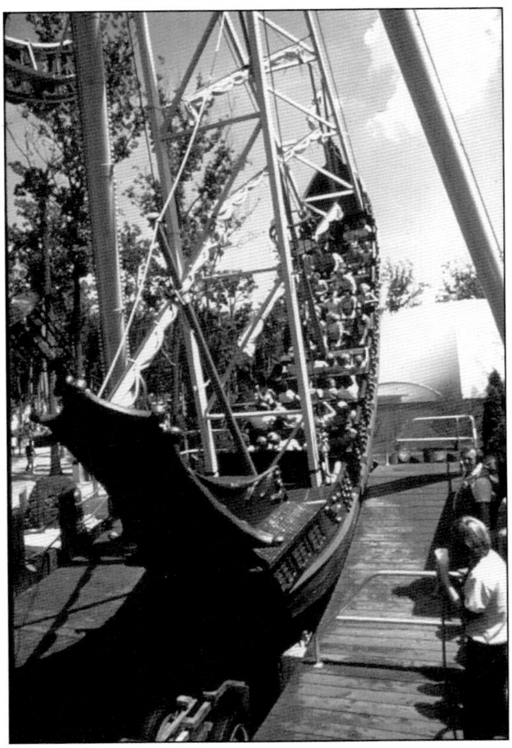

The Buccaneer was one of the first "swinging ship" style rides in the United States, and although considered tame by today's standards, it was a state-of-the-art thrill ride at the time. Guests waited in long lines to try the new ride, with some waiting extra time for the end rows of seats, which swung the highest.

For many years, Delta Airlines sponsored the Skyride, with the cars painted white and bearing the Delta logo on their doors. On the bottom of the cars were advertisements for the airline, which could be seen by guests walking below. The cars featured several advertisements, each mentioning different cities Delta served.

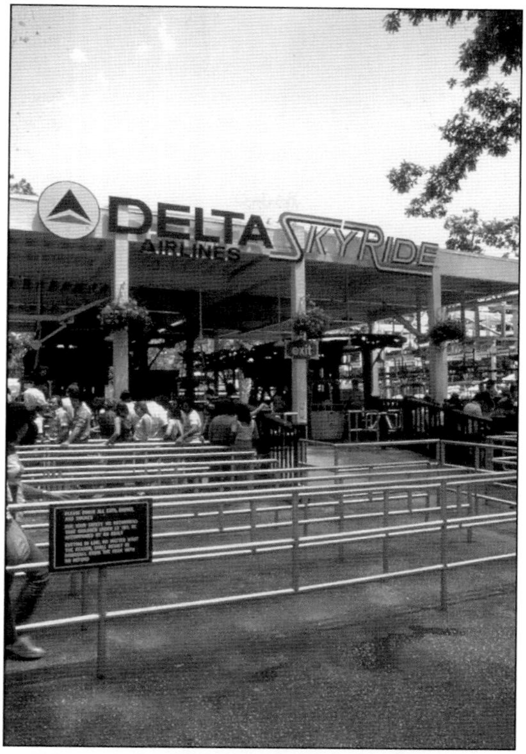

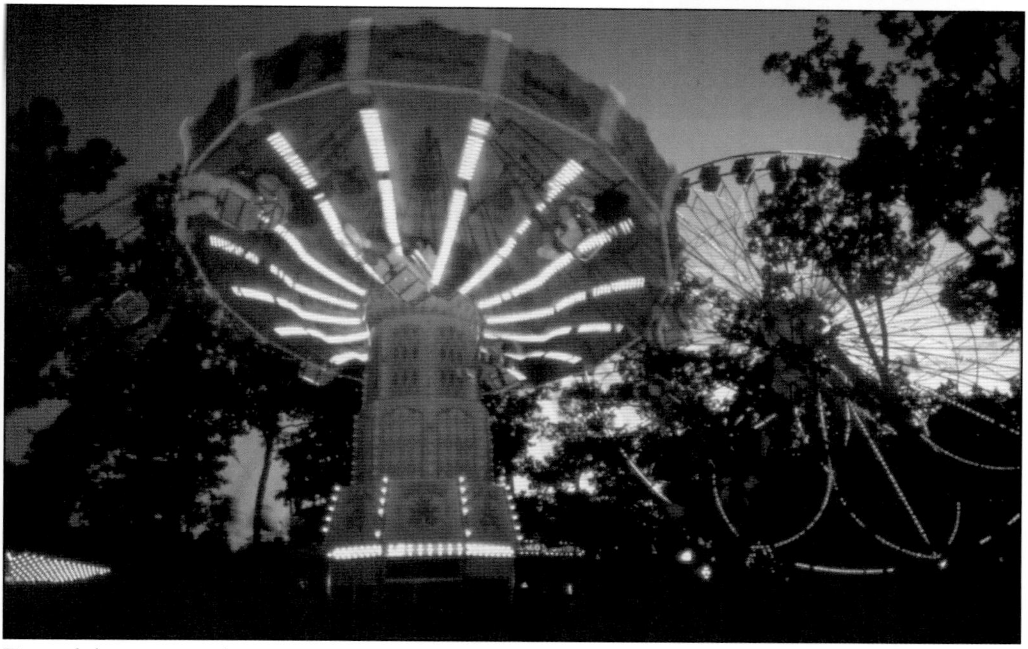

Two of the most striking attractions by day or by night were the Giant Wheel and the Flying Wave. Side by side, the classic rides delighted families since the park opened, with their hundreds of lights spinning in patterns. Together with the lights in the surrounding trees, the park became an even more magical place after dark with "Magic 'til Midnight."

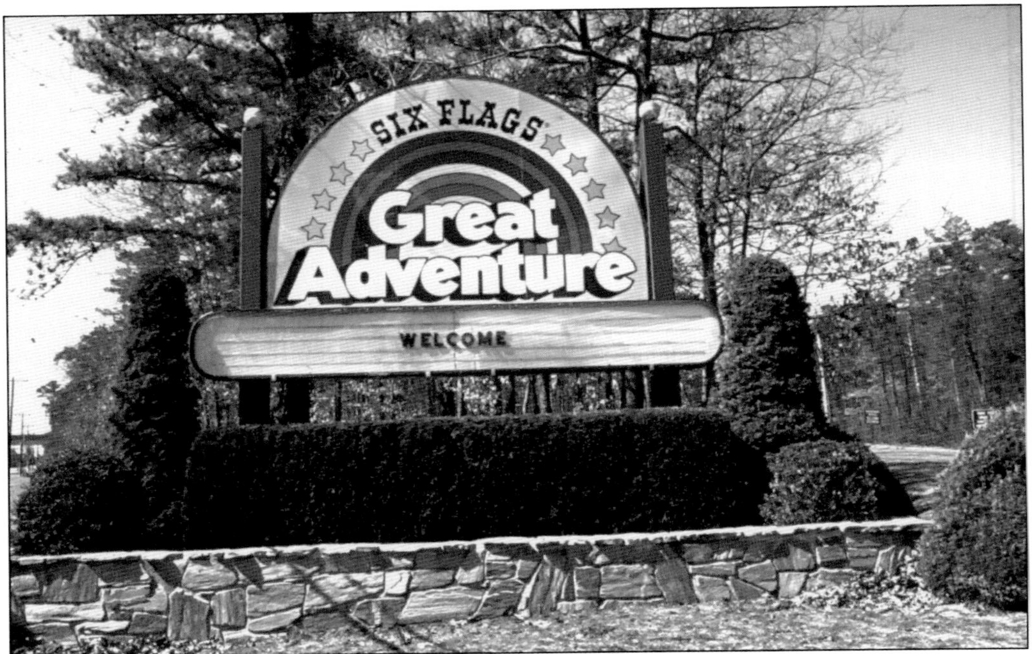

With the acquisition of the park by Six Flags, the original lion sign was moved into the park and placed near the Safari entrance plaza. A new marquee was built on Route 537, featuring the park's rainbow logo that was used into the early 1990s. The marquee was updated daily with the concerts, events, and groups the park was hosting each day.

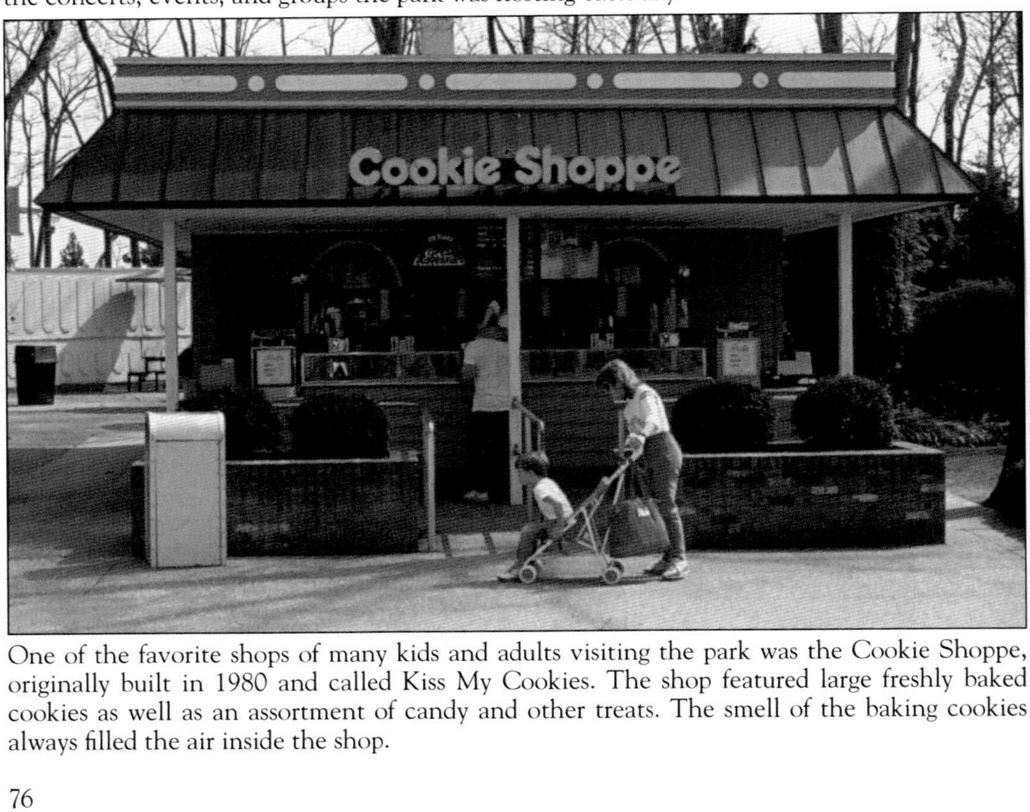

One of the favorite shops of many kids and adults visiting the park was the Cookie Shoppe, originally built in 1980 and called Kiss My Cookies. The shop featured large freshly baked cookies as well as an assortment of candy and other treats. The smell of the baking cookies always filled the air inside the shop.

The Hocus Pocus Magic Shop was a fun store where guests could buy practical joke kits, magic tricks, lots of glow-in-the-dark posters, a large assortment of masks, and other oddities. The building was unique with its octagonal shape, and the window facing the street always had enticing displays.

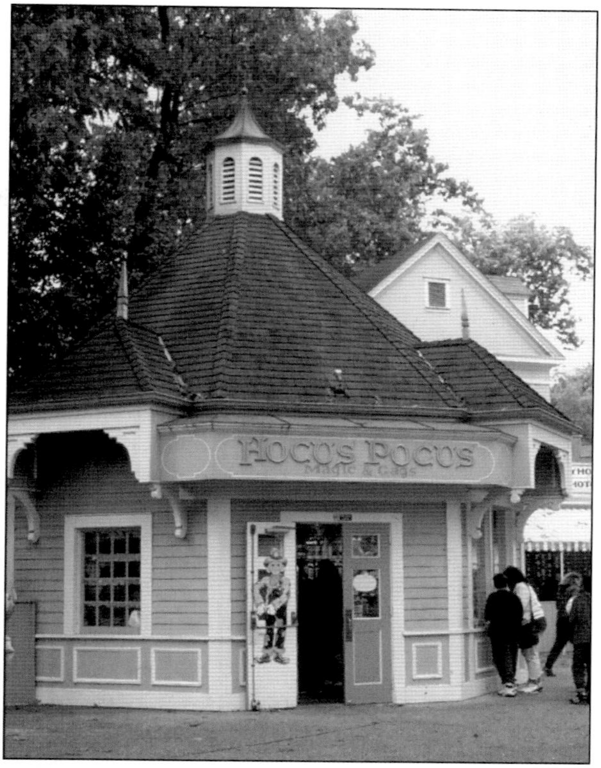

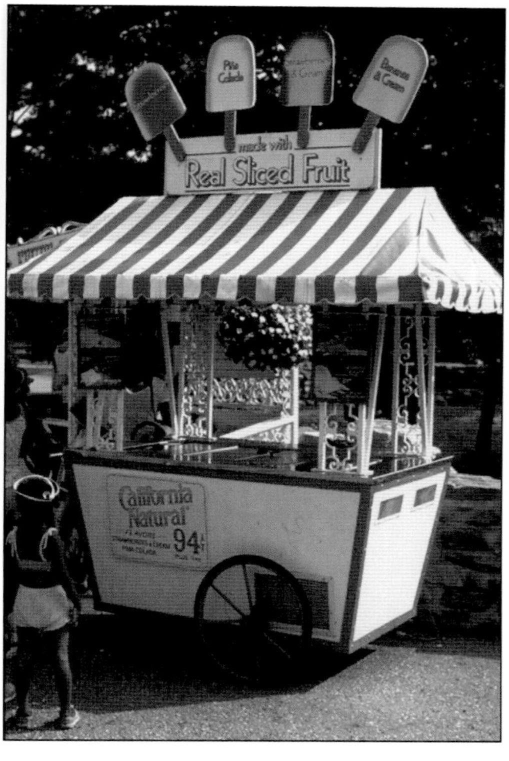

Throughout the park, carts sold ice-cream novelties, Italian ices, and fruit juices. Some of the most unique things were the plastic juice bottles that were shaped like the juice they held (oranges, grapes, lemons, and pineapples that were filled with fruit punch). Each one came with a clear plastic crazy straw, making them a must-have for every kid.

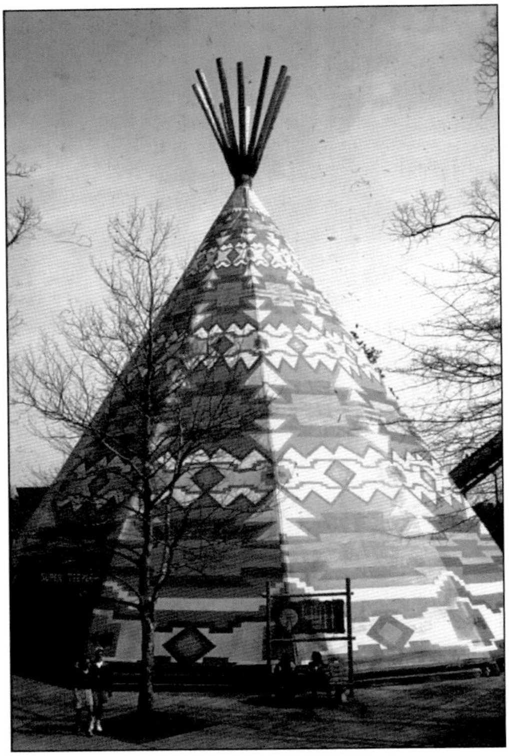

The 70-foot-high and 93-foot-diameter Super Teepee was a gift shop that originally sold all kinds of western clothing, jewelry, and an array of Native American and southwestern-themed souvenirs. The colorful larger-than-life structure stood out in the park and was one of the focal points of the western area opening with the park in 1974.

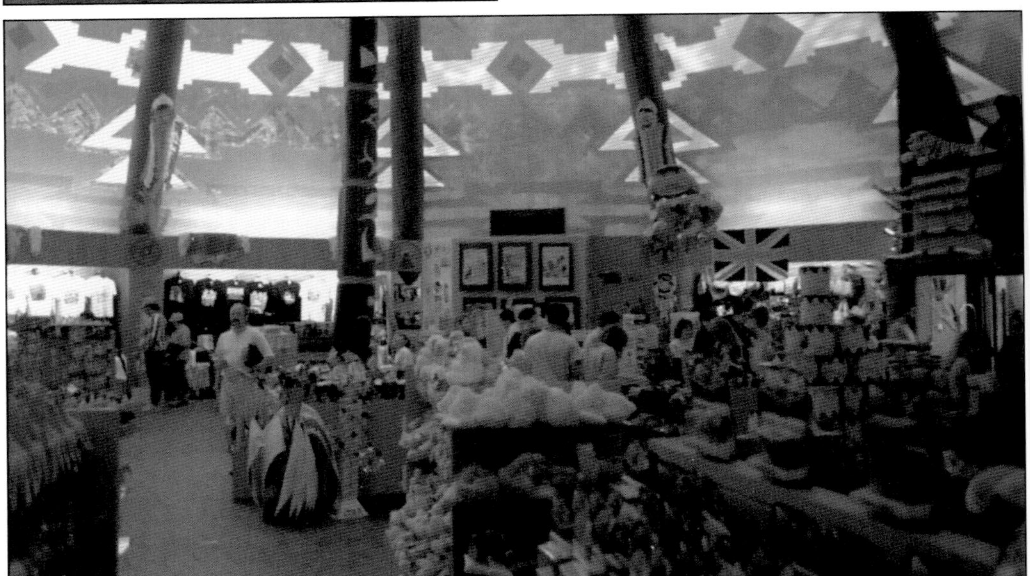

The inside of the Super Teepee was just as colorful as the outside, with Native American headdresses, tomahawks, and drums along with assortments of western-themed ashtrays, paperweights, mugs, and other souvenirs. The building featured a unique 60-foot-tall and 20-foot-wide chandelier hanging from its apex. Although the interior of the Super Teepee's canvas skin was yellow, the vibrant paint colors shone through in a kaleidoscopic rainbow of hues. (GreatAdventureHistory.com collection.)

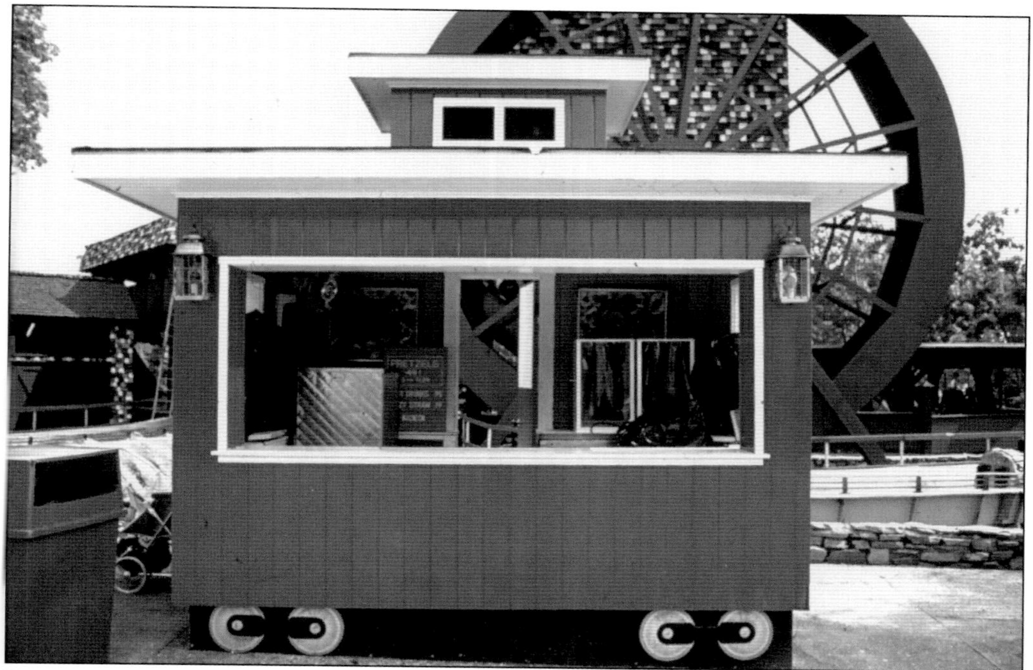

Tuscan Dairies was a longtime sponsor in the park and was the host of the Runaway Mine Train and the Yum Yum Palace for many seasons. It also ran the Tuscan Caboose, located right across from the Runaway Mine Train entrance, which sold ice cream and other snacks.

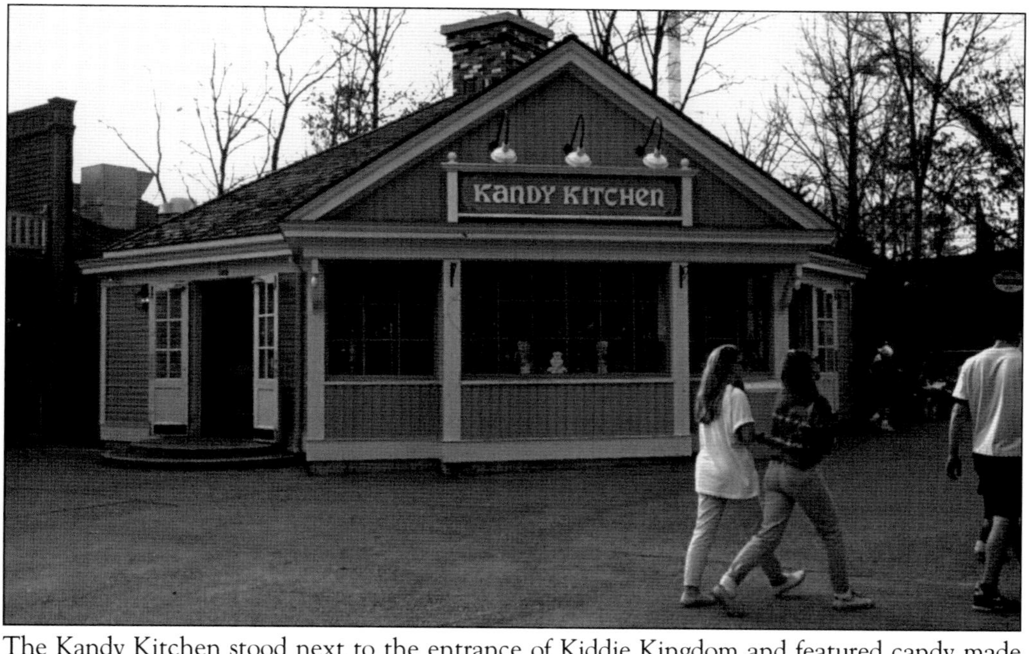

The Kandy Kitchen stood next to the entrance of Kiddie Kingdom and featured candy made on premises. The most popular item was its peanut brittle, which was sold in little plastic bags in the bins on the front of the candy counter. A big copper kettle was used to make the peanut brittle, fudge, and candy apples all day long.

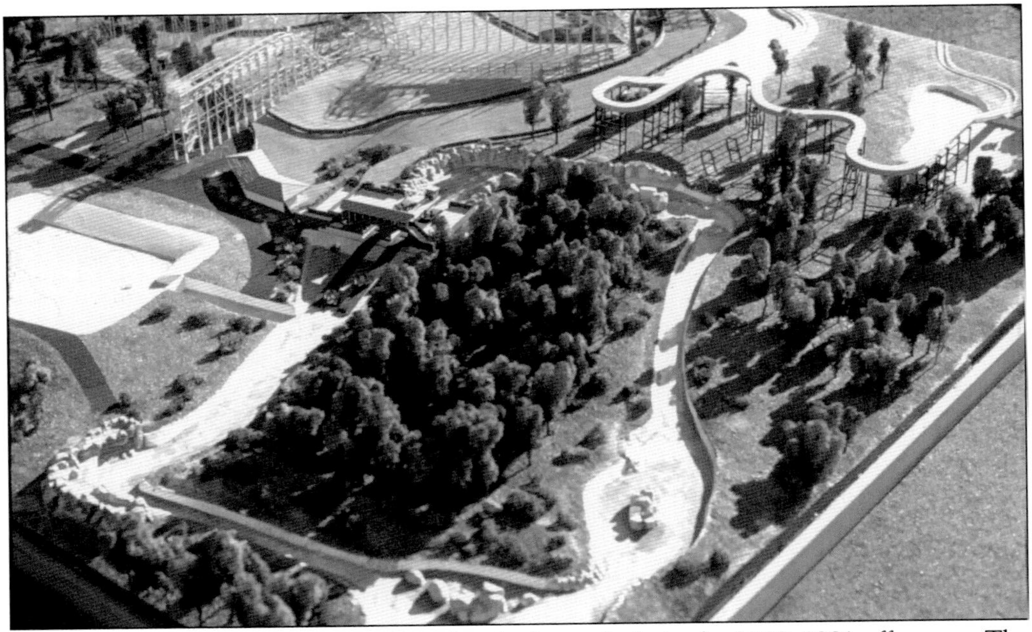

Seen here is the model of Roaring Rapids, which was built in the 1980–1981 off-season. The ride featured rapids, waterfalls, and wave pools along its quarter-mile-long "river" and occupied more than five acres. The river's 12-foot elevation change created the current that pulled the boats over the turbulent rapids along the route.

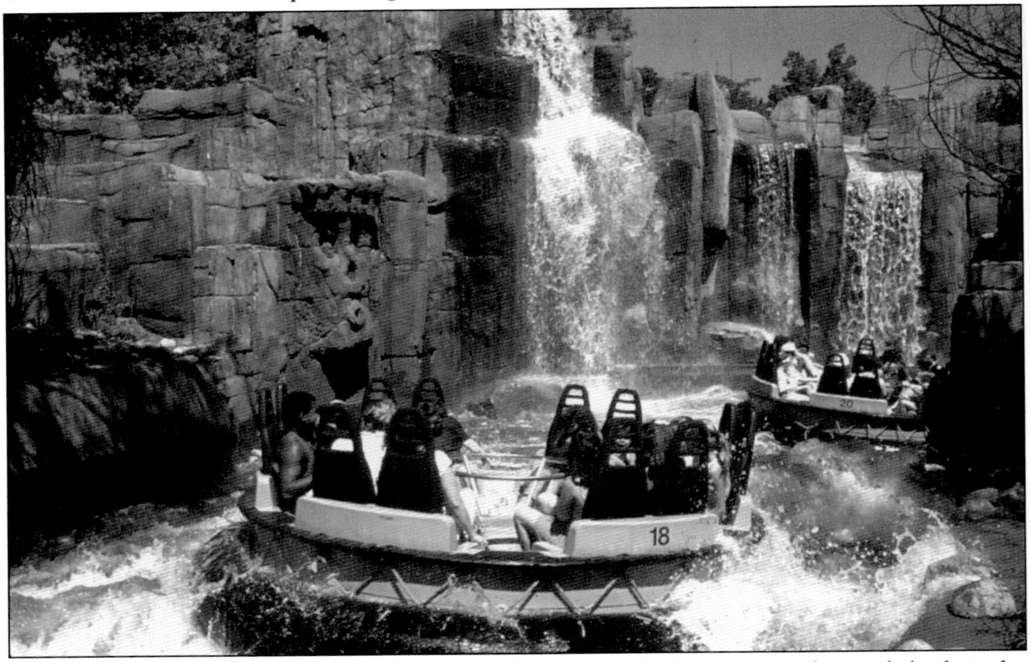

When the park added Roaring Rapids, it was only the second white-water rafting ride built in the world. Six Flags developed the ride in cooperation with INTAMIN AG of Switzerland the year before and opened the first one at Six Flags Astroworld in Houston. Astroworld's overwhelming success led to Six Flags adding the ride in its parks coast to coast.

In the 1982 off-season, the new Goodtime Alley was built to replace the Fortune Festival games area. Part of the new Goodtime Alley was a new flat ride called the Joust-A-Bout, which was placed at the far end of the games area. The unique ride was the only one of its kind in the United States.

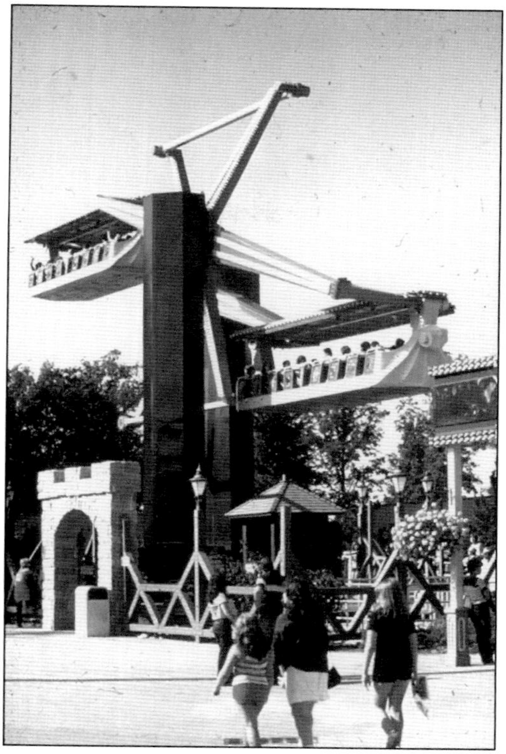

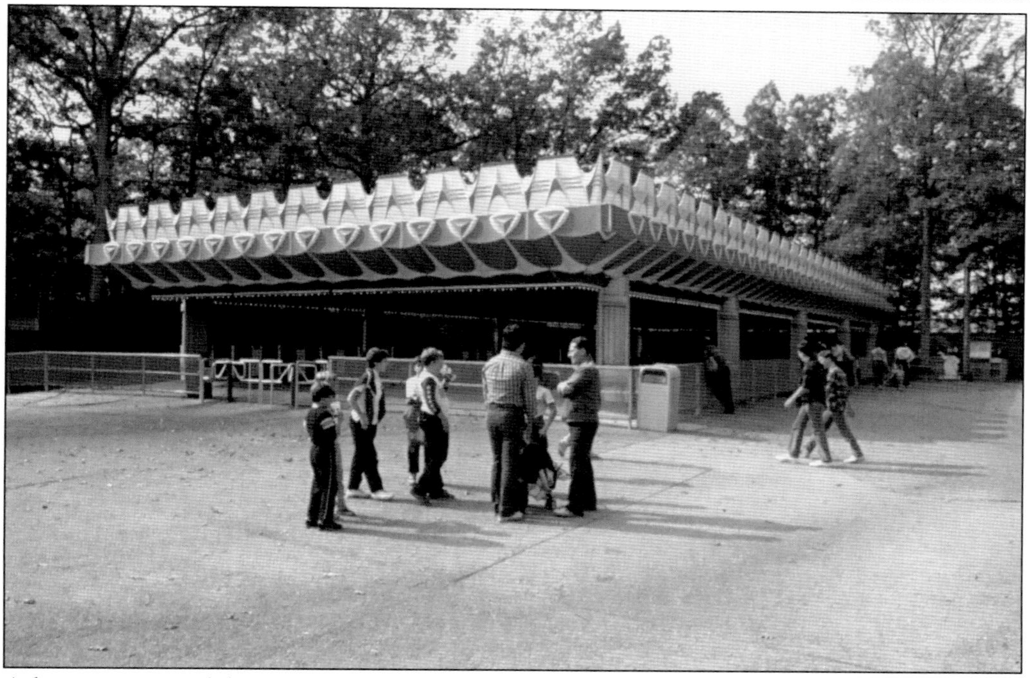

A larger version of the Traffic Jam, the Fender Bender bumper cars were part of the Fun Fair area. The ride was often overlooked, being the more isolated bumper car ride, but in 1983, it got a new neighbor that would bring a lot more attention to the area with the arrival of Freefall.

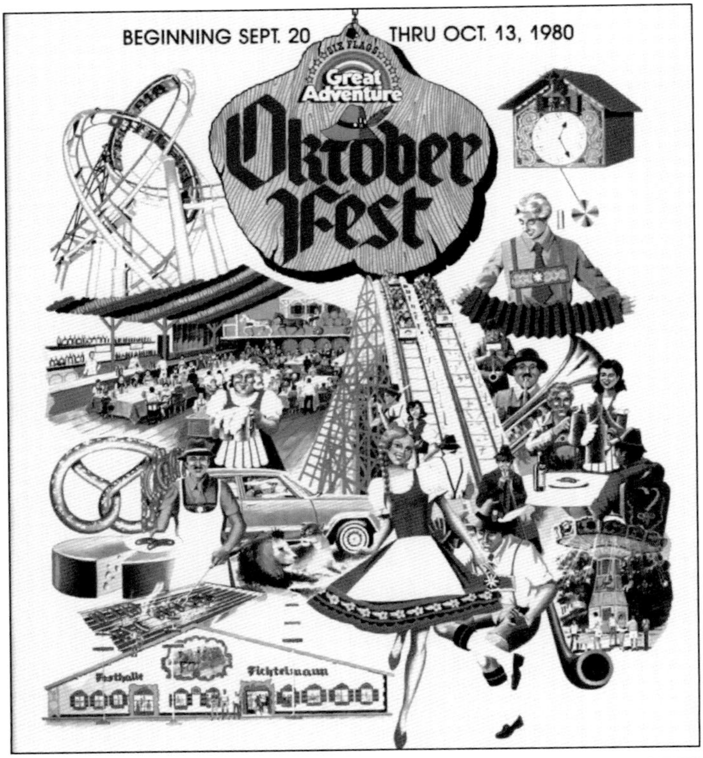

Always looking to expand the operating season and bring more value to guests, the park began a yearly Oktoberfest, which generally ran from mid-September until the park closed in mid-October. The event was held from 1980 to 1982 and was later revived from 1989 to 1992. The event featured traditional German music, dancing, and of course, Bavarian food.

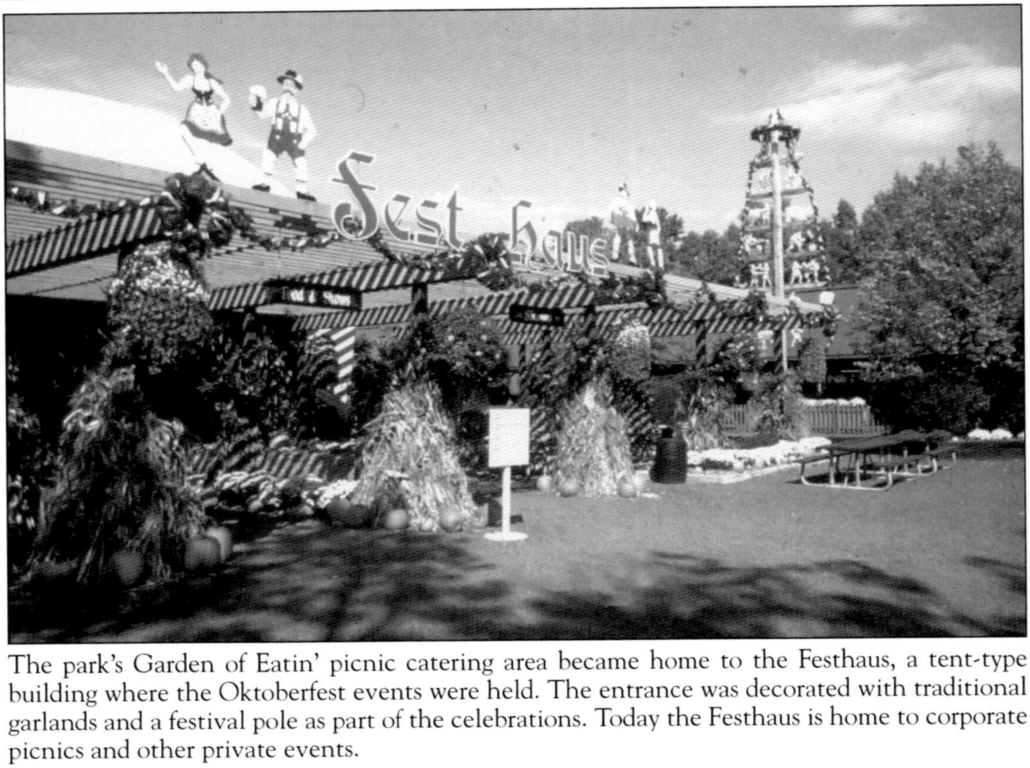

The park's Garden of Eatin' picnic catering area became home to the Festhaus, a tent-type building where the Oktoberfest events were held. The entrance was decorated with traditional garlands and a festival pole as part of the celebrations. Today the Festhaus is home to corporate picnics and other private events.

In 1982, the New Jersey State Fair was moved to the park, taking over a section of the parking lot adjacent to the Garden of Eatin' and utilizing the picnic area as well. Other fair exhibits were located within the park, making use of the show venues and some of the ride buildings. As part of the event, a Miss New Jersey State Fair pageant was held.

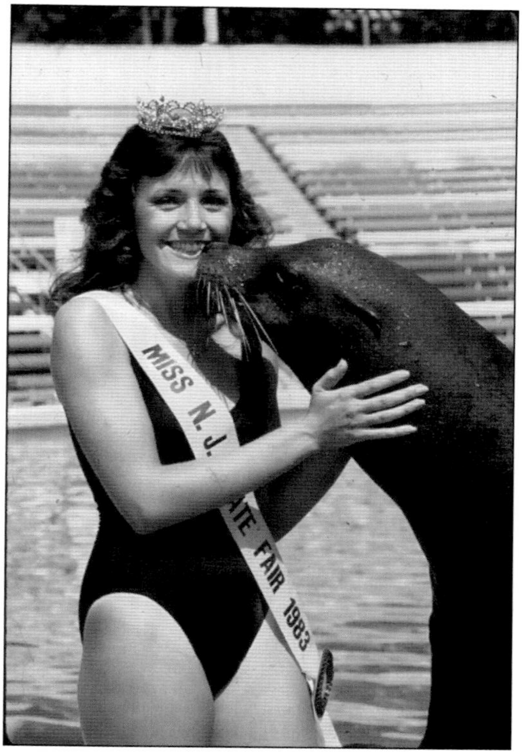

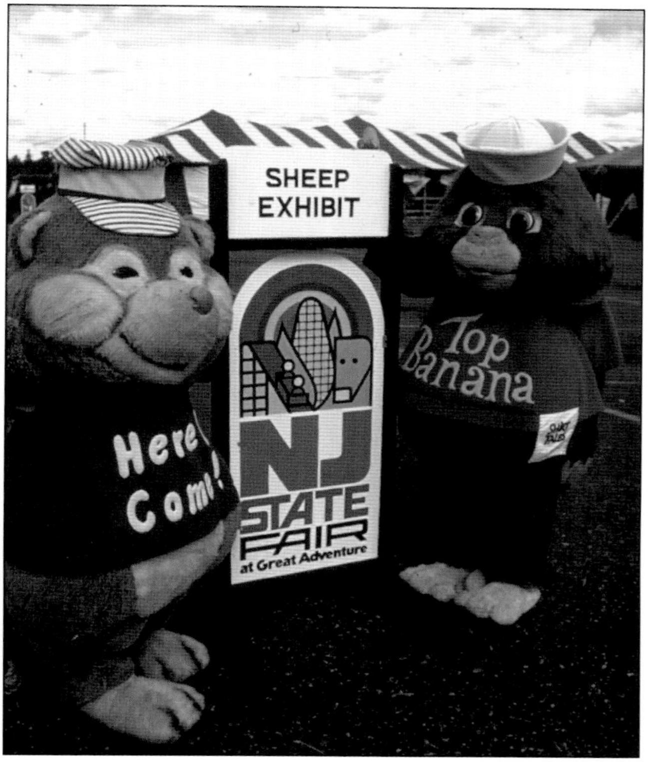

Traditional livestock exhibits were a part of the fair as well, filling the tents in the parking lot. For the 1983 season, the park became home to the Shirt Tales characters, who posed for photographs all around the fair as publicity for the addition of the new Shirt Tales Land in 1984.

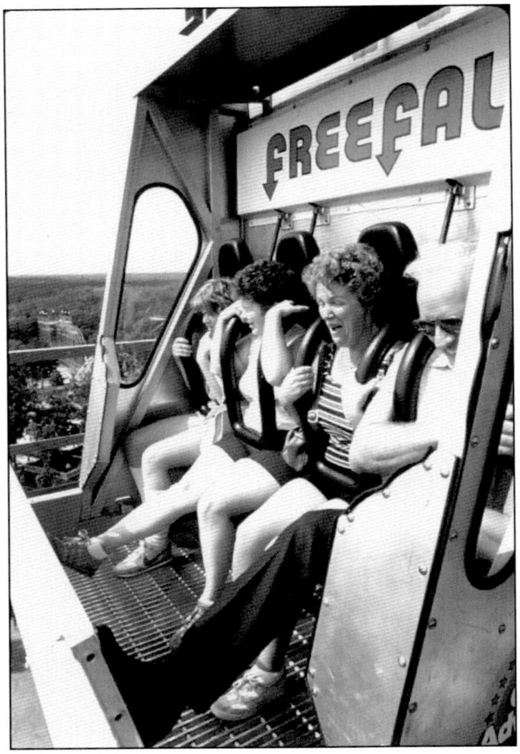

Adding state-of-the-art thrill rides was always the Six Flags tradition, and for 1983, the cutting edge of thrills was the Freefall. Built by INTAMIN AG, the 13-story tower dropped riders who got to experience (what was then) an amazing two seconds of true free fall.

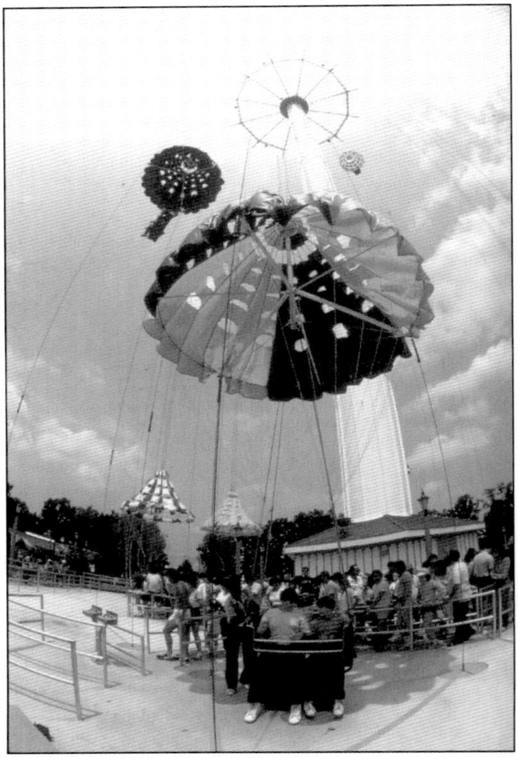

A second ride added for the 1983 season was the Parachuter's Perch, the world's tallest amusement ride at the time, towering 250 feet. The ride, which was also manufactured by INTAMIN AG, was moved to Great Adventure from Six Flags Over Mid-America in St. Louis where it had operated for five seasons as the Sky Chuter before moving east.

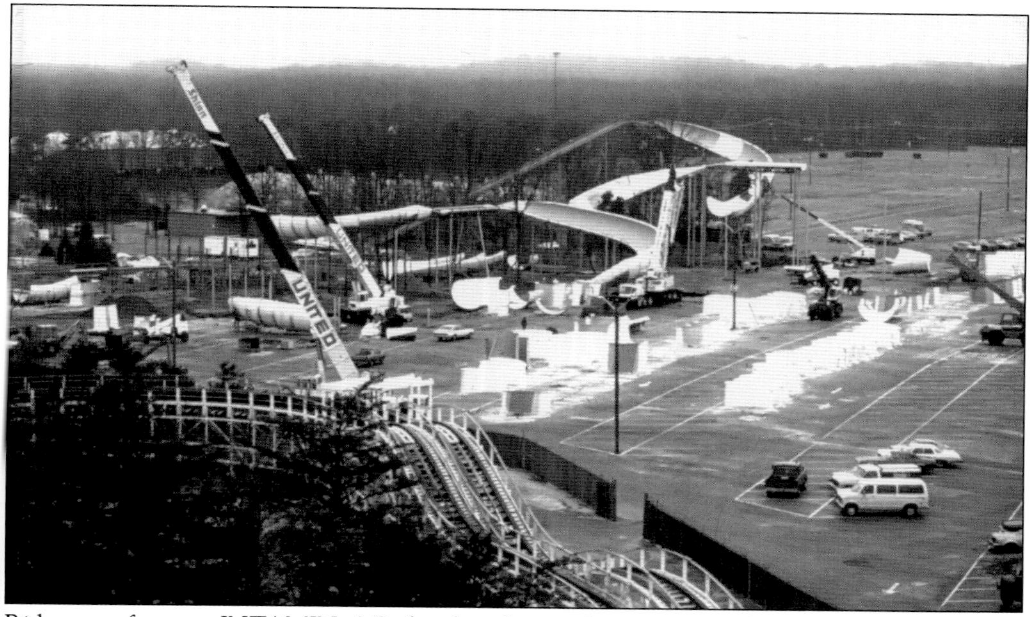

Ride manufacturer INTAMIN AG developed a modern version of the classic bobsled-style roller coaster, and Six Flags was one of the first companies to add the new coasters, choosing Great Adventure as one of the first parks to receive one. Here the Sarajevo Bobsled is under construction in the spring of 1984.

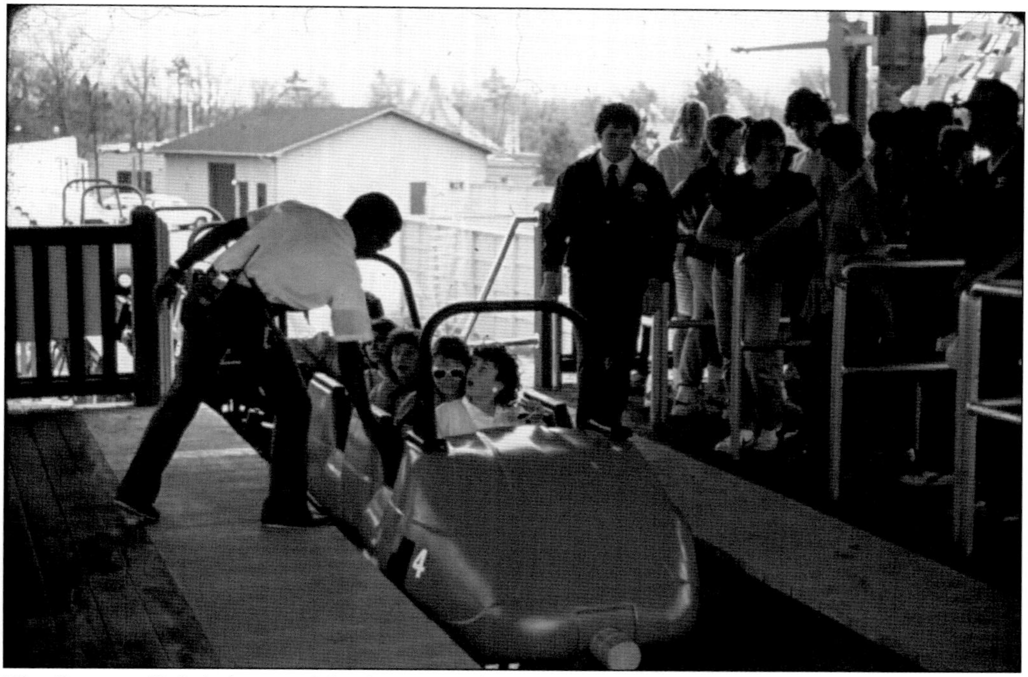

The Sarajevo Bobsled, named for the 1984 Olympic Winter Games held in Sarajevo, Yugoslavia, over the previous winter, offered a chance to experience a very realistic bobsled run. The fun, family-friendly coaster, which was built at the end of the Goodtime Alley games square, suffered from low capacity with its six-person ride vehicles and closures for rain.

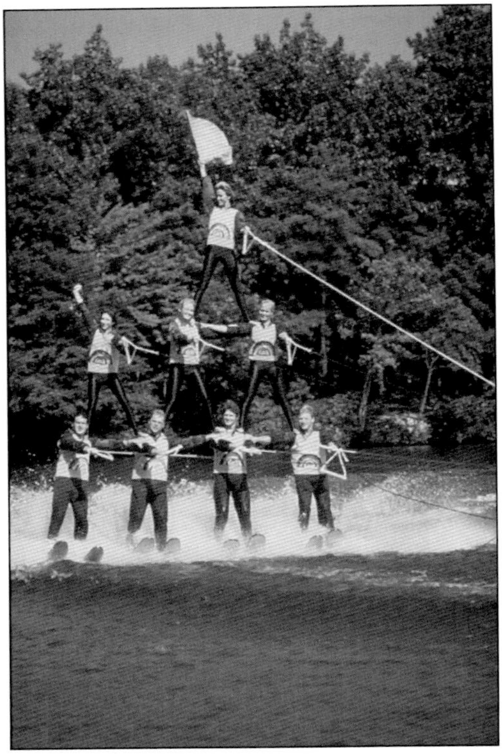

At the close of the 1982 season, the Great Lake was drained in order to reprofile it and remove submerged stumps for the arrival of the Water Ski Spectacular for the 1983 season. The addition of the show also included the construction of the Great Lake Grandstand, which doubled as home to the park's frequent fireworks shows.

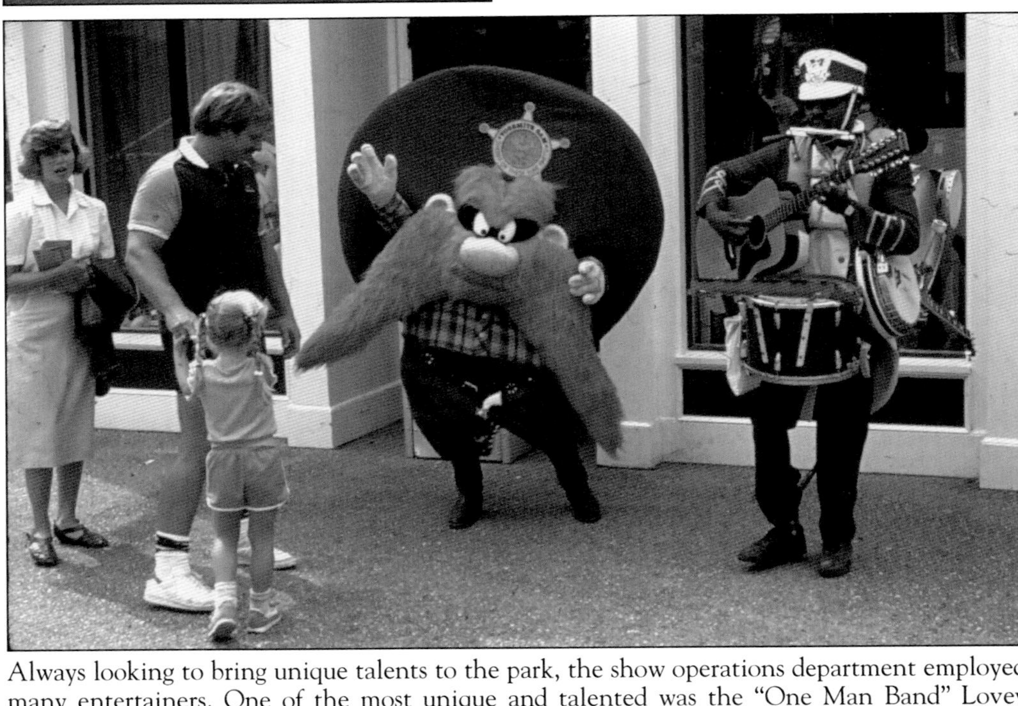

Always looking to bring unique talents to the park, the show operations department employed many entertainers. One of the most unique and talented was the "One Man Band" Lovey Williams, who strolled through the park playing music on guitar, banjo, drums, and harmonica, as well as singing.

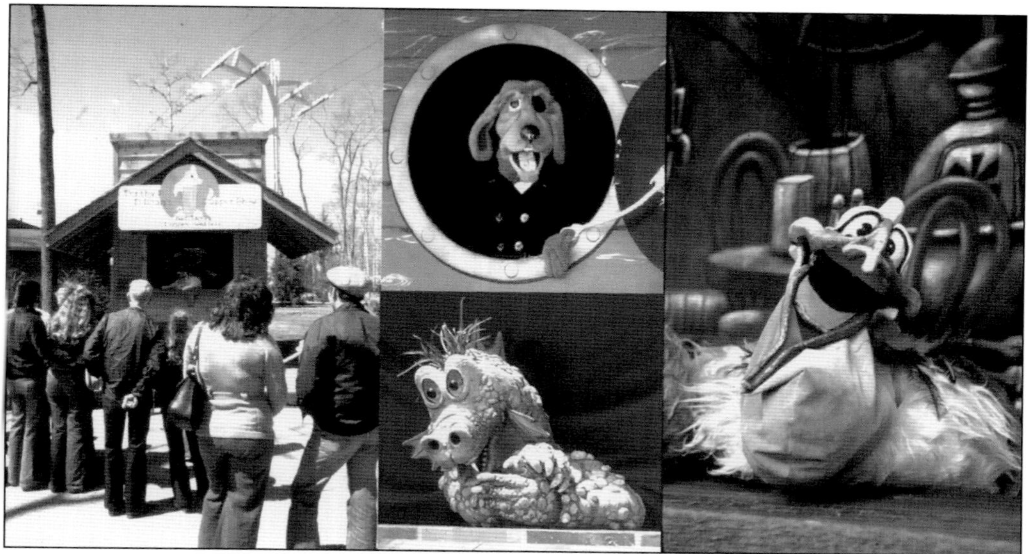

One of the longest-running shows in the park was the puppet show that had been located in the Neptune's Kingdom area of the park. Originally the show featured Perthy P. Pelican, who was later replaced by Salty Dog and finally Dastardly Dragon. All three characters performed comedy interactions with the audience members and were voiced by quick-witted performers.

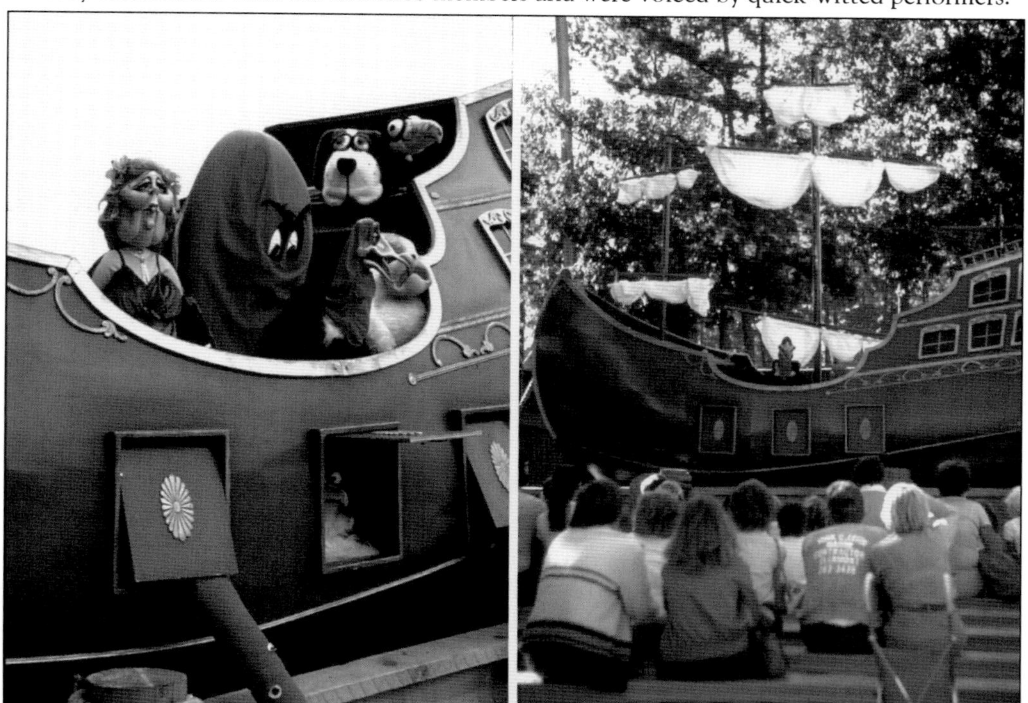

Kiddie Kingdom had a unique ship-shaped puppet theater that was added as part of the new King's Sandbox in 1982. The Foghorn Follies featured a unique array of odd-looking characters. The puppets appeared on the ship's deck as well as through the portholes and the hatches at children's eye level.

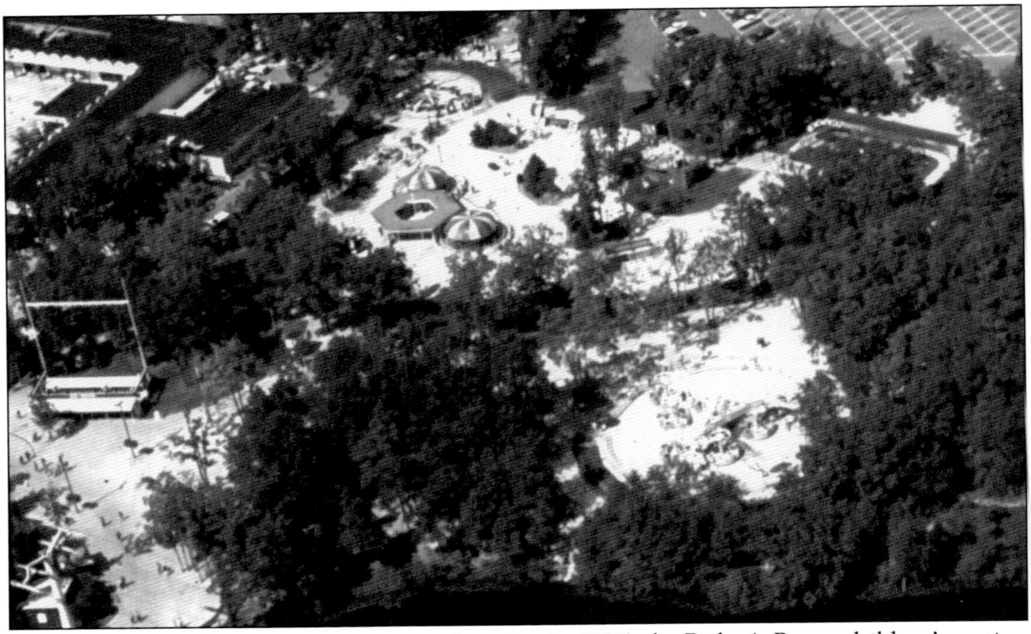

After moving the front gate to its present location in 1976, the Ride-A-Rama children's section was moved to the old entrance plaza area, becoming Kiddie Kingdom. Themed updates to the area included Shirt Tales Land in 1984, then Looney Tunes Land in 1985 when Six Flags acquired Great America in Gurnee, Illinois, from the Marriot Corporation and with it the license to the Looney Tunes Characters.

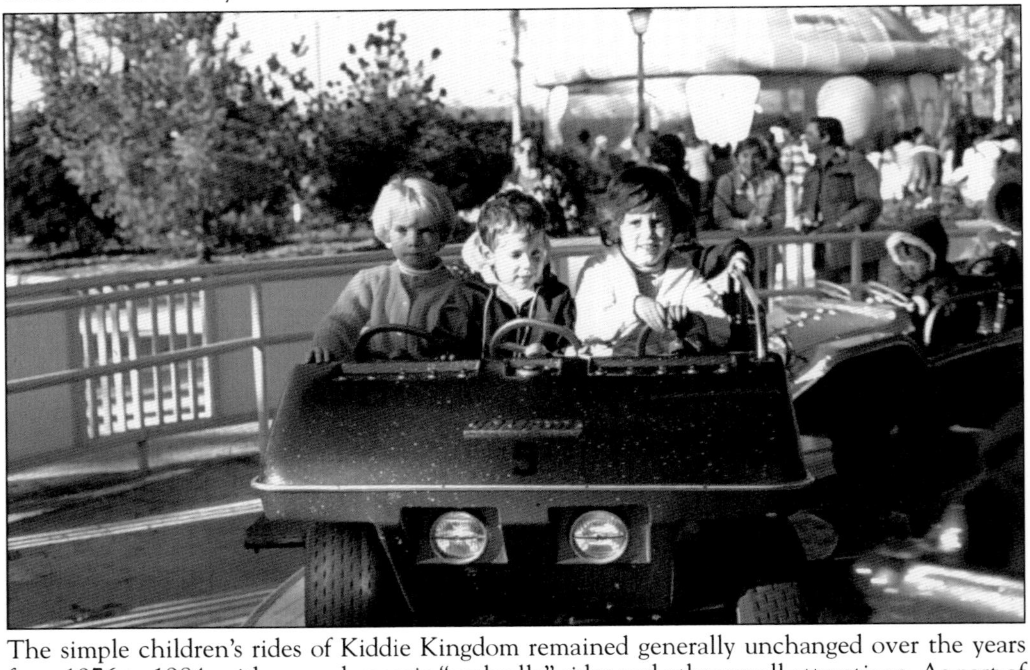

The simple children's rides of Kiddie Kingdom remained generally unchanged over the years from 1976 to 1984, with several generic "umbrella" rides and other small attractions. As part of the Shirt Tales Land retheme, more activity elements were added, like net climbs and ball crawls. These were adapted with the arrival of the Looney Tunes characters the following season.

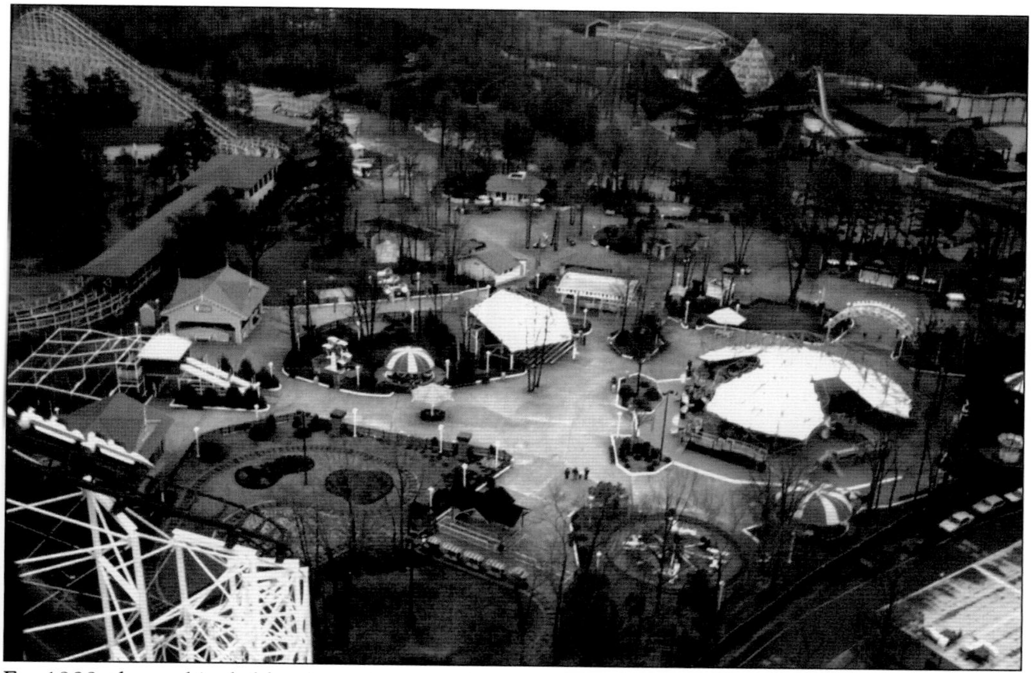

For 1988, the park's children's section was given a total upgrade and makeover and became Bugs Bunny Land, with new, modern interactive elements and rides. The makeover included play equipment built on a spongy ground covering for safety, new shade structures, and a new covered Bugs Bunny Land theater. (GreatAdventureHistory.com collection.)

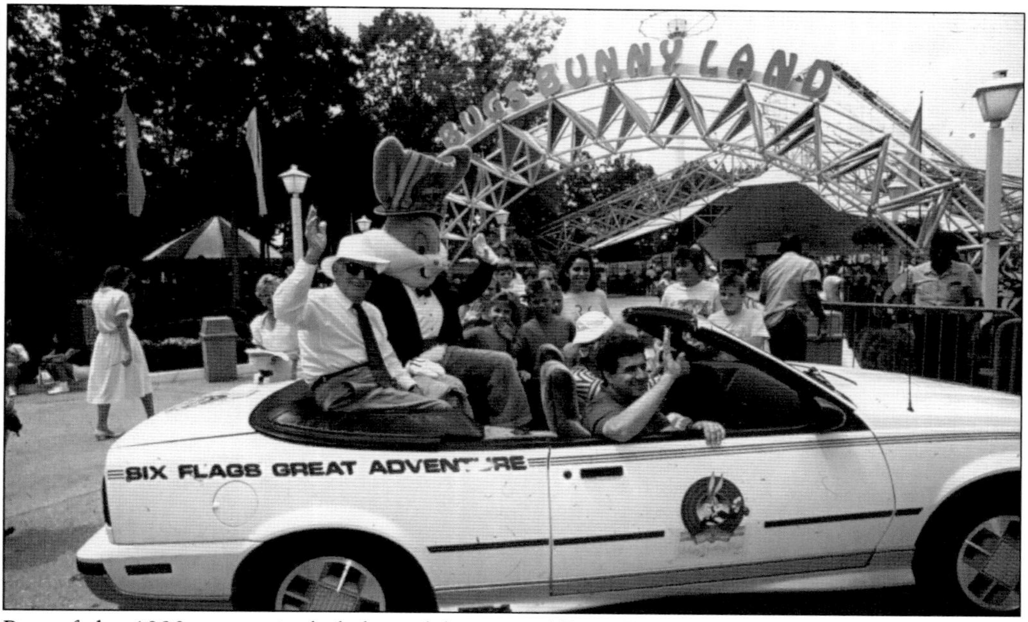

Part of the 1990 season included a celebration of Bugs Bunny's 50th birthday. Festivities in the park included a parade, which featured one of Bugs Bunny's creators, Friz Freleng, as well as the voice of Bugs Bunny, Jeff Bergman, who took over after the death of Mel Blanc the previous year.

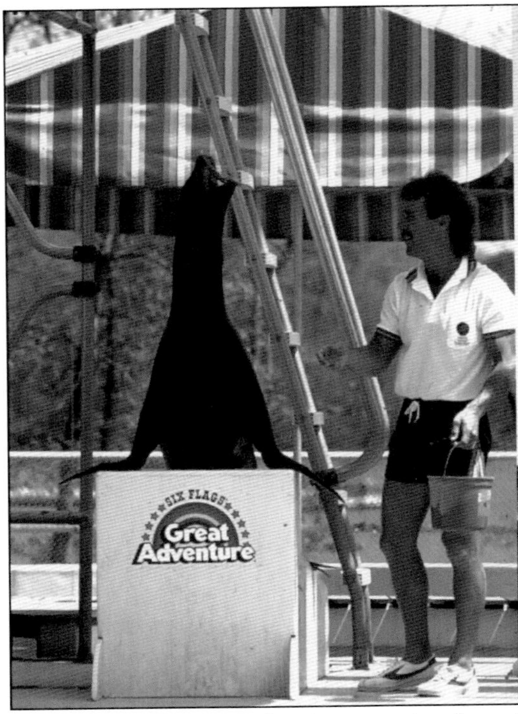

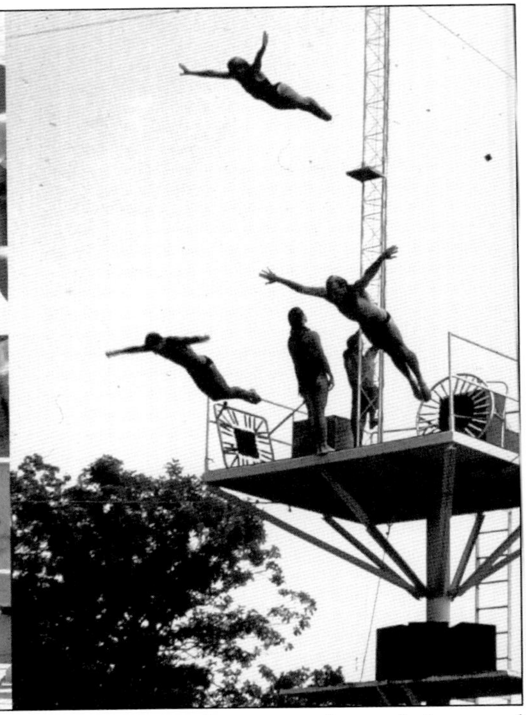

Throughout the years the shows at the Aqua Stadium remained very popular and alternated throughout the day between the Great American High Dive Team and the dolphin and sea lion shows. Over the seasons the shows changed very little with slightly updated joke references and music selections with each passing year.

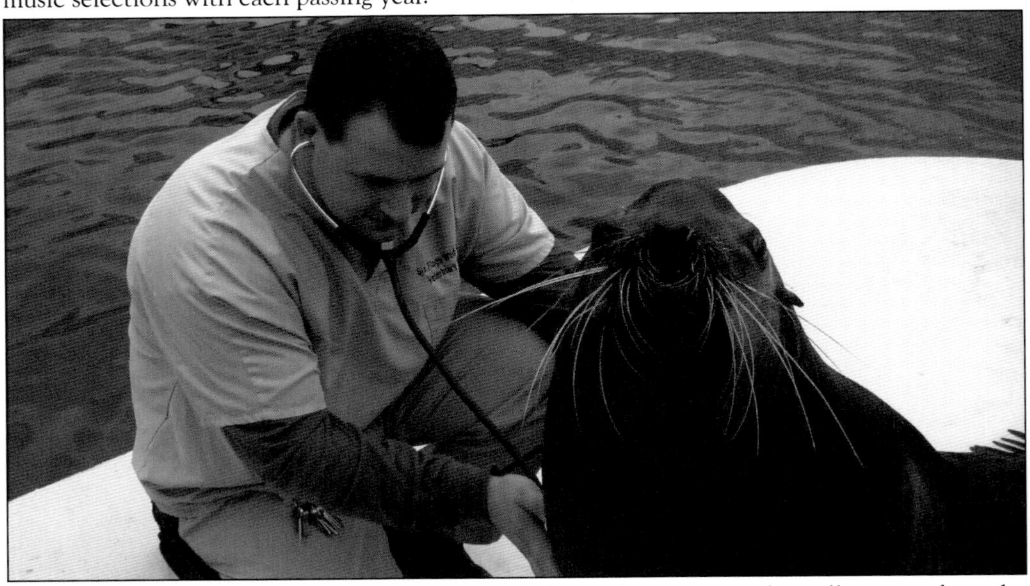

In the Aqua Stadium, the park's marine mammals have always received excellent care from the veterinary staff and trainers. The health and well-being of the animals has always been the top priority, with trainers and veterinarians building a strong bond with the animals and conducting expert training through positive reinforcement.

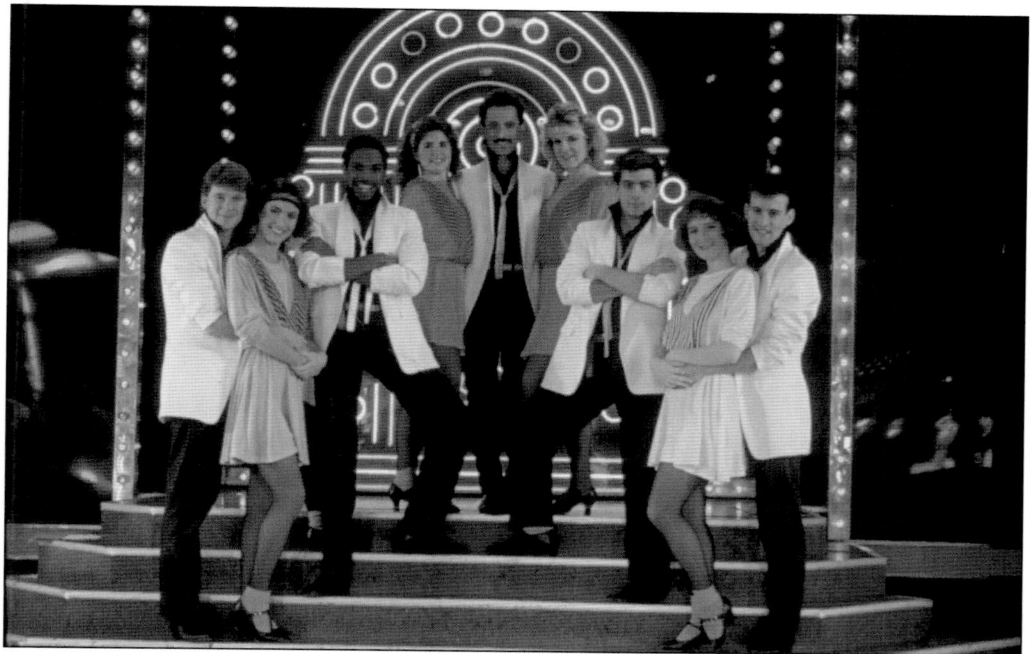

The Bandstand by the Lake was always one of the park's main show venues, generally hosting musical revues. The stage featured a large neon jukebox as part of the backdrop and generally a cast of six to eight singers and dancers performing lively retrospectives of varying styles of music.

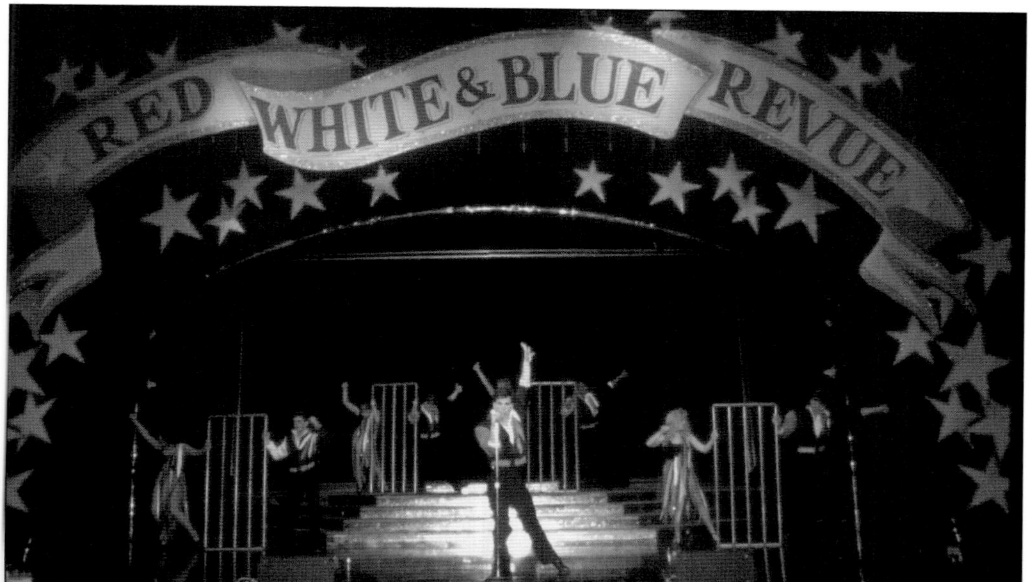

Six Flags had been one of the innovators of Broadway-style revue shows, and Great Adventure's Showcase Theater was the home to many of these. One of the more memorable featured productions from the late 1980s was the Red White and Blue Revue, a tribute to American music through the years.

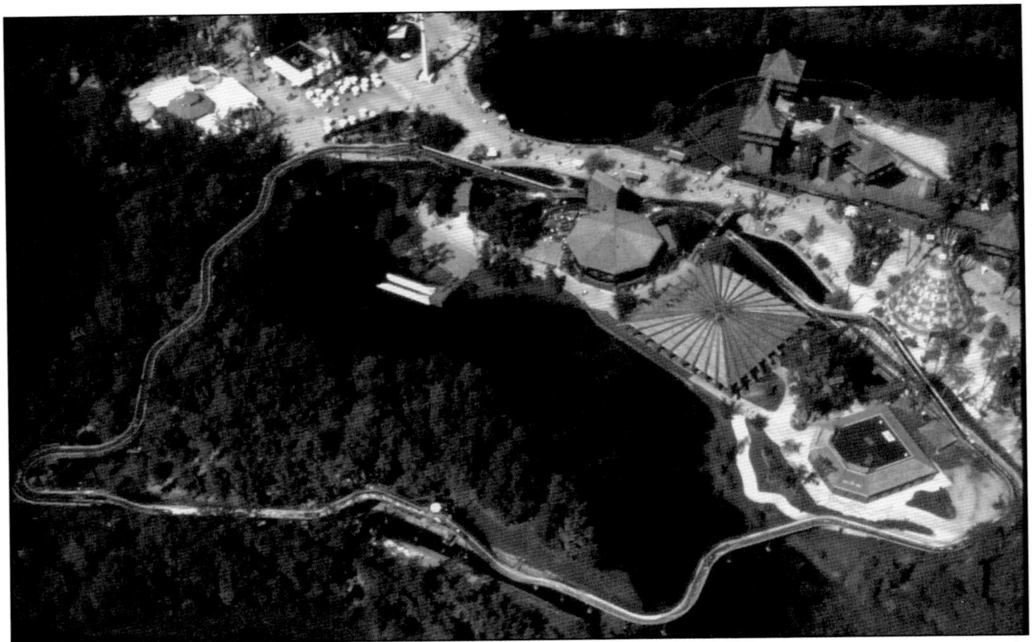

The park's western section has always been one of the most picturesque areas. The oversized buildings and the exciting family rides set on the naturally beautiful lakeside have always been the perfect combination and a favorite of guests throughout the years. Here the entire 2,160-foot-long flume can be seen as it winds through the treetops.

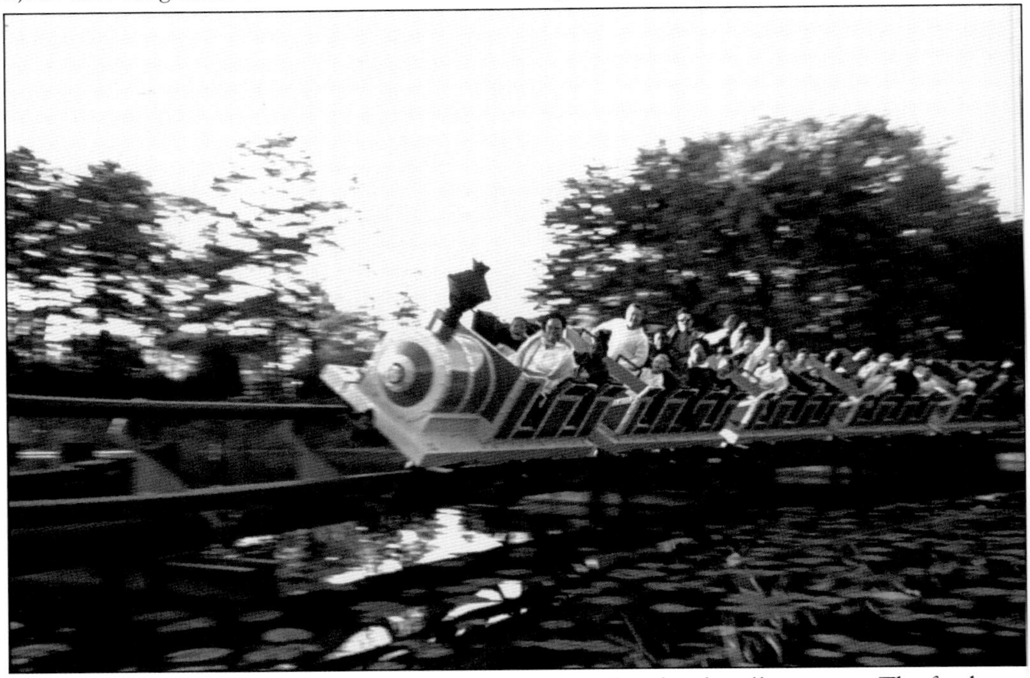

The Runaway Mine Train's hills and turns create the perfect family roller coaster. The final turn in the 2,429-foot-long track, which takes place over the water in front of the Fort, has always been one of the best picture spots in the park as the colorful trains speed back into the station.

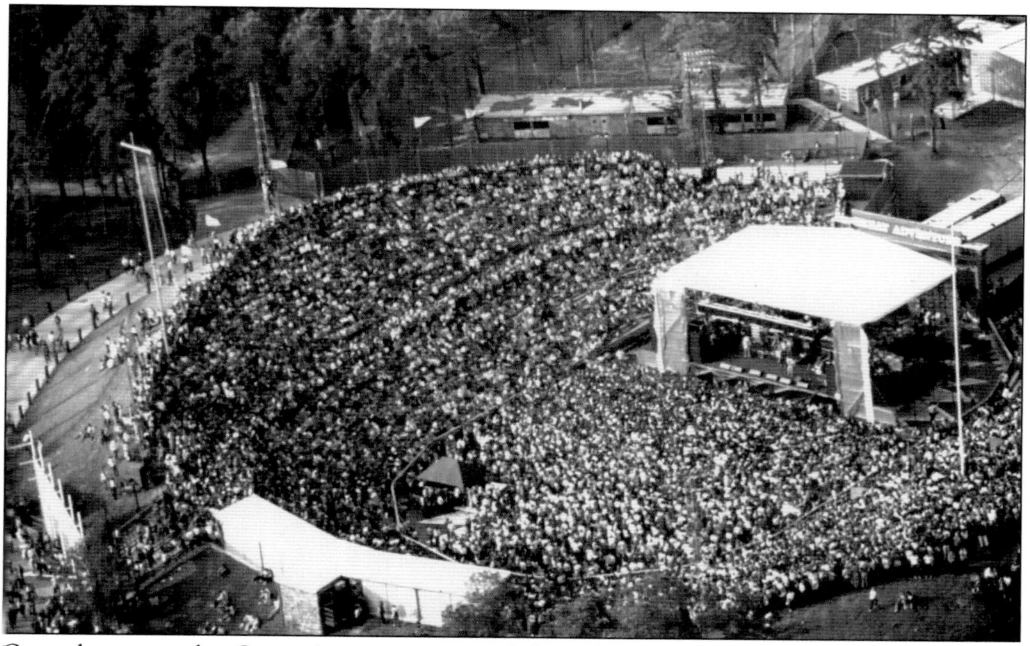

Over the years, the Great Arena transitioned from show venue to concert venue, hosting big-name music acts and other special events. Here a capacity crowd of more than 12,000 guests can be seen enjoying one of the hundreds of great concerts the park has hosted in its history.

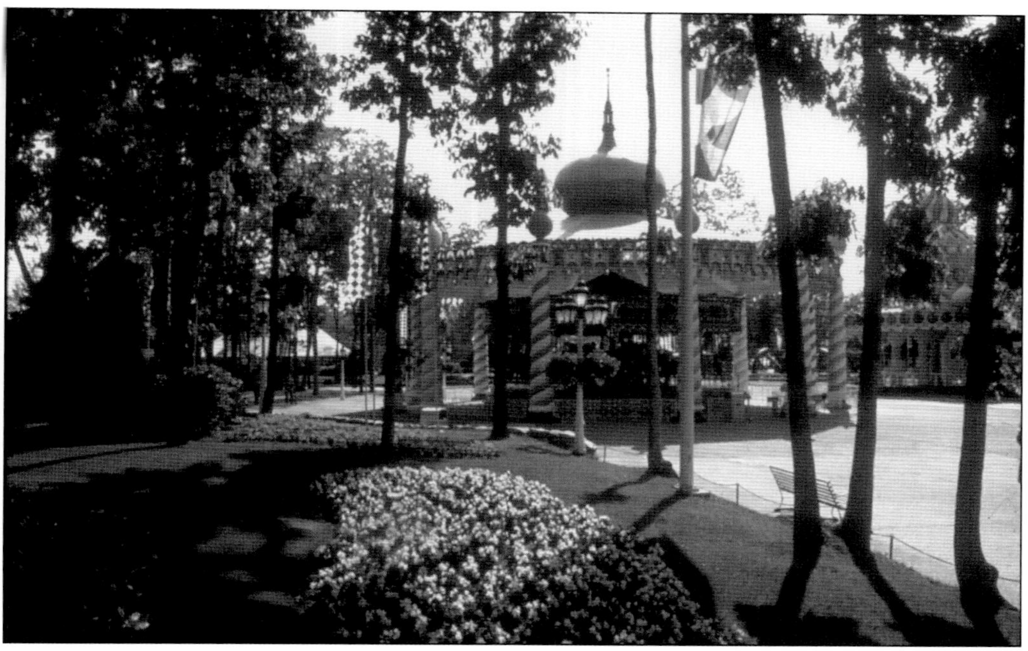

The park's landscaping crews strive to create beautiful displays throughout the property. The beautiful flower beds seen here along Dream Street are the perfect complement to the ornate carousel pavilion and Yum Yum Palace just beyond. Throughout the operating year, the flower beds receive fresh plantings with each season to provide vivid color and endless beauty.

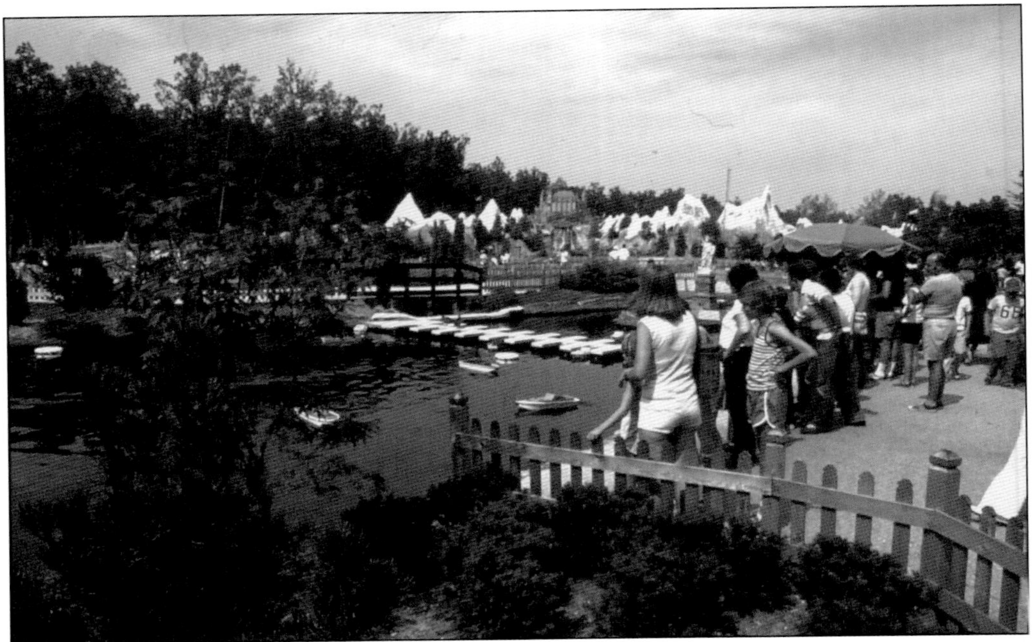

The original buildings of the Garden of Marvels area were leased, and after 1978, when the contract for them expired, the area was transformed into an expansive miniature golf course. The ponds became home to radio-controlled boats, and later remote-control cars were also added to the entrance area of the section.

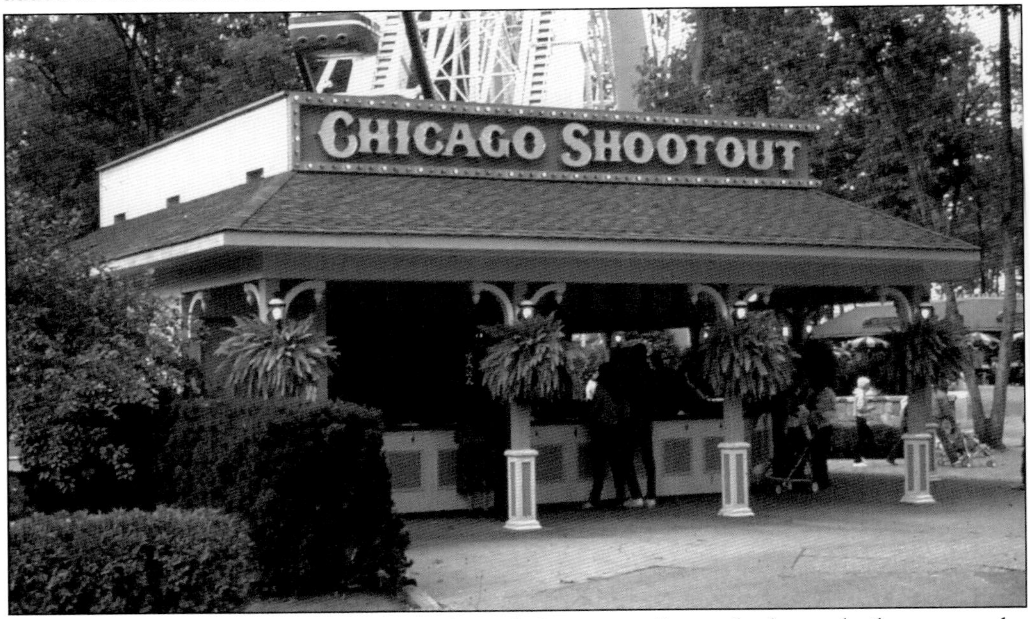

The Chicago Shootout was a gangster-themed shooting gallery, which was built next to the Big Wheel. The elaborately themed targets and props included a full-size antique car and mannequins dressed as 1920s gangsters. Just like the other shooting galleries, the targets were triggered by flashes of light, so flash photography would set off all the targets at once, creating a cacophony of sound and movement.

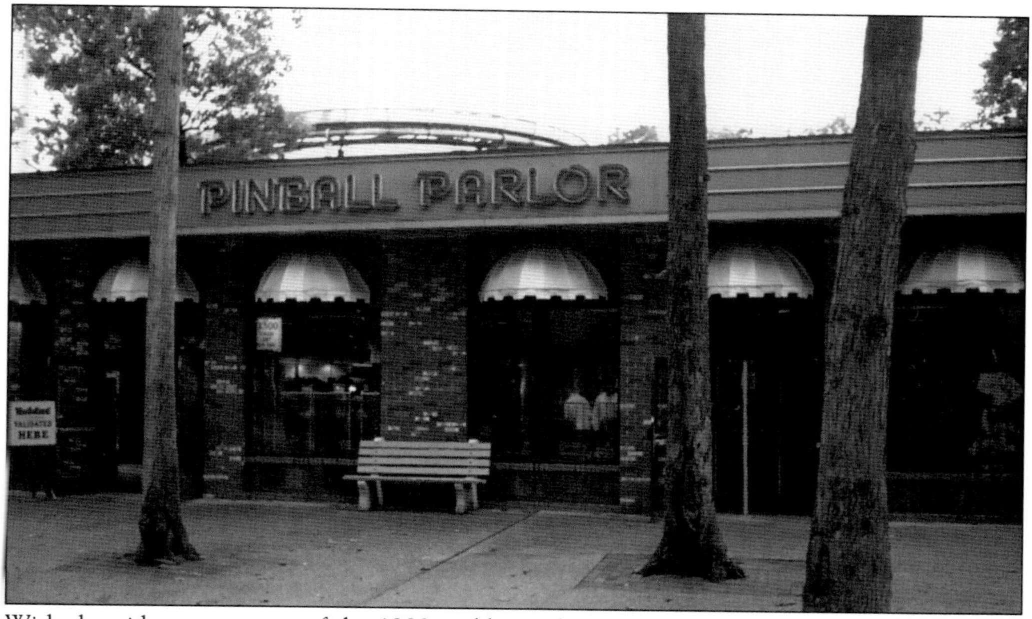

With the video game craze of the 1980s, additional space was needed for arcade machines, so the Pinball Parlor was constructed near the Big Wheel. Pinball Parlor in addition to the Dream Street Arcade located in the red tent building featured all the hottest video games of the day. (GreatAdventureHistory.com collection.)

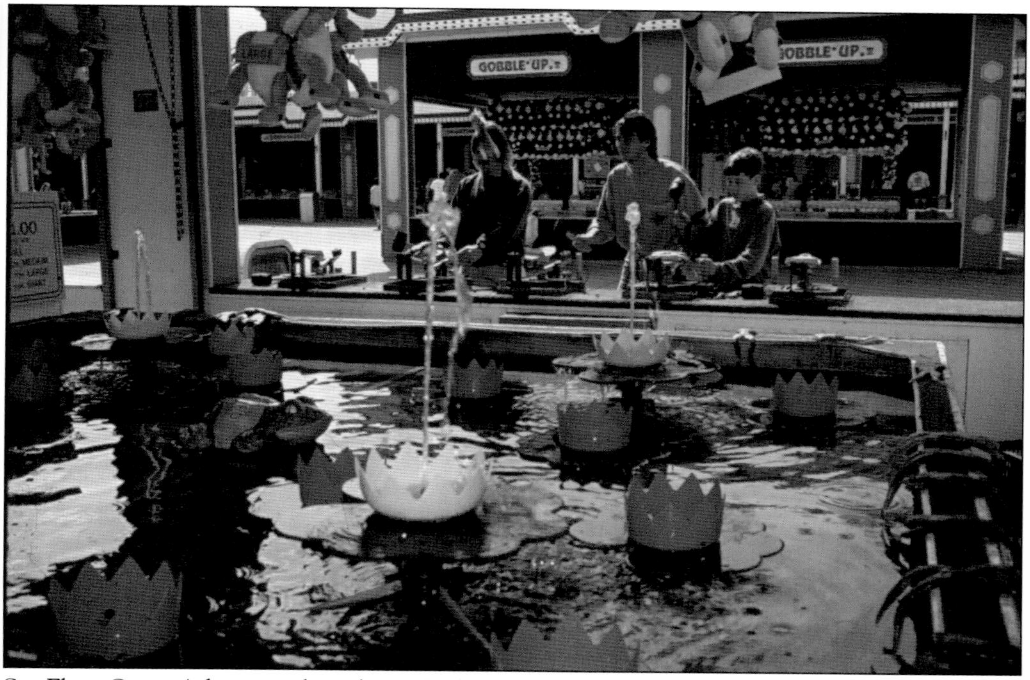

Six Flags Great Adventure has always had the very latest in games of skill, adding new games with each season and each new trend. Games like Whac-A-Mole and Frog Bog were so popular that they often required the addition of a second similar game with a variation on the theme, spawning Smack-A-Shark and Chicken in the Pot games.

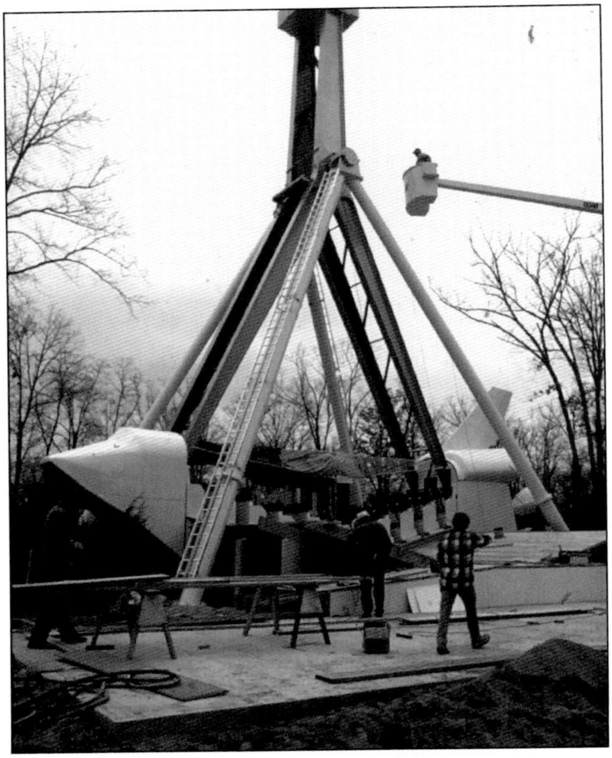

Another of the rides that were added as part of the changing trends and developments in the theme park industry was the Looping Starship, which came to the park in 1985. The ride was a variation on the swinging ship–type ride, with this version performing complete 360-degree loops.

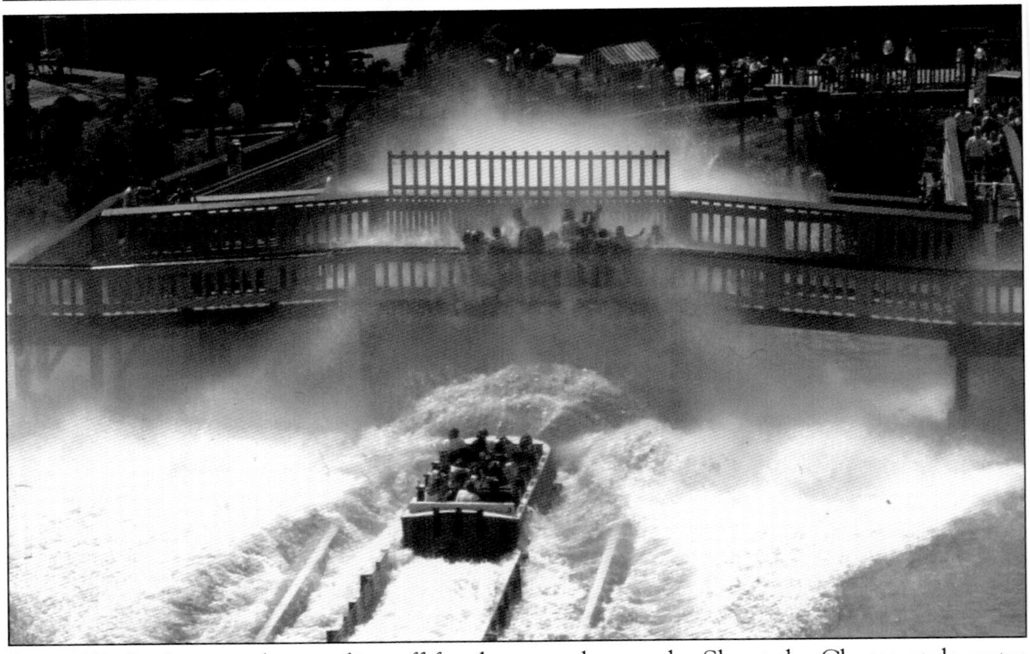

For 1987, the hot trend in cooling off for theme parks was the Shoot the Chutes–style water ride, and Six Flags Great Adventure added Splashwater Falls. Guests were mesmerized by the enormous wall of water the boats produced and looked forward to getting completely soaked both on the boat and on the exit ramp bridge on hot days.

Six Flags Great Adventure was always on the cutting edge of roller coaster technology, and for the 1986 season, the new twist was the Ultra Twister. Ultra Twister was the only one of its kind in the United States and one of the first of its kind in the world. The ride was unique in all aspects from start to finish. (GreatAdventureHistory.com collection.)

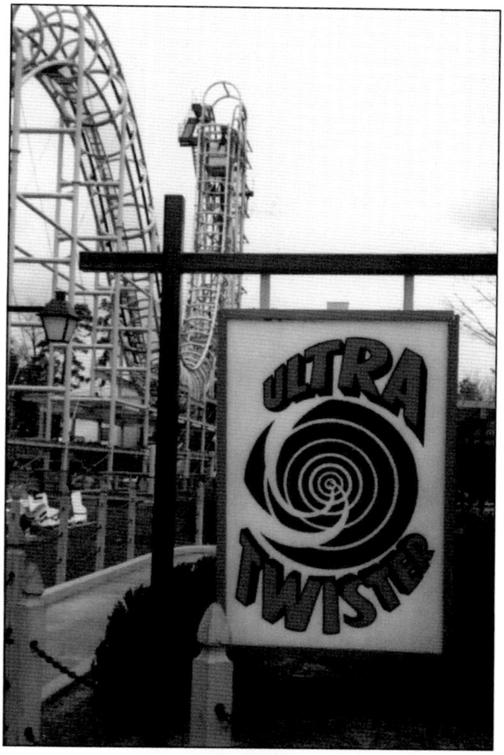

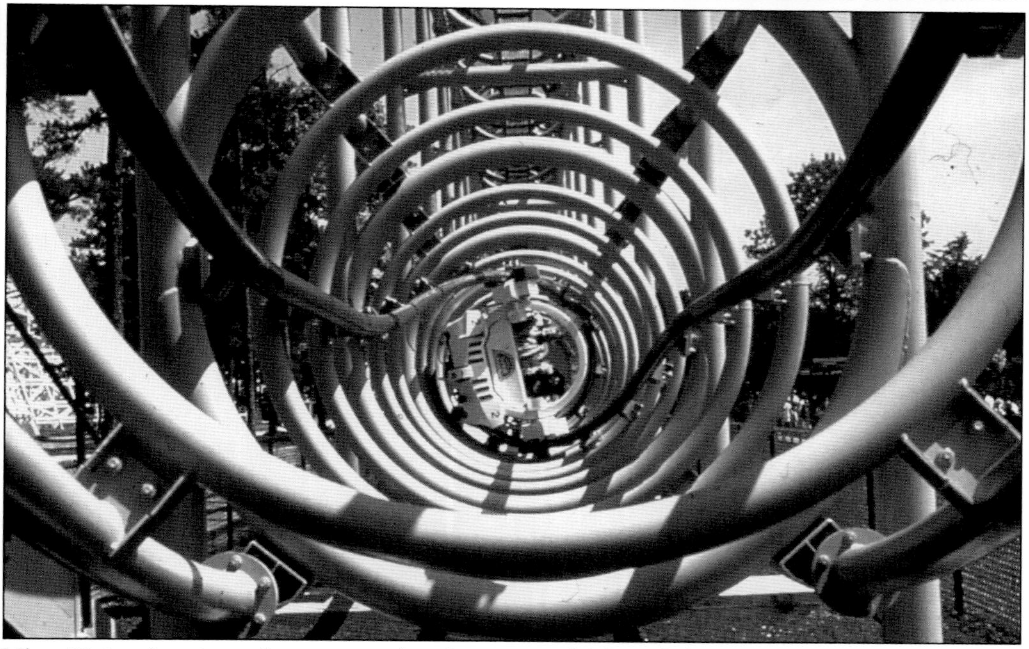

Ultra Twister's unique design started with a vertical lift and drop, and it was the first roller coaster in the world to perform a "heartline spiral" where the track spirals around the cars, keeping the riders bodies centered throughout the inversion. Another unique feature of the ride was the switch track mechanism that shuttled the cars from the upper to the lower track.

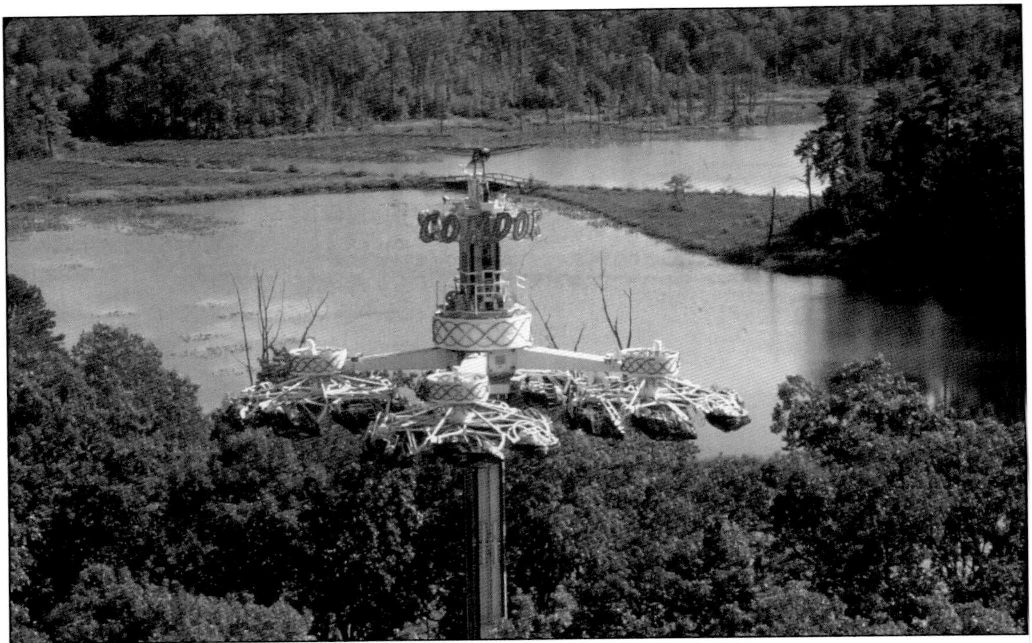

For 1988, the park introduced the new Bugs Bunny Land along with another brand-new innovation in rides, the Condor. Condor's ride combined both the rotations of a Scrambler-type ride with the added thrill of climbing a 100-foot tower. The ride provided both thrills and a spectacular view.

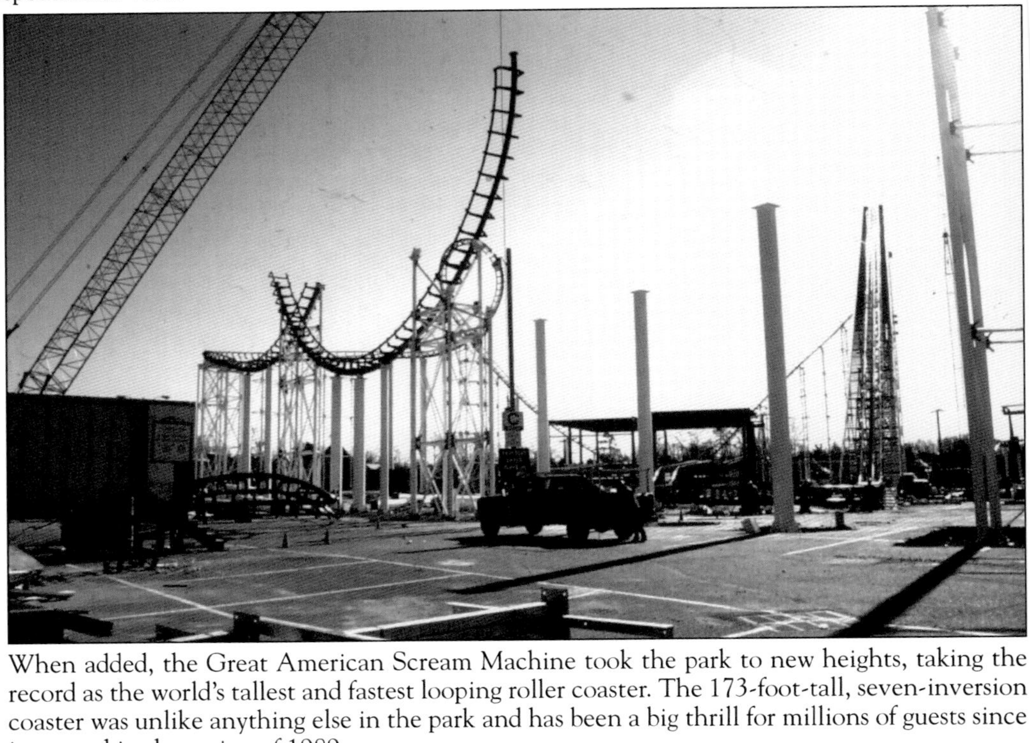

When added, the Great American Scream Machine took the park to new heights, taking the record as the world's tallest and fastest looping roller coaster. The 173-foot-tall, seven-inversion coaster was unlike anything else in the park and has been a big thrill for millions of guests since it opened in the spring of 1989.

For 1990, Six Flags Great Adventure challenged thrill seekers to stand up to the Shockwave, a roller coaster that took standing riders through a fast-paced ride down a 90-foot drop and into a vertical loop and around a compact twisted course. The ride was the first in the park to feature four-abreast coaster vehicles.

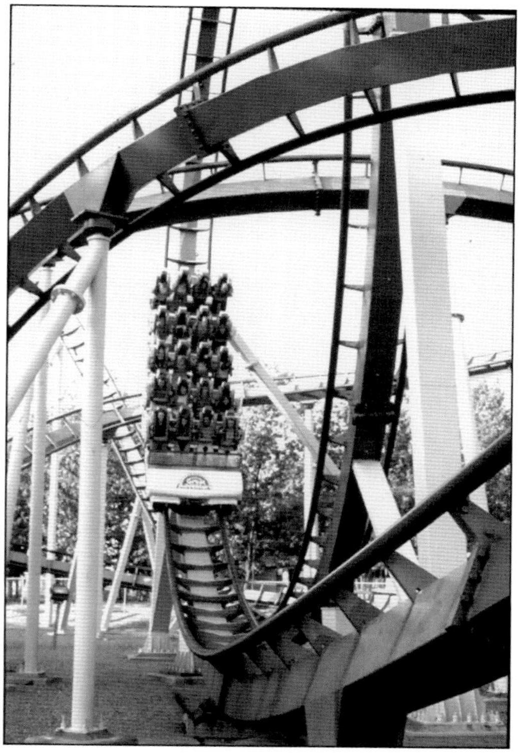

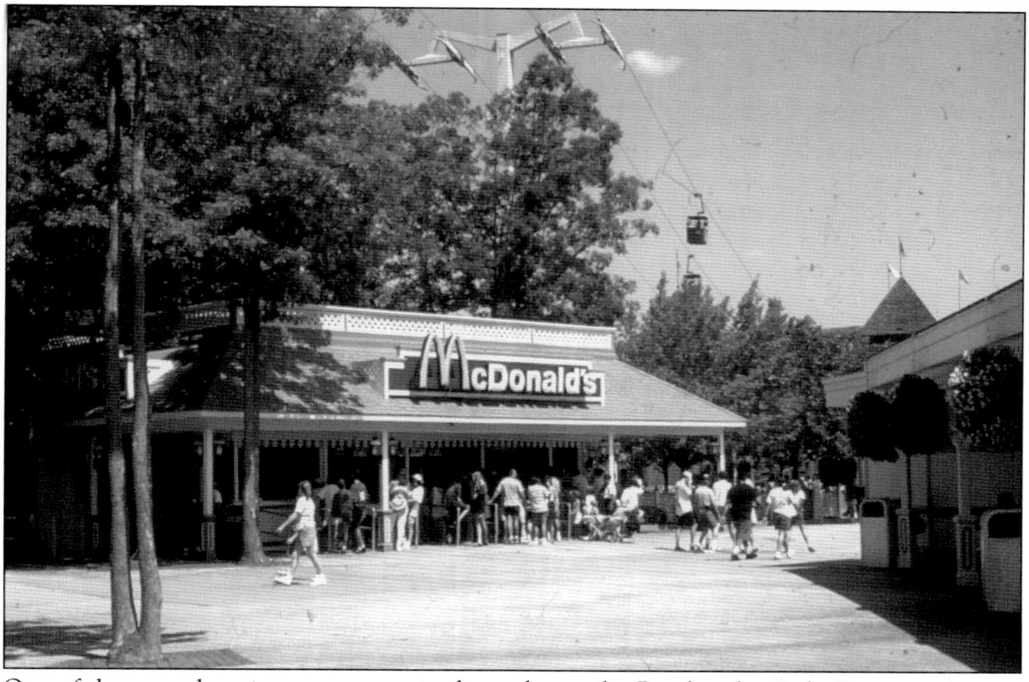

One of the ever-changing restaurants in the park was the Bandtandza Café. For several years, the location operated as a McDonald's, the first brand-name fast food in the park. Later the restaurant became the Showtime Café and now operates as the Looney Tunes Camp Kitchen.

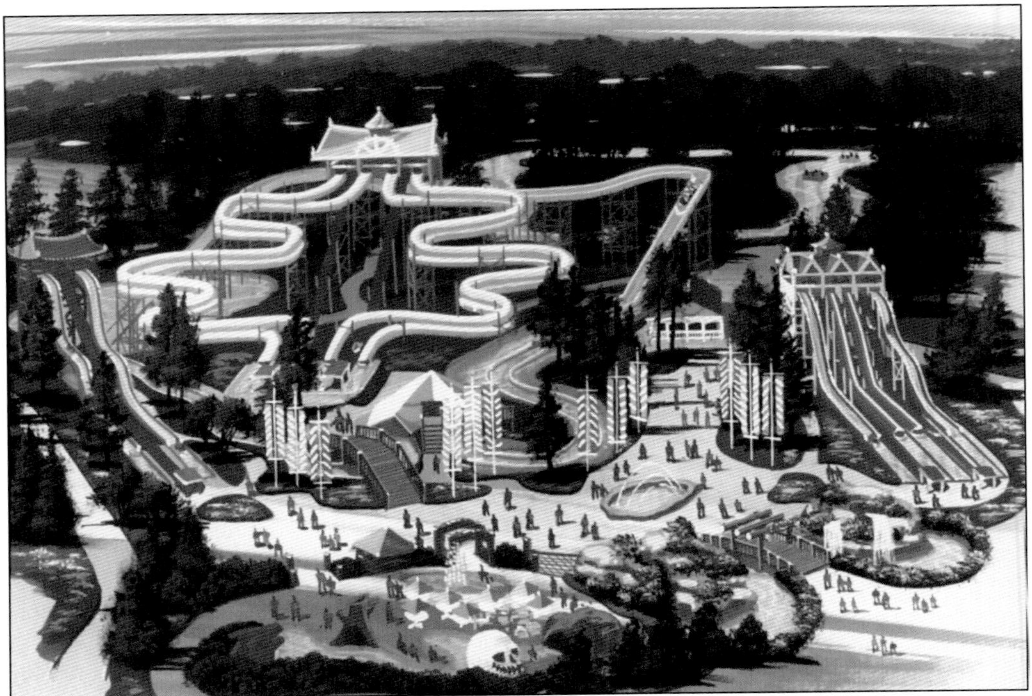

The 1991 season was an exciting one, with the addition of an entirely new themed area of the park, Adventure Rivers. The concept was an area of water rides themed to the rivers of the world. Originally the children's Koala Canyon section was planned for the entrance of the area but was relocated to the back of the section when constructed.

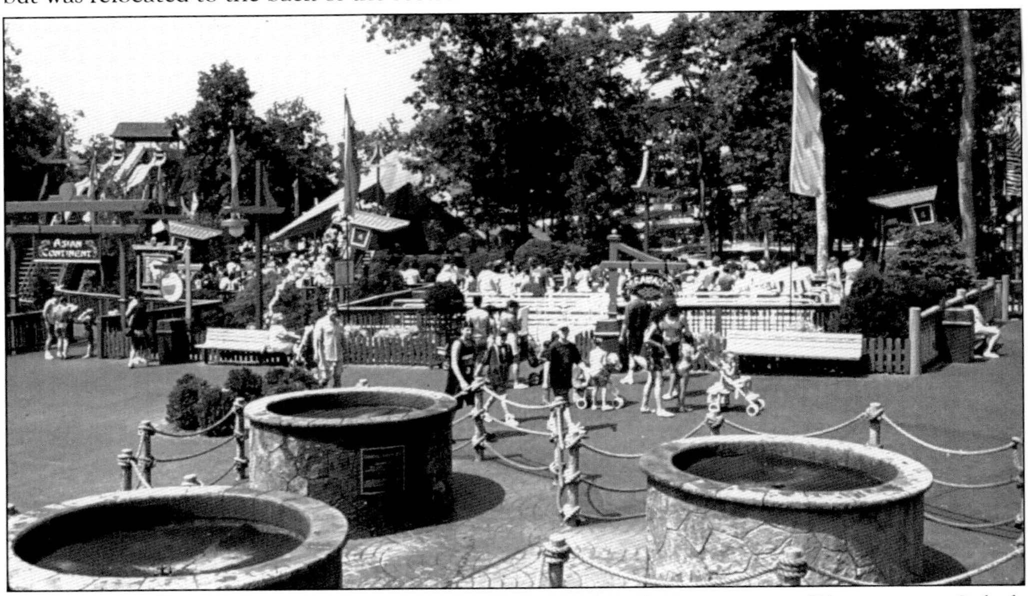

The Adventure Rivers area was beautifully landscaped and very inviting. The existing Splash Down flume (Moon Flume) and Roaring Rapids rides were included in the section, taking on the new names Irrawaddy Riptide and Congo Rapids, respectively. Adventure Rivers even featured a "jumping fountain" in the entrance plaza, seen here in the foreground.

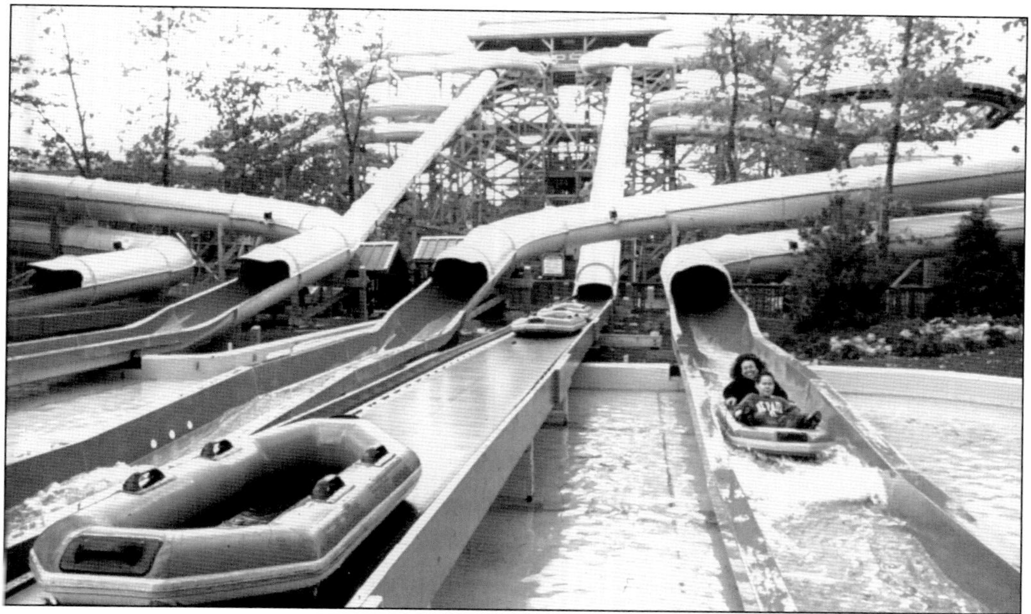

The dominant feature of Adventure Rivers was the Asian Tower, with its four bright yellow enclosed twisting tubes. Combined with the African and the North American Rivers slide complexes, the 10 slides added were "dry slides," not requiring guests to wear swimsuits since they rode in small rubber rafts.

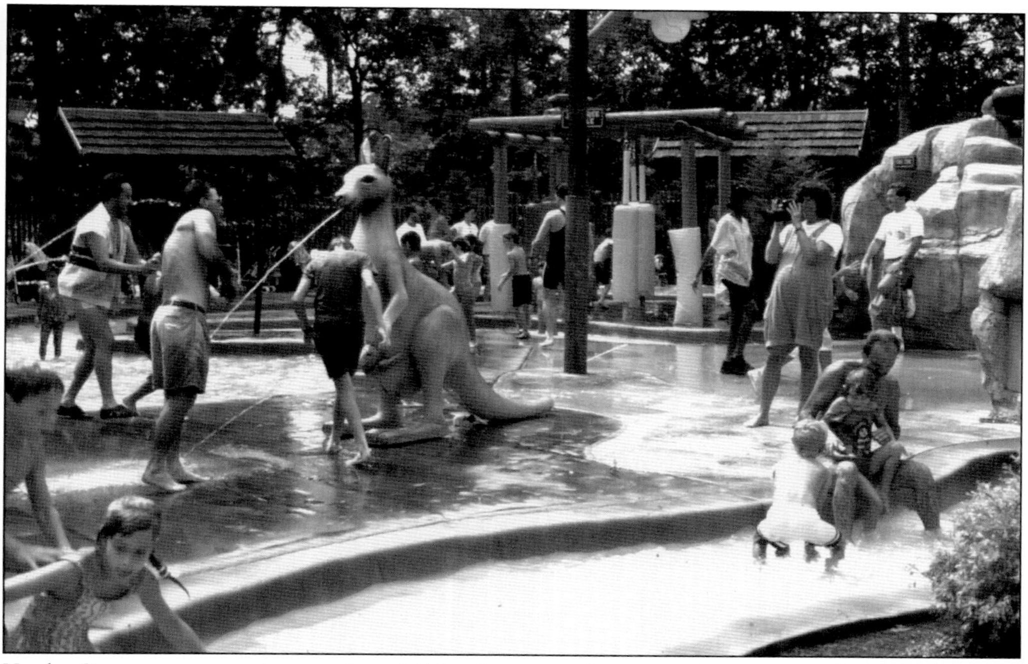

Koala Canyon was an interactive children's water play area, featuring wading pools, water cannons, and huge rubber Australian creatures. The entire area was covered with rubber padding to keep the playing kids safe, and an adjoining changing facility, restrooms, and a first aid station were built as part of the section.

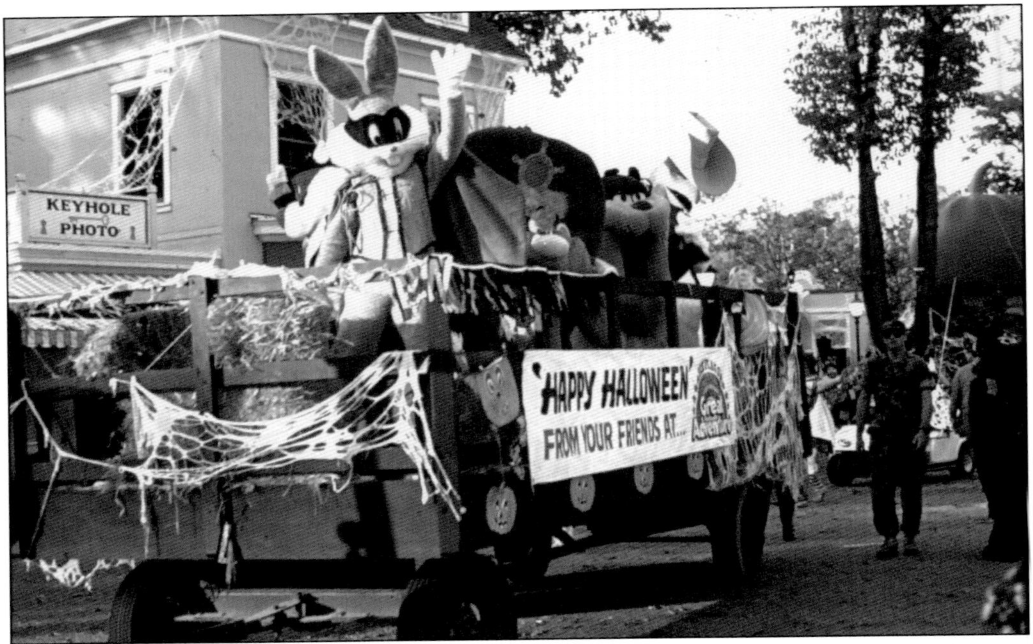

In 1989, the park began to extend the season with Halloweekends, the precursor to Fright Fest. Early events included a simple parade featuring the Looney Tunes characters in Halloween costumes riding on a hay wagon. The park's workers who dressed up in their own costumes were encouraged to join the parade as well.

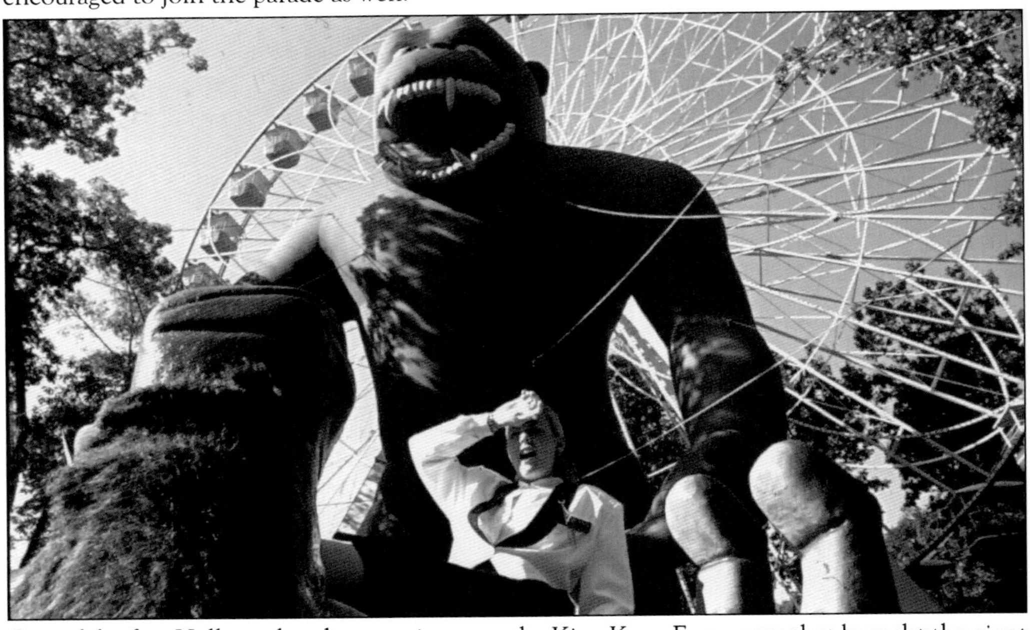

One of the first Halloweekends attractions was the King Kong Encounter that brought the giant inflatable ape to the theme park. This 70-foot-tall figure had been hung on the Empire State Building in 1983 as part of a celebration of the movie's 50th anniversary. Kong stood in front of the Big Wheel, and a life-size King Kong hand, once used for the park's Kong Photo booth, was available for pictures.

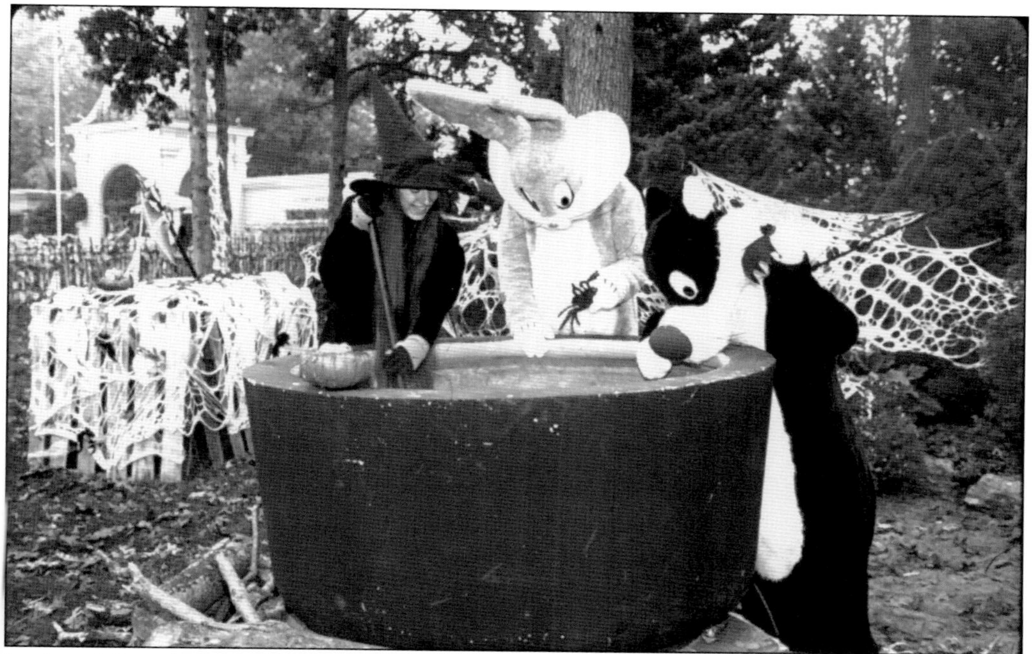

In this 1991 publicity photograph, the park's resident witch brews up some Halloweekends fun with Bugs Bunny and Sylvester. Each year's celebrations became more and more elaborate with more props and more special Halloween-themed attractions to satisfy the growing crowds. This year marked the beginning of the elaborate spiderweb decorations that have become synonymous with the park's Halloween celebrations through the years.

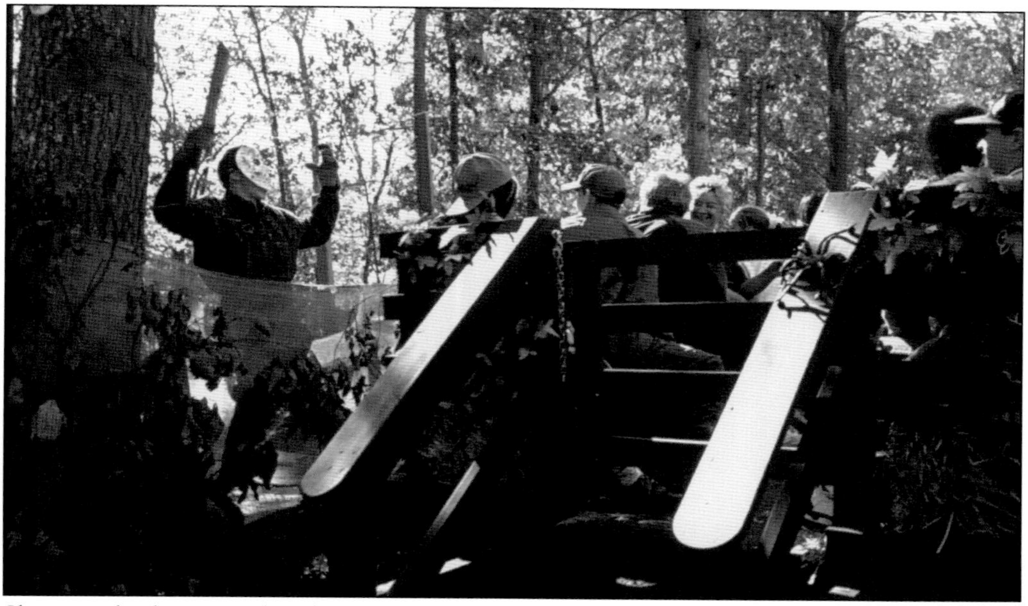

Shows and other special Halloween attractions were developed for the event, which became Fright Fest in 1992. Some of the featured additions were the indoor stage show, Thriller, and the very popular hayride. The hayrides drew long lines and often took guests into backstage areas that became journeys into the macabre.

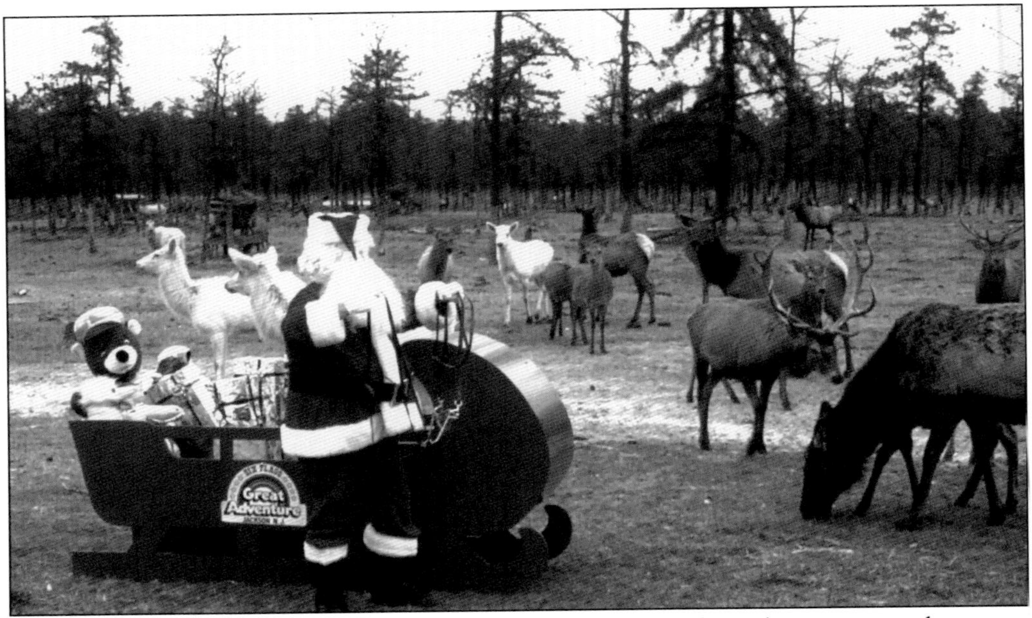

Santa brought his sleigh for a special visit to the Safari just before Christmas, spending some time visiting the cousins of the reindeer. The Safari's animals reside in the park year-round and are provided with shelter for the winter's coldest days. A full-time staff of more than 23 takes care of them all year long.

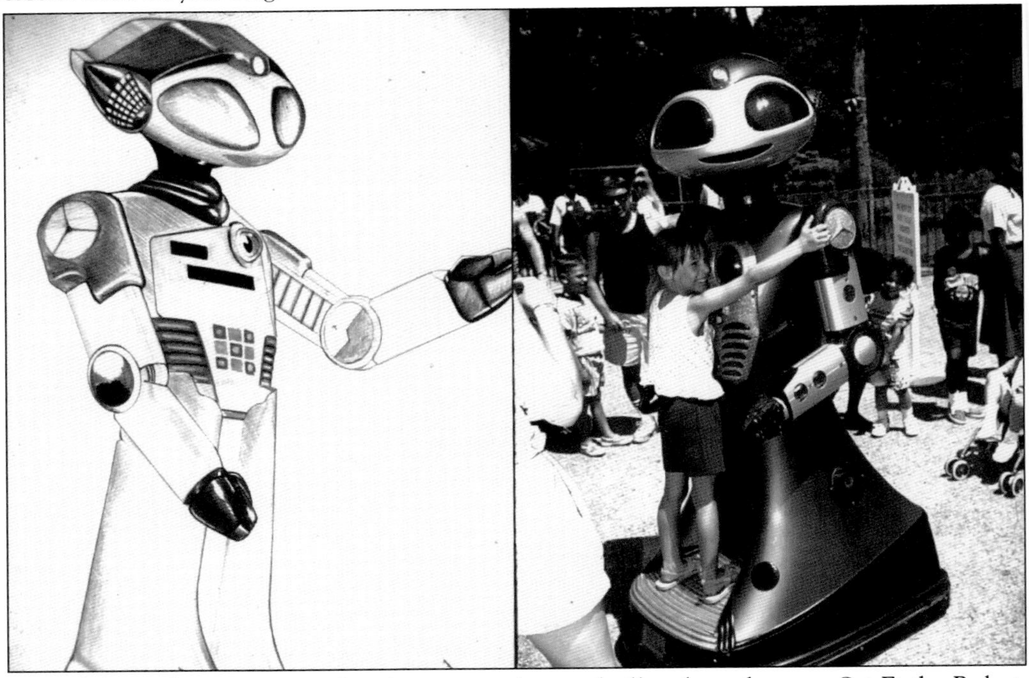

One of the park's most unusual and most popular goodwill ambassadors was Sci-Fi the Robot, introduced in the late 1980s. Sci-Fi appeared in the park and also traveled to schools and events throughout the Northeast with kids clamoring to stand on his platform as he sang and danced with them.

Four

It's Playtime!

In 1993, Time Warner acquired the Six Flags chain, and a total transformation of the parks began, which brought the magic of the Warner Brothers movies, television shows, and publications to Great Adventure. A renewed emphasis on bringing the "theme" elements back to the park took place, transforming some areas of the park that had no discernible theme into cohesive sections.

Themed rides like Batman: The Ride, the Right Stuff Mach 1 Adventure, Viper, and Skull Mountain were introduced under Time Warner's ownership. Later under the ownership of Premier Parks, world-class roller coasters were introduced, including Medusa, Nitro, and Superman Ultimate Flight, taking thrills to all new levels. Also added during this period was Six Flags Hurricane Harbor, an entirely new water park joining Six Flags Great Adventure and Six Flags Wild Safari Animal Park.

It was during this time that Fright Fest evolved into the hugely popular annual event it has become. Each year, more elaborate shows and attractions were added to the Halloween celebration, and each year, the event became more and more popular, growing into the largest Halloween event in the Northeast.

For the 2005 season, Six Flags took the "coaster arms race" that had been going on for the last 20 years to a whole new level, taking the title of the world's tallest and fastest roller coaster with Kingda Ka's 128-miles-per-hour race 456 feet into the sky. Kingda Ka was the cornerstone of a brand-new themed area of the park, the Golden Kingdom, which combined rides, shows, animals, and elaborate tropical theme elements.

Later that year, Six Flags management changed when Mark Shapiro, a former ESPN executive, took over as chief executive officer, and with that change in management came a change in focus, bringing back the priorities of cleanliness, courtesy, and creating a family-friendly atmosphere. A renewed emphasis on staff training and enforcement of a code of conduct made the park better than ever, with guest satisfaction levels at all-time highs, assuring that Six Flags Great Adventure will continue to delight future generations of visitors to this magical place.

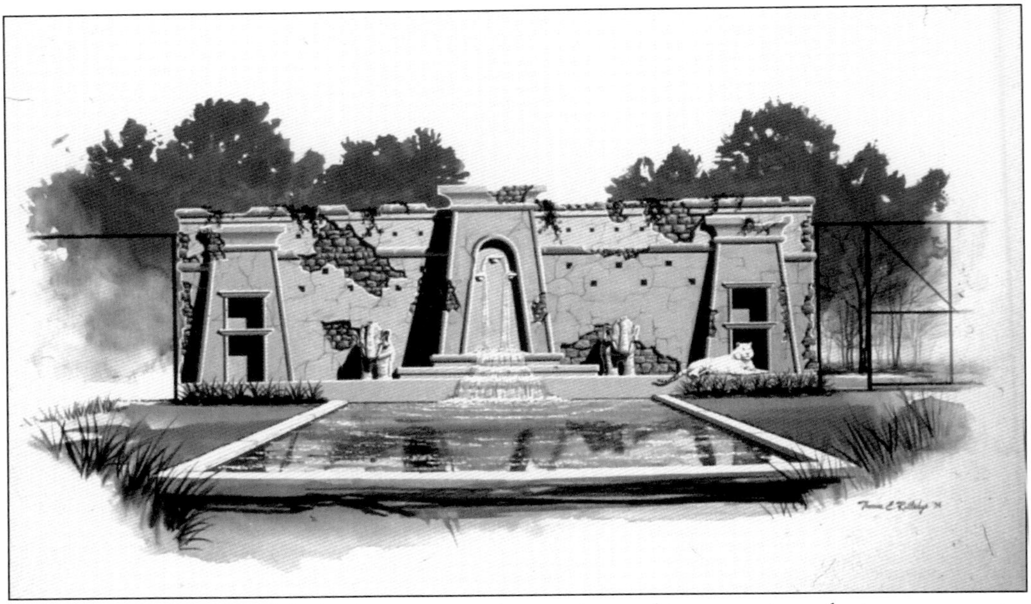

Over the years, the Wild Safari has continued to evolve and improve, introducing new species and exhibits. Rare and exotic white tigers came to the park in 1994, and they were given a unique temple-themed habitat reflecting the culture of their native India. Their habitat was added to the existing Siberian tiger section and was the first major structural addition to the Safari in the park's history.

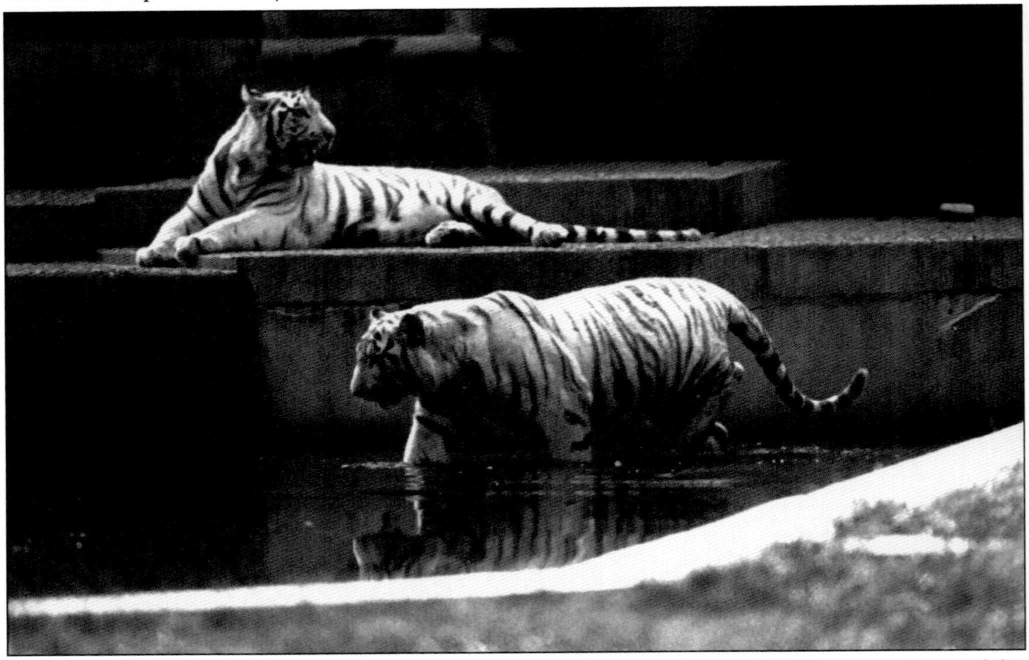

The white Bengal tigers were an instant hit with the crowds, with guests lingering in front of the habitat for extended periods of time watching them play in the water or bask in the sunshine. White Bengal tigers are an endangered species and have a longer life span in captivity. Their coat coloring, the result of a genetic mutation, makes them vulnerable in the wild.

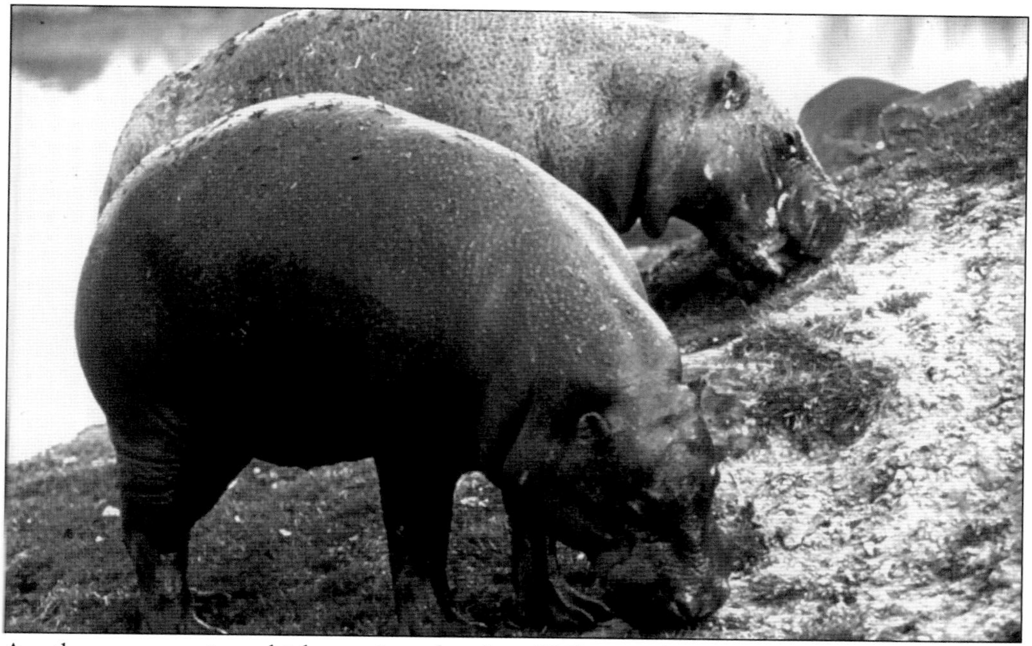

Another new species, which was introduced in 2000, was the pygmy hippo, although many guests never got to see them. The small hippos spent most of their day submerged, with only their nostrils breaking the water's surface. Infrequently these natives of West Africa could be found wandering on land when they emerged for meals.

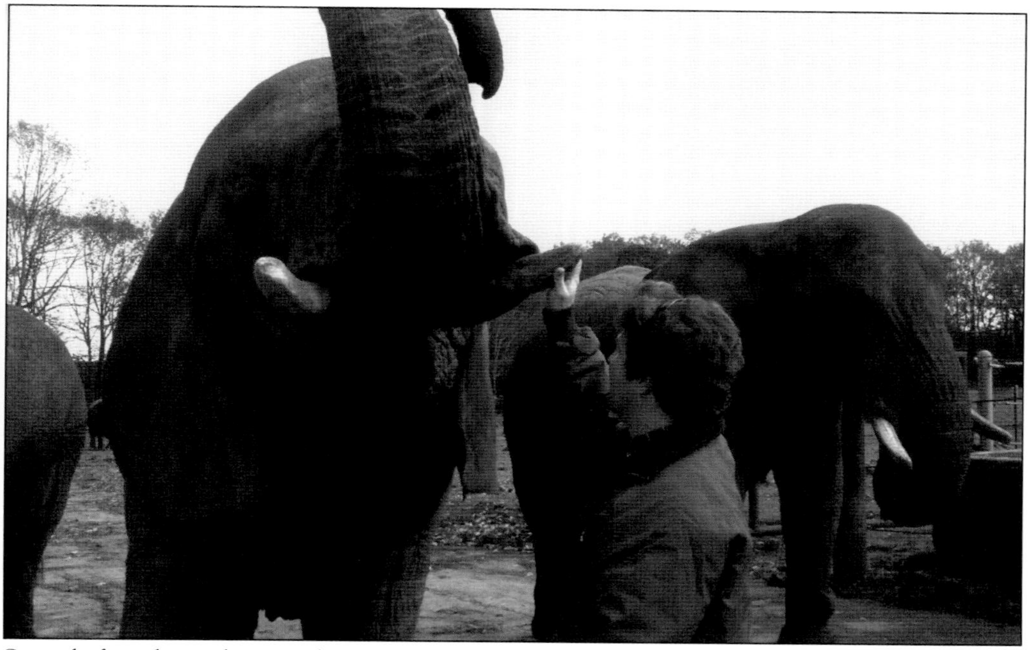

Since before the park opened, caring for the animals has always been a top priority. The Wild Safari veterinary staff specializes in the care of the many species of animals and attends to their needs. The care has resulted in thriving herds of animals and continued new generations of animals being born.

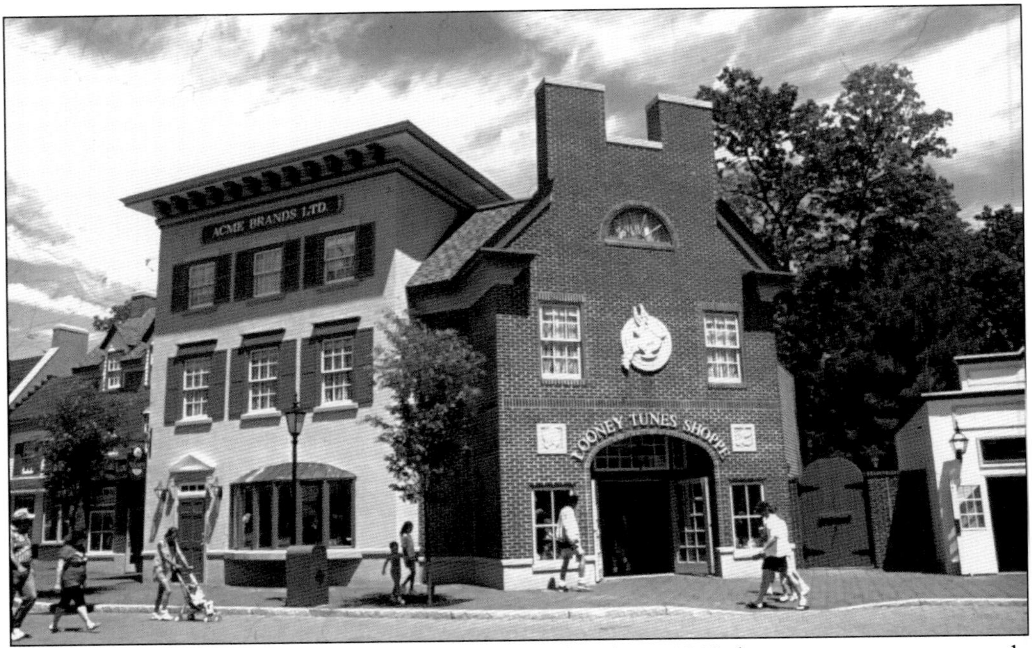

When Time Warner acquired the Six Flags chain of parks in 1992, big investments were made in all the parks to bring the "theme" back to theme parks. At Great Adventure, part of the effort included additional shops and other theme elements being added to Main Street, including the huge new Looney Tunes Shoppe, which prominently featured the Warner Brothers characters throughout.

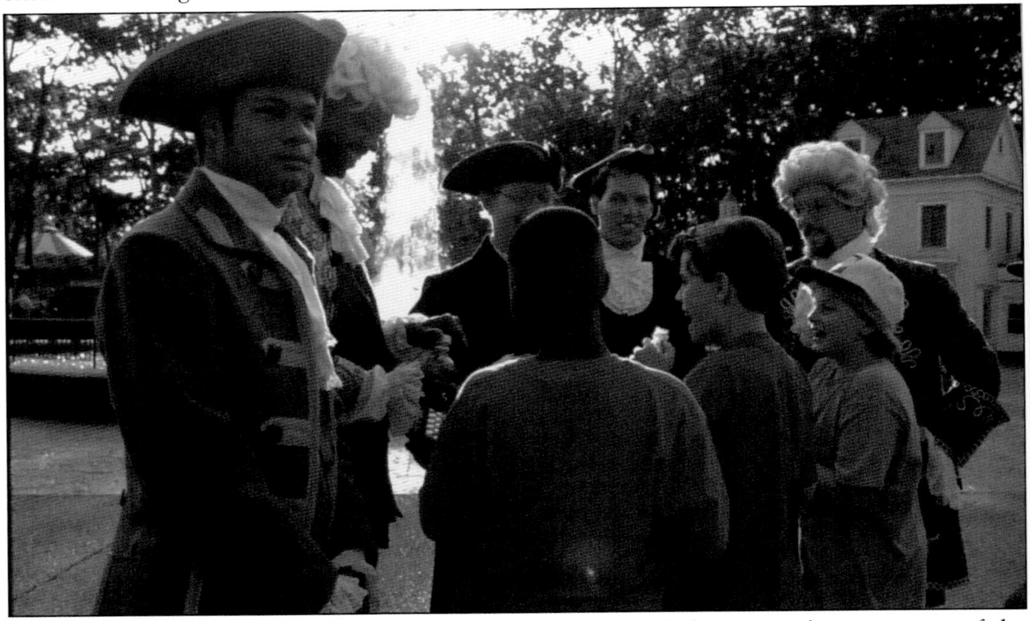

Other new additions to Main Street included new costumed characters that were part of the new Colonial/patriotic style of the entrance plaza. Sometimes these performers even included a fife-and-drum band. The Main Street area was expanded to include the shops and restaurants around the fountain and the Aqua Stadium, which was renamed Fort Independence.

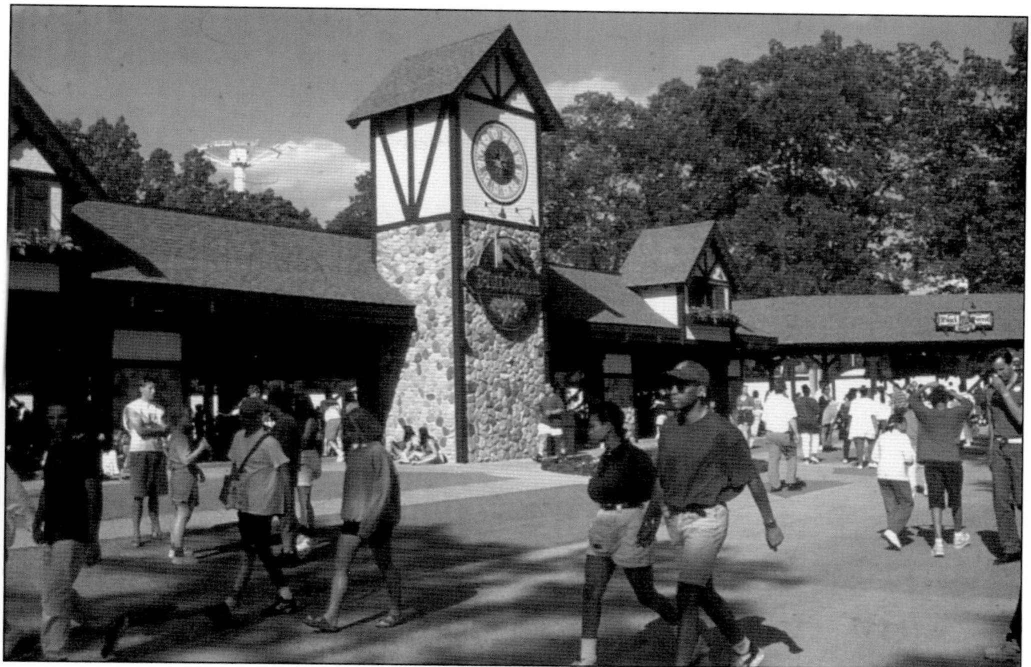

One section of the park, which had never had a true theme to it, was the area that became Old Country. The Enterprise, waffle cone stand, and Musik Express already had a slight European appearance to them, which was enhanced with the addition the Autobahn bumper cars and surrounding new games. This along with a name change from Enterprise to Spin Meister further solidified the Old Country as a cohesively themed area.

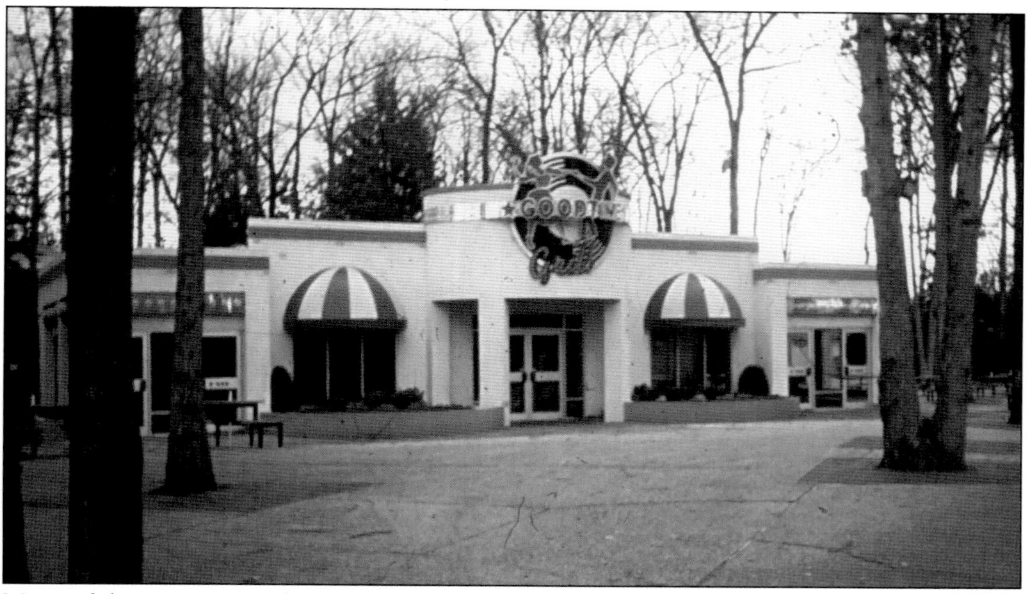

Many of the very generic buildings that had been added to the park over the years were given makeovers to help them fit the areas they were part of. One example of this was the Big Wheel Burger restaurant, which was expanded, improved, and given a 1950s-diner-style makeover to become the Goodtime Grill.

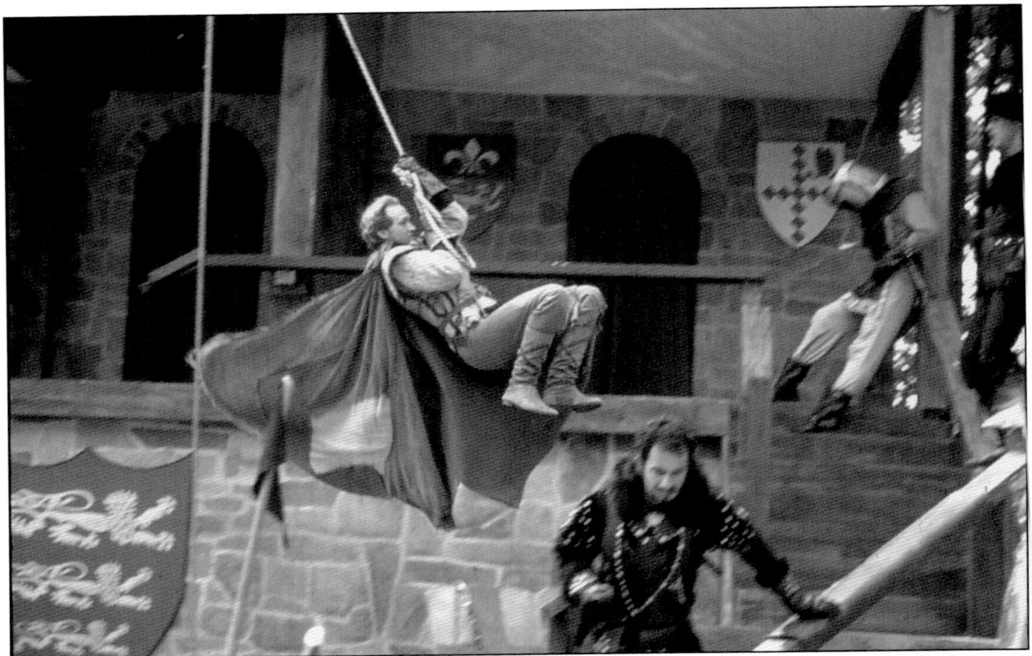

Time Warner sought to promote its movies and brands throughout the Six Flags parks, and Great Adventure was one of the first to debut a stunt show. The Robin Hood: Prince of Thieves show debuted in the summer of 1991, promoting the Kevin Costner film of the same name. The action-packed show played on a temporary stage built next to the Yum Yum Palace.

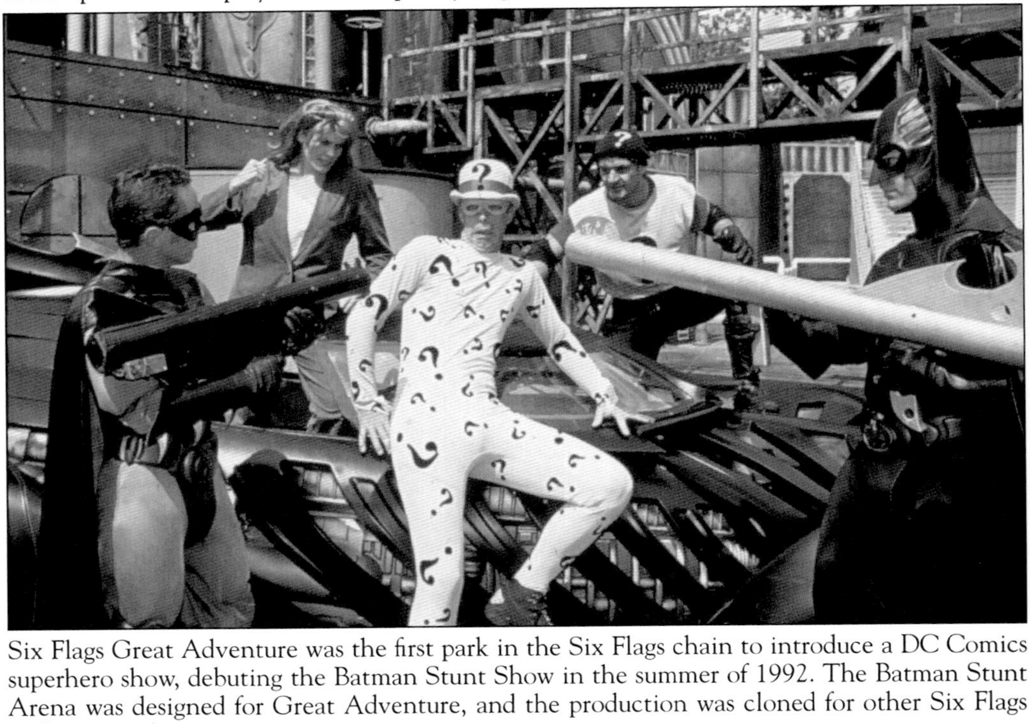

Six Flags Great Adventure was the first park in the Six Flags chain to introduce a DC Comics superhero show, debuting the Batman Stunt Show in the summer of 1992. The Batman Stunt Arena was designed for Great Adventure, and the production was cloned for other Six Flags parks across the country.

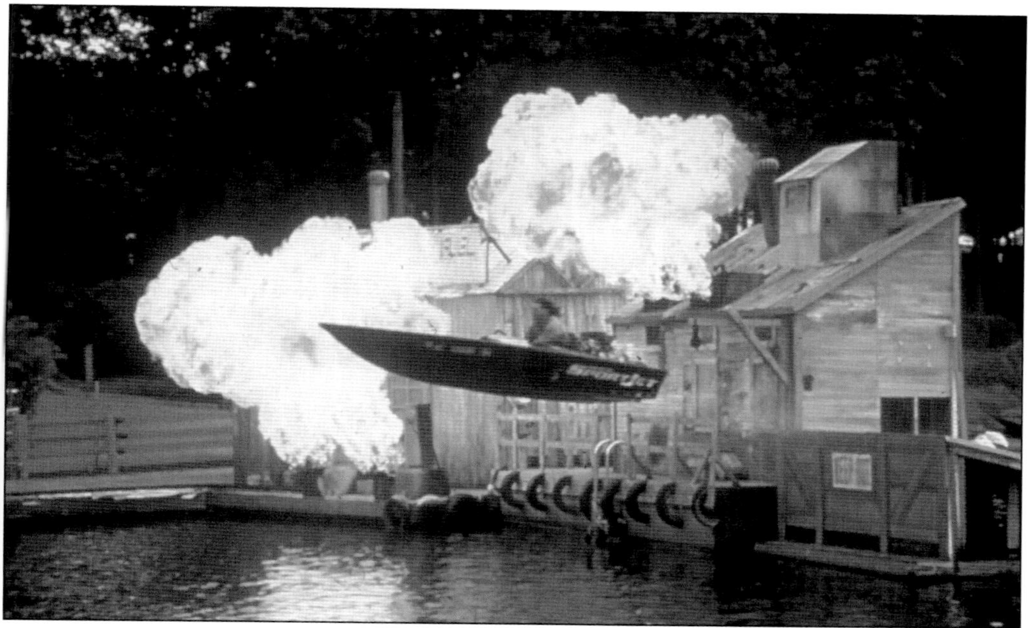

Following the success of the Batman Stunt Show, in 1996, the park's Great Lake became home to the Lethal Weapon Stunt Spectacular. Expertly trained daredevils on Jet Skis and in boats performed a variety of stunts both on water and on land. The show featured impressive pyrotechnic explosions that wowed audiences.

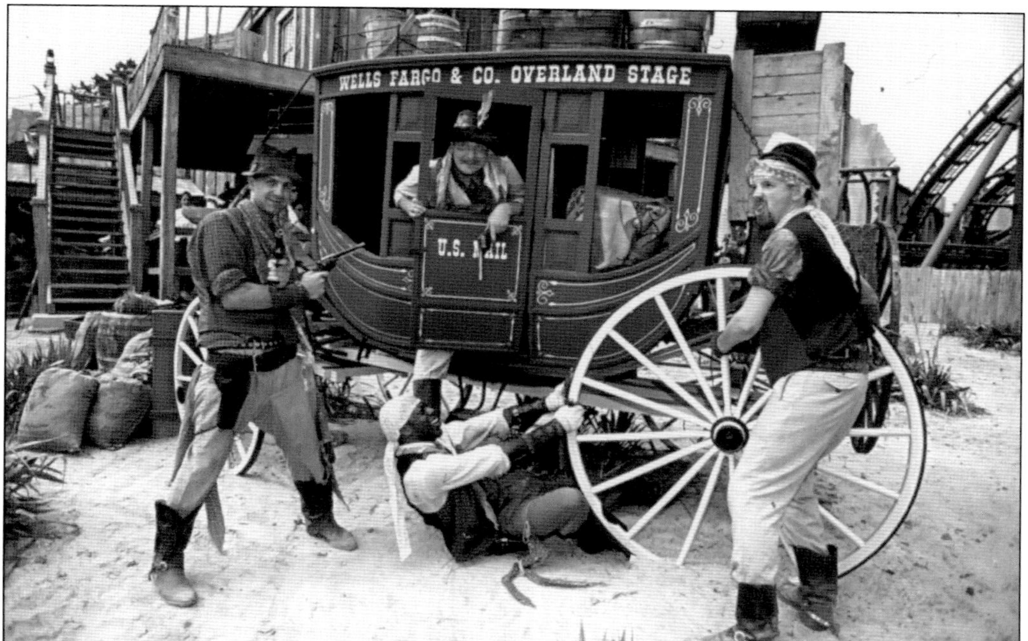

With the addition of the old west–themed Viper roller coaster for the 1995 season, a comedy western show was soon added in the desert area alongside the ride's ghost town–themed queue, which doubled as a backdrop. The stagecoach pictured here was once part of the Great Arena's Wild, Wild West Show, which debuted when the park opened in 1974.

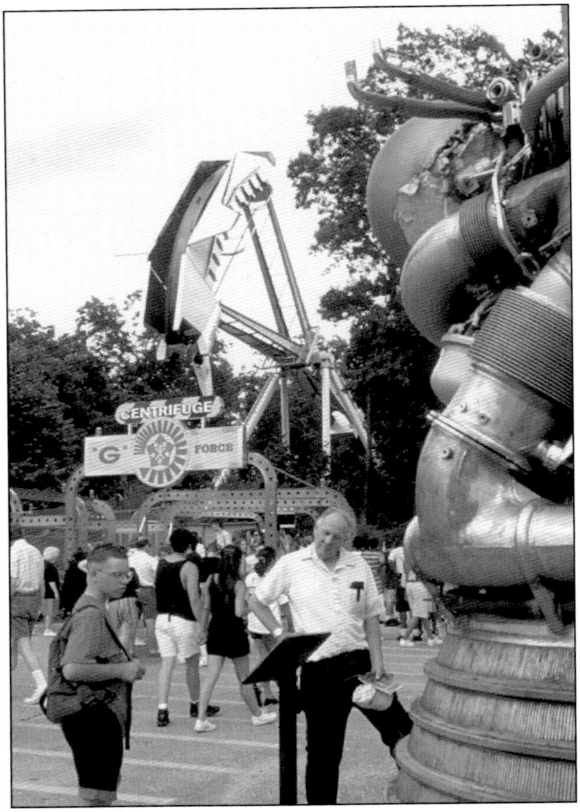

The biggest changes in the park while Time Warner was running the show occurred in the former Fun Fair area, which was completely revamped, becoming Action Town for 1992 and then Movietown for the 1993 season. Existing rides were given movie themes with the Space Shuttle and Centrifuge G-Force being themed to *The Right Stuff*, complete with space capsule and rocket engine props.

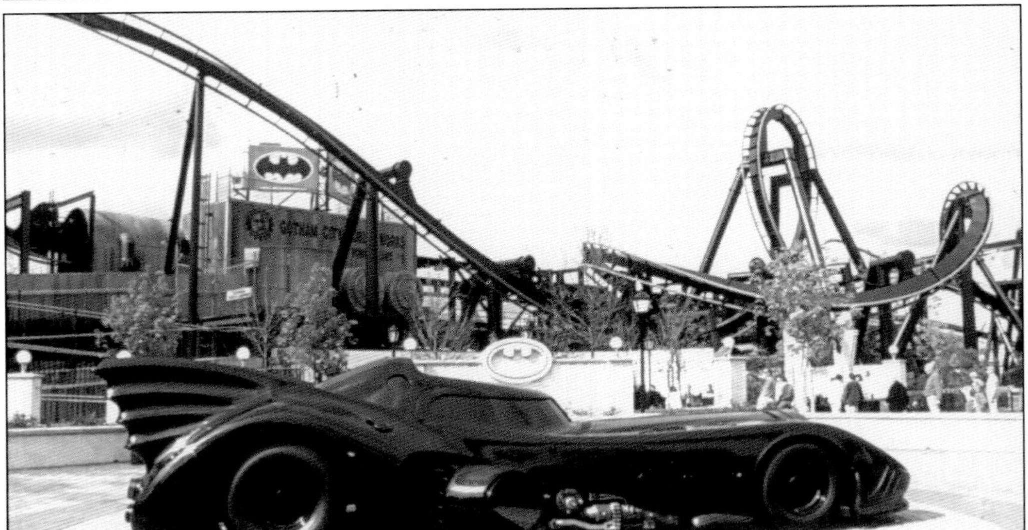

The new addition that really changed Movietown was Batman: The Ride, one of the first inverted roller coasters ever built. The coaster was a huge success and went beyond being a run-of-the-mill attraction, with immersive theme elements throughout the queue, taking riders into the depths of Gotham City.

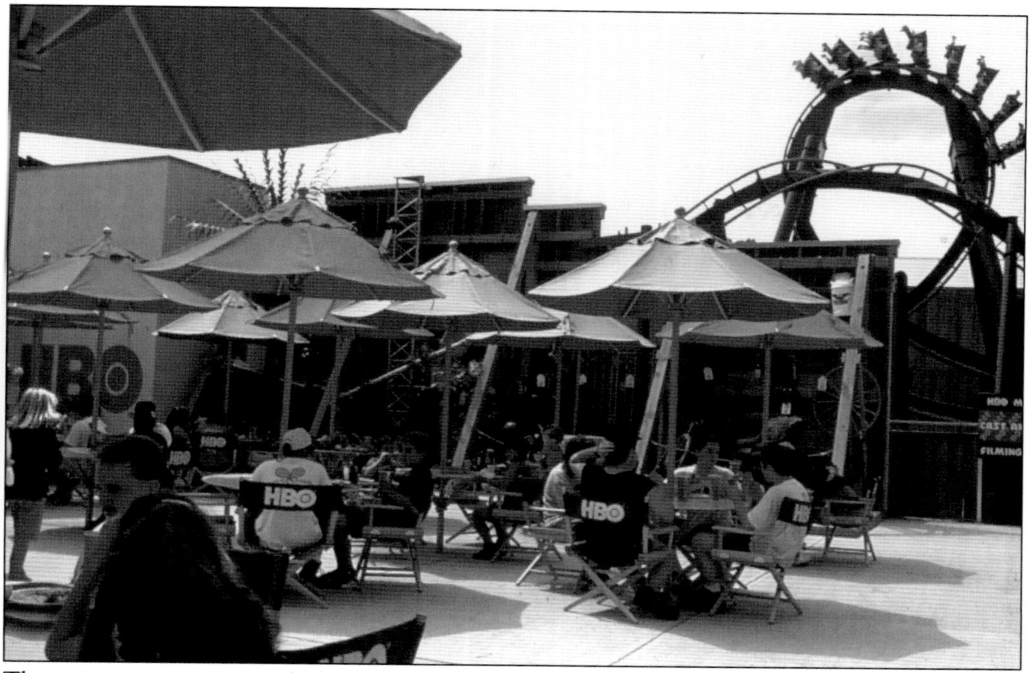

The existing restaurants of Movietown were given a movie makeover, along with all the rides in the section. The pair of restaurants and the patio between them became the HBO Backlot Commissary and were fitted with director chair–style seating and surrounded with movie props of all shapes and sizes.

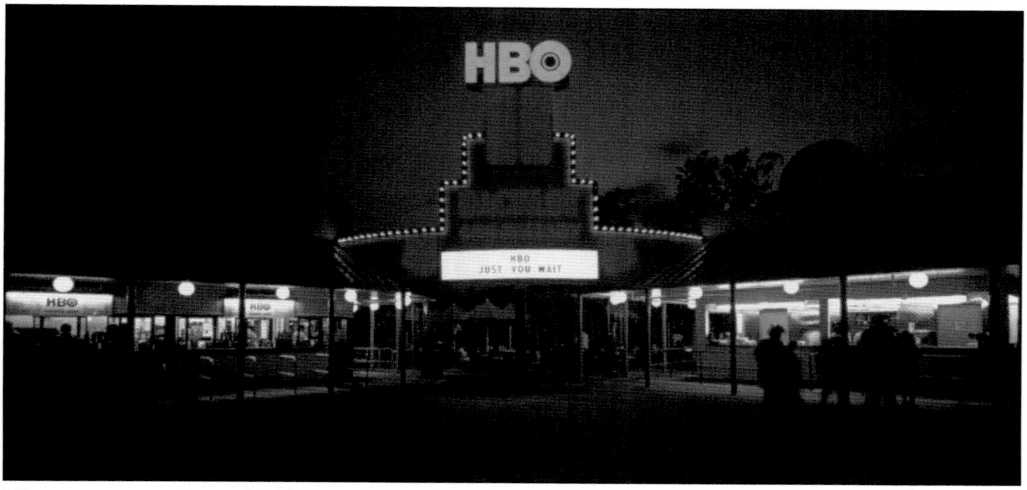

The premium channel HBO was another division of Time Warner, and the HBO Backlot Commissary was part of the cross promotion of the company's brands. The restaurants formerly known as La Pizzeria and Splashwater Snacks were connected with a Hollywood-style neon marquee covered with lights.

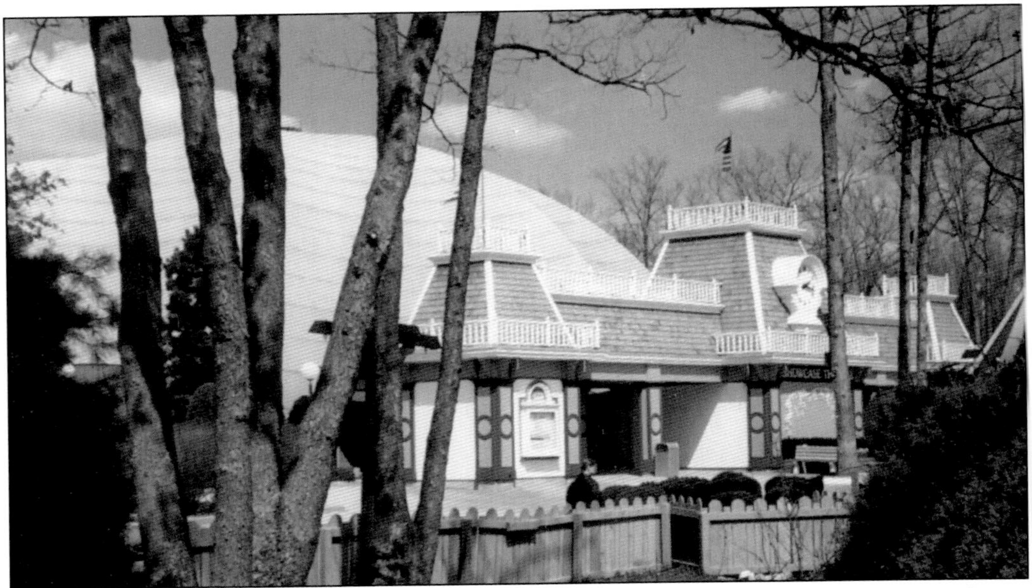

The 1,162-seat Showcase Theater, originally named the Americana Music Hall, was home to several Warner Brothers–themed stage shows as part of Movietown. Some of the shows included a *Dennis the Menace* screen test, a pictorial history of the making of the motion picture *Maverick*, and the Music of Warner Brothers, a retrospective of movie soundtracks. (GreatAdventureHistory.com collection.)

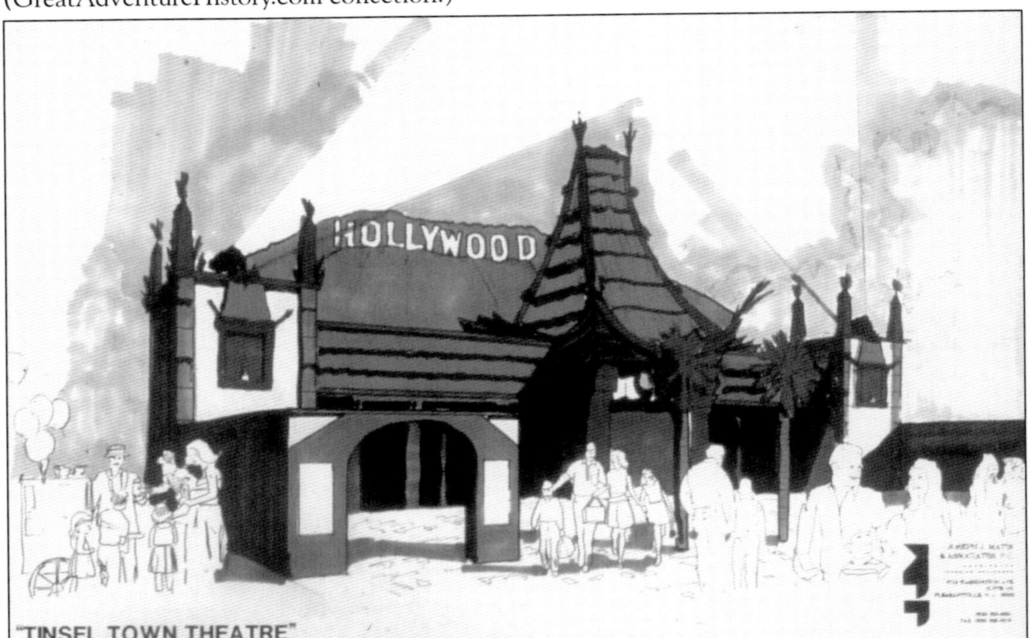

One of the plans for reinventing the attractions of Movietown that never came to fruition was renaming the Showcase Theater and adding a new facade to the building. The rendering above shows a new Grauman's Chinese Theater–style roof being added and the addition of a Hollywood sign on the "hill" formed by the tent building, turning the facility into the Tinsel Town Theatre.

The Time Warner Boutique was the new gift shop added to Movietown, and it featured products from all of Time Warner's many brands, including movies, music, and publishing. Many of the products sold were upscale and not the typical theme park souvenirs. The exterior of the building featured movie posters of current Warner Brothers films.

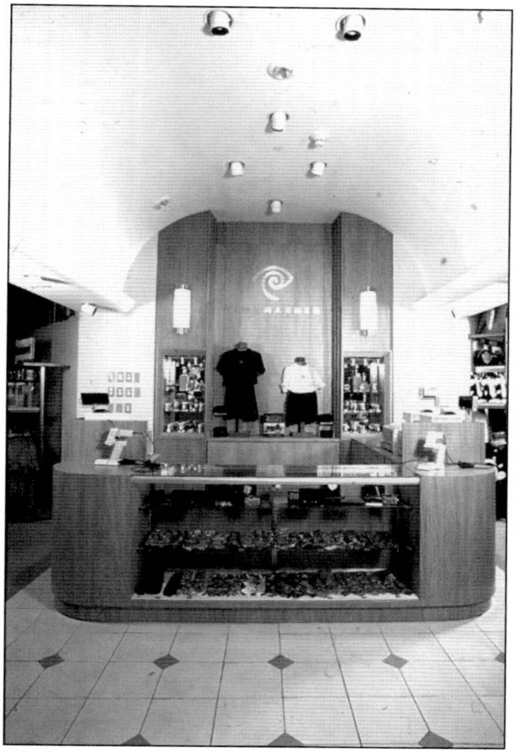

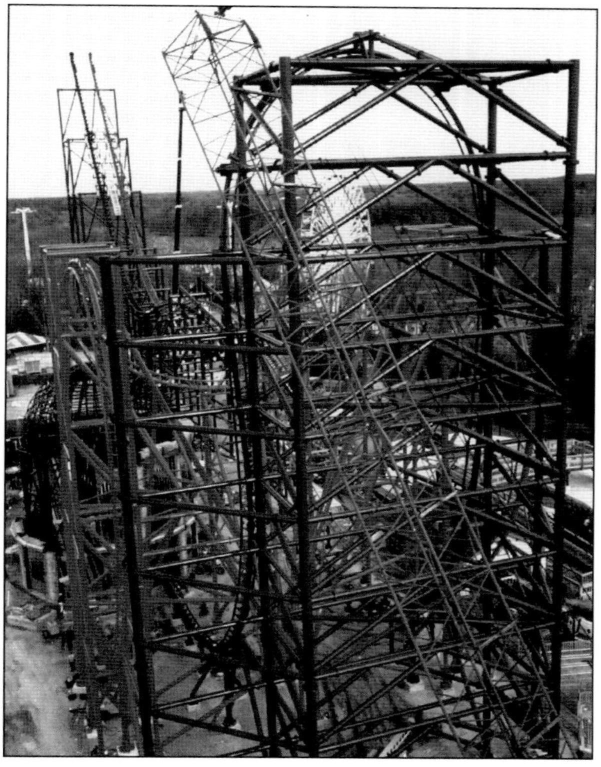

Built in 1997 to coincide with the release of the *Batman and Robin* movie, Batman and Robin: The Chiller was a first-of-its-kind dual-launching, linear induction coaster. While in the park, the ride was modified several times, with the over-the-shoulder restraints being replaced to enhance rider comfort, and the track itself receiving modifications before the ride's removal to make way for future attractions in Movietown.

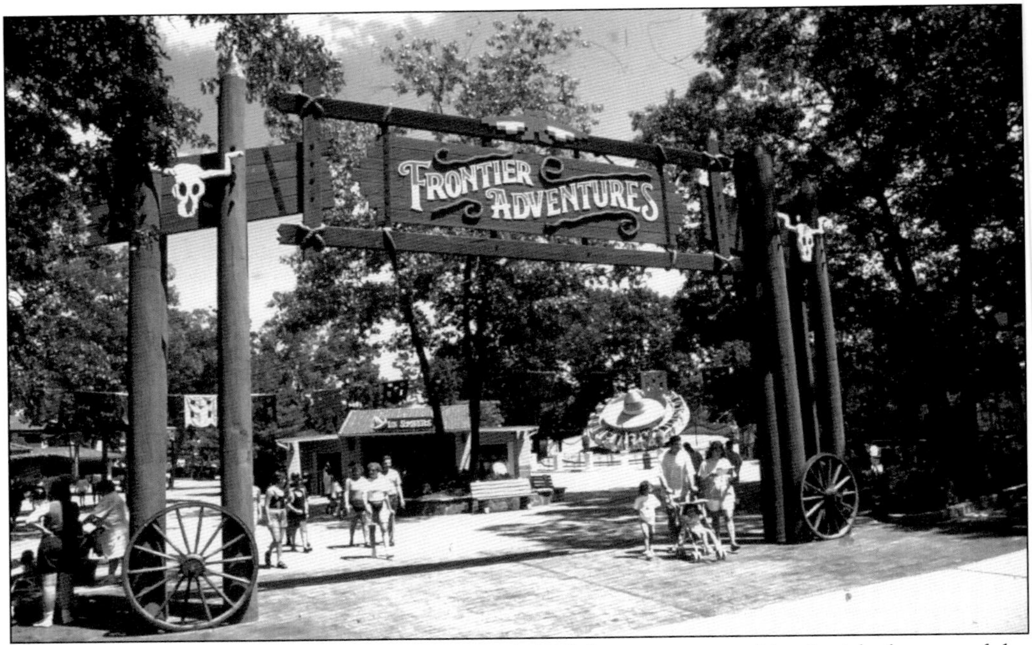

The section of the park that had been Hernando's Hideaway was combined with the rest of the park's western section to form Frontier Adventures. Additional attractions and theme elements were added, including a new fountain, the Dry Gulch Shooting Gallery, and the relocated Schwabinchen ride, which was rethemed as El Sombrero.

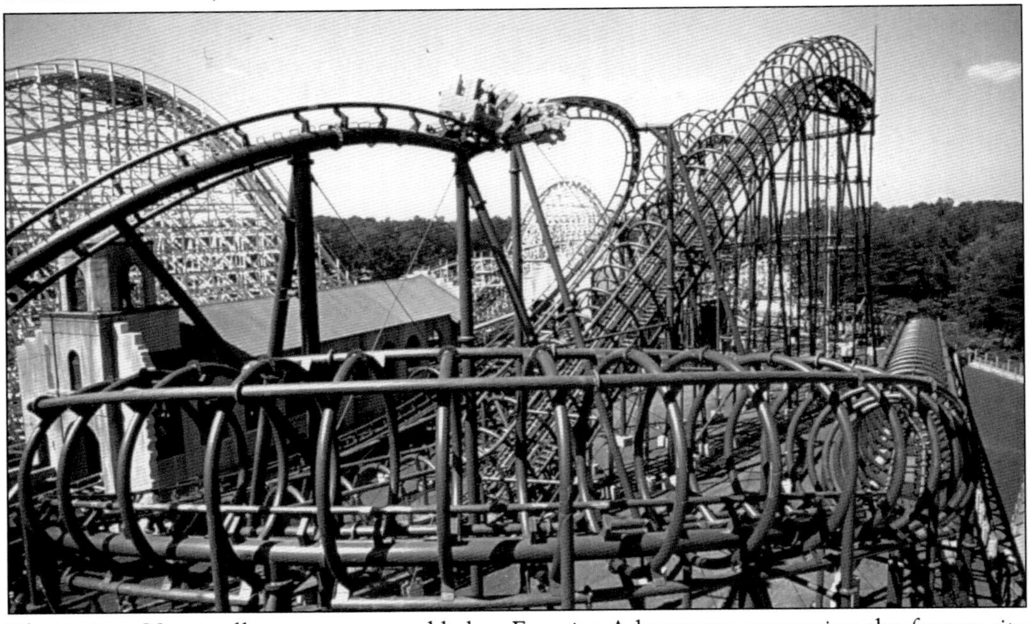

The unique Viper roller coaster was added to Frontier Adventures, occupying the former site of Ultra Twister and bringing new life to what had been a deserted area. The coaster was a prototype that had been brought to Great Adventure for the 1995 season, and the ride's station and queue were given impressive old west–style theme elements to fit the snakelike appearance of the ride.

Bugs Bunny Land was given a revamped entrance as part of the retheme efforts throughout the park. A giant tree stump replaced the original rainbow-colored archway, and a second tree was added under the central shade structure, with leaves painted on the canvas roof above. Decorative cartoon-style backdrops were installed on the area's perimeter fence as part of the makeover.

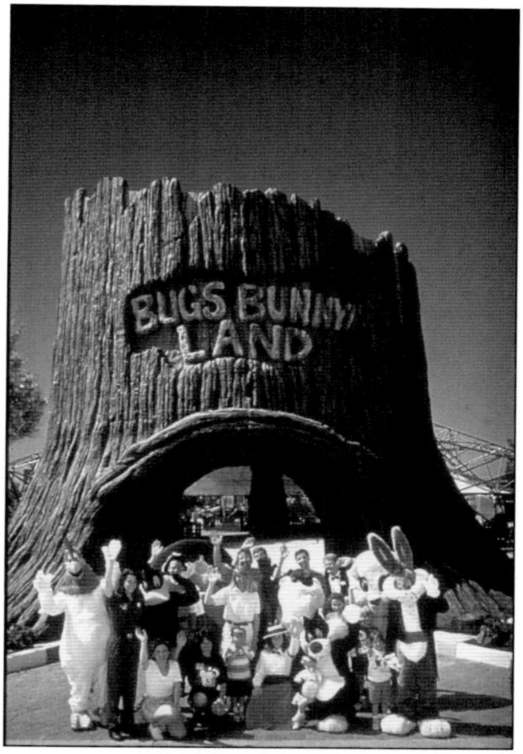

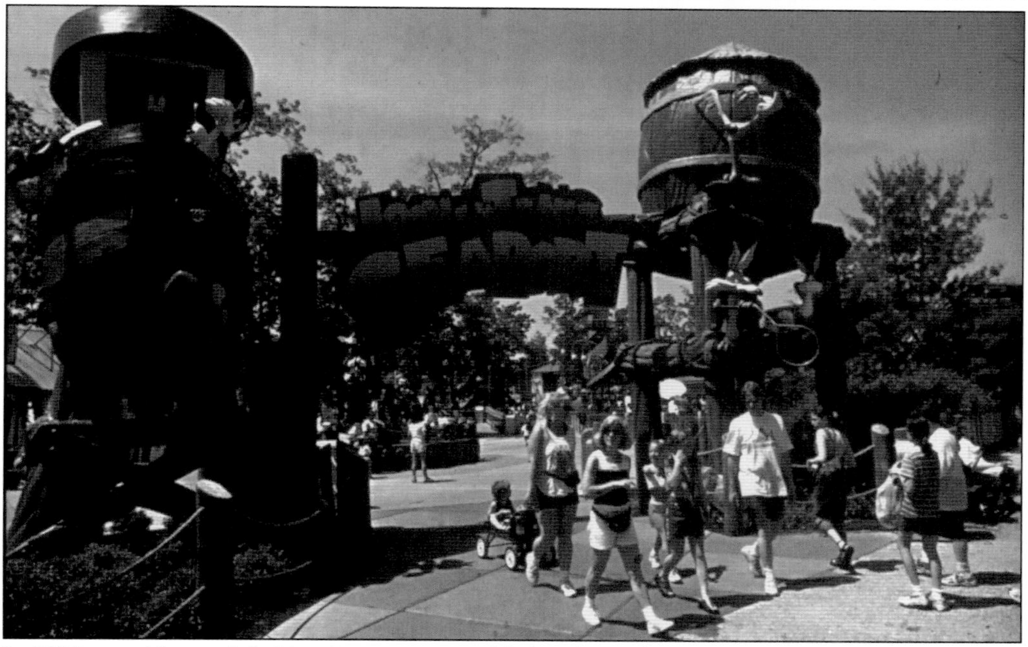

In 1999, an additional children's section was added to the park, taking the place of the Adventure Rivers slides. Looney Tunes Seaport was part of the 1999 "War on Lines, " which brought more than 25 new attractions to the park in one season. The Koala Canyon, a children's water play area, was incorporated into the new Seaport section.

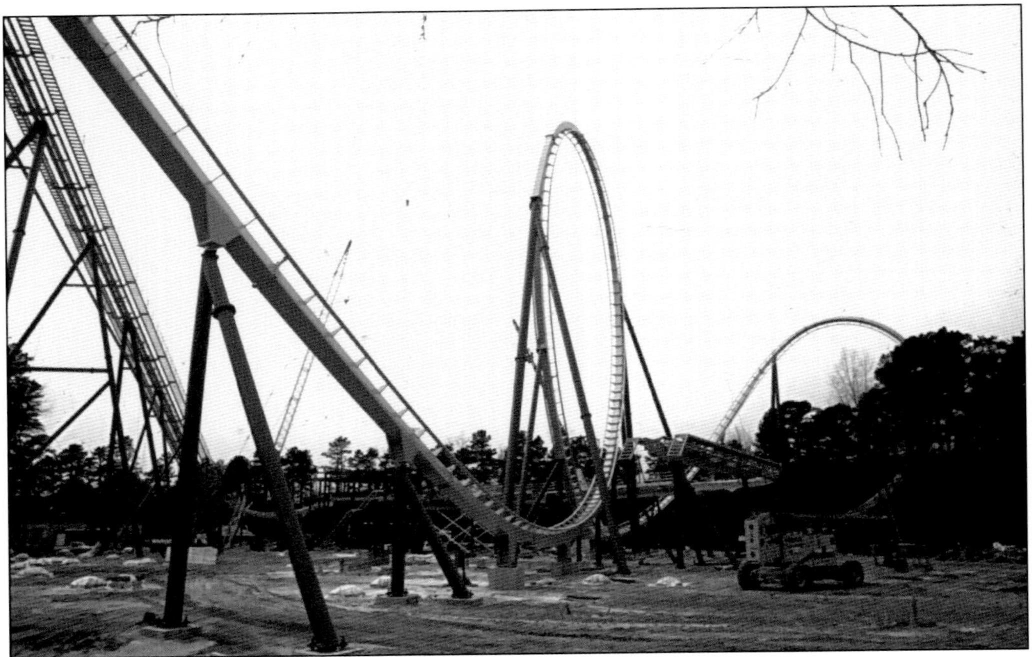

The largest of the new attractions of the 1999 season was Medusa, which was the world's first "floorless" roller coaster and built by the creators of Batman: The Ride, Bolliger and Mabillard. The bright green and purple coaster was added to the Frontier Adventures section and given a backstory of the legend of the Medusa Mine.

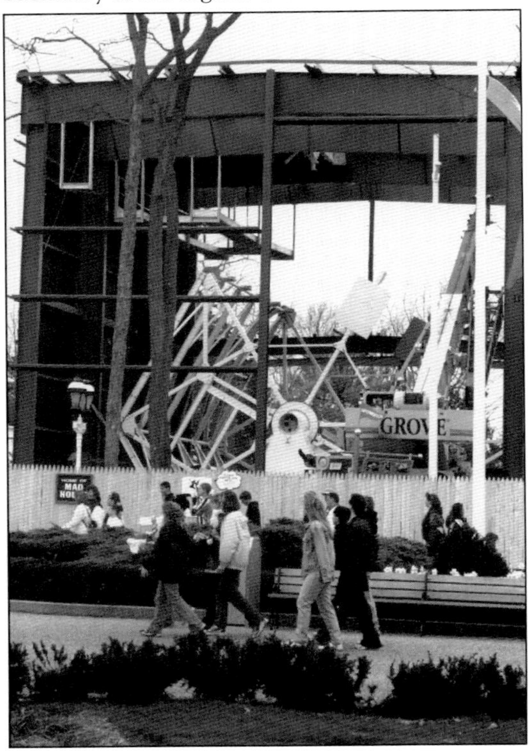

The most unique ride added in 1999 was Houdini's Great Escape, a "mad house" ride that created the illusion the riders were turning upside down inside a room. Seen here under construction, the white framework is the drum that forms the room that rotated around the riders to create the effect. (GreatAdventureHistory.com collection.)

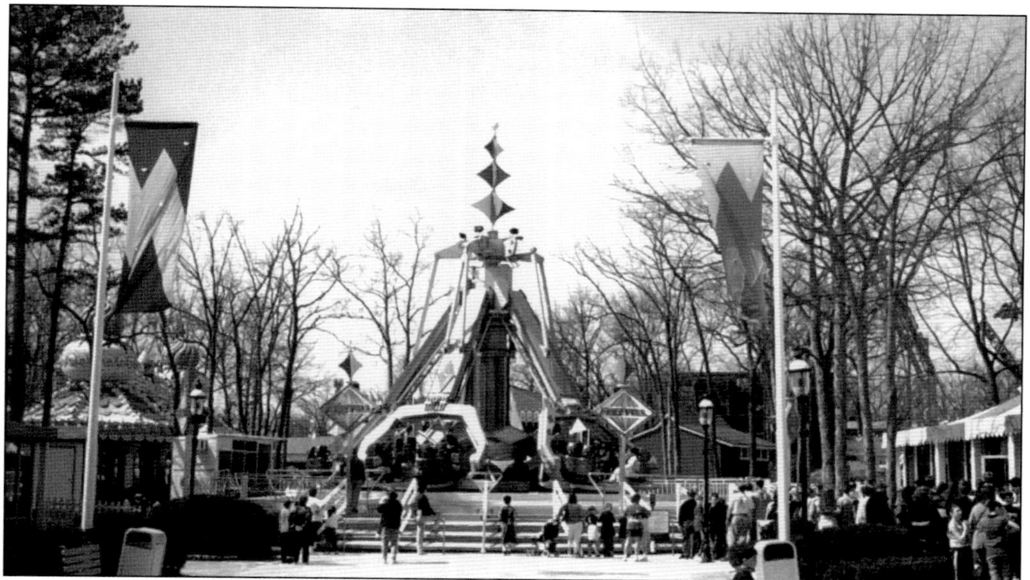

Always on the cutting edge of thrills, Six Flags brought several first-of-their-kind attractions to the park with the War on Lines. One of the most visible of the new rides was Jumpin' Jack Flash, a unique ride that spun riders while lifting and dropping them at random intervals. The ride was visually stunning but suffered many growing pains that resulted in downtime. (GreatAdventureHistory.com collection.)

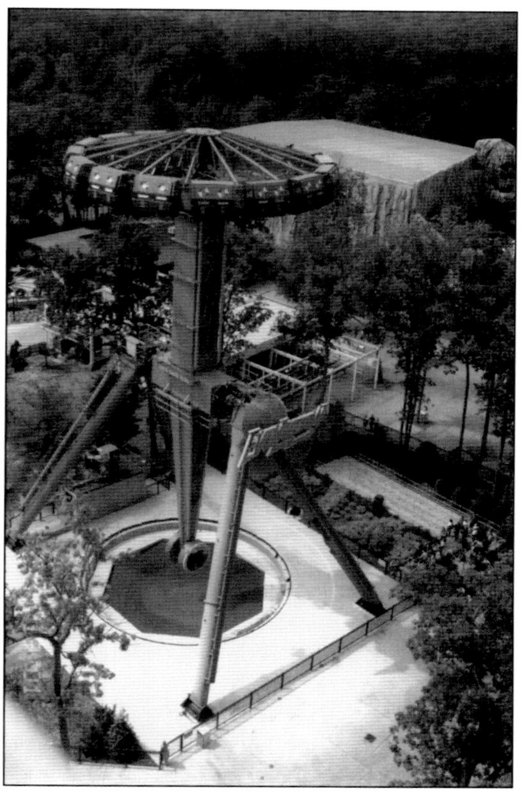

The largest of the flat rides introduced in 1999 was Evolution, another prototype that had been operated on the European fair circuit before coming to the park. Evolution was impressive to watch as the huge wheel spun at the end of the long arm, turning a full 360 degrees. (GreatAdventureHistory.com collection.)

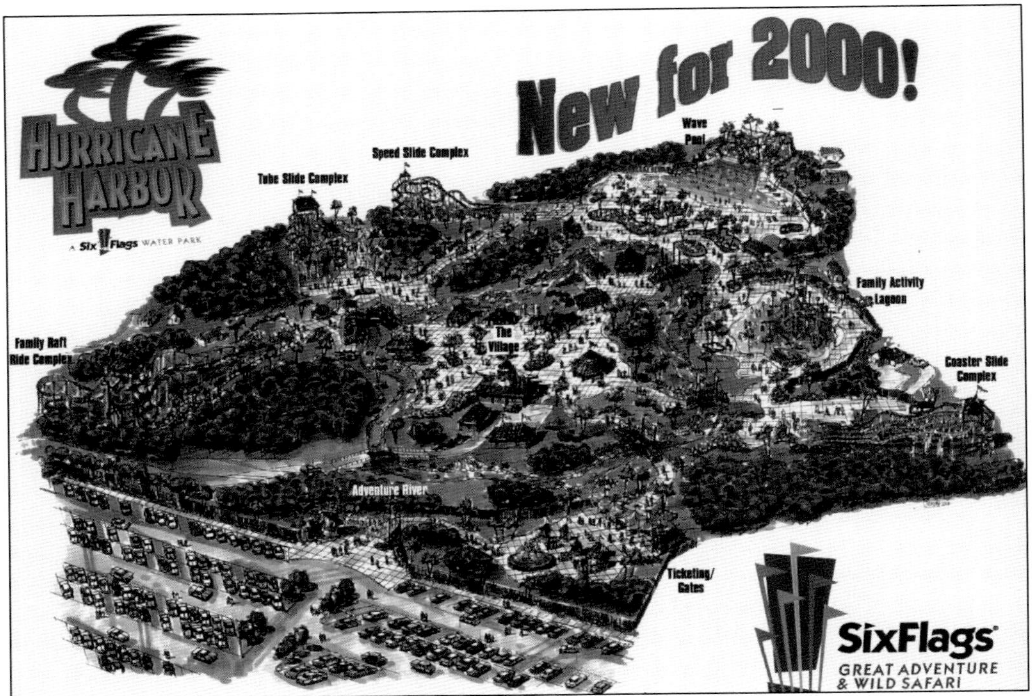

For the 2000 season, Six Flags Great Adventure added an entirely new park to the lineup, with Six Flags Hurricane Harbor water park joining the Wild Safari Animal Park and Great Adventure theme park. The park was designed to be a lush tropical oasis, with crystal clear water, white sand, and lush shady foliage.

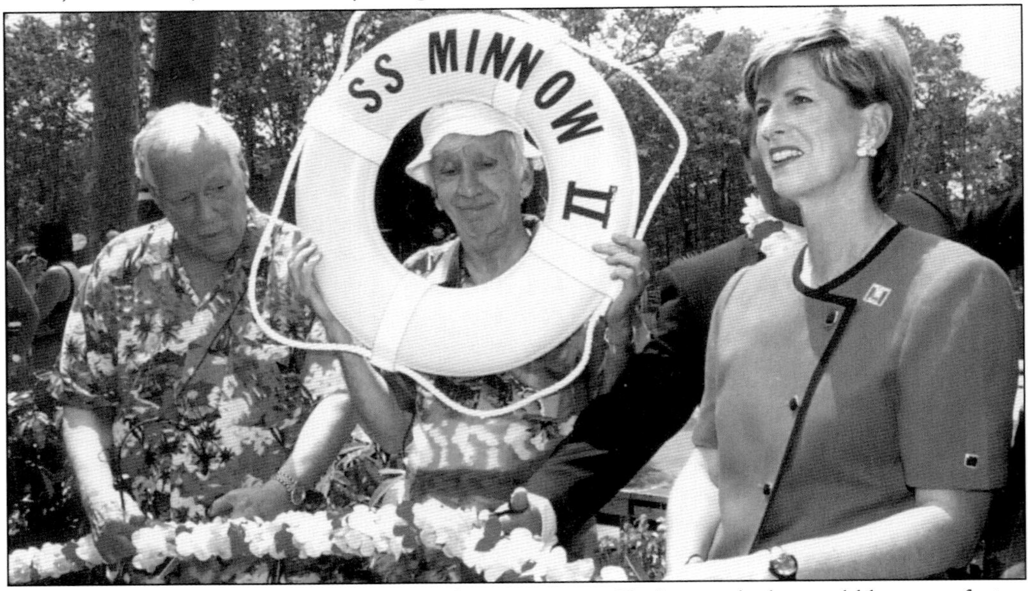

Celebrities were brought in to open Six Flags Hurricane Harbor, and who could be more fitting to open a tropical island water park than the cast of *Gilligan's Island*? Russell Johnson (the Professor), Dawn Wells (Mary Ann), and Bob Denver (Gilligan) were there to cut the ribbon along with then New Jersey governor Christine Todd Whitman.

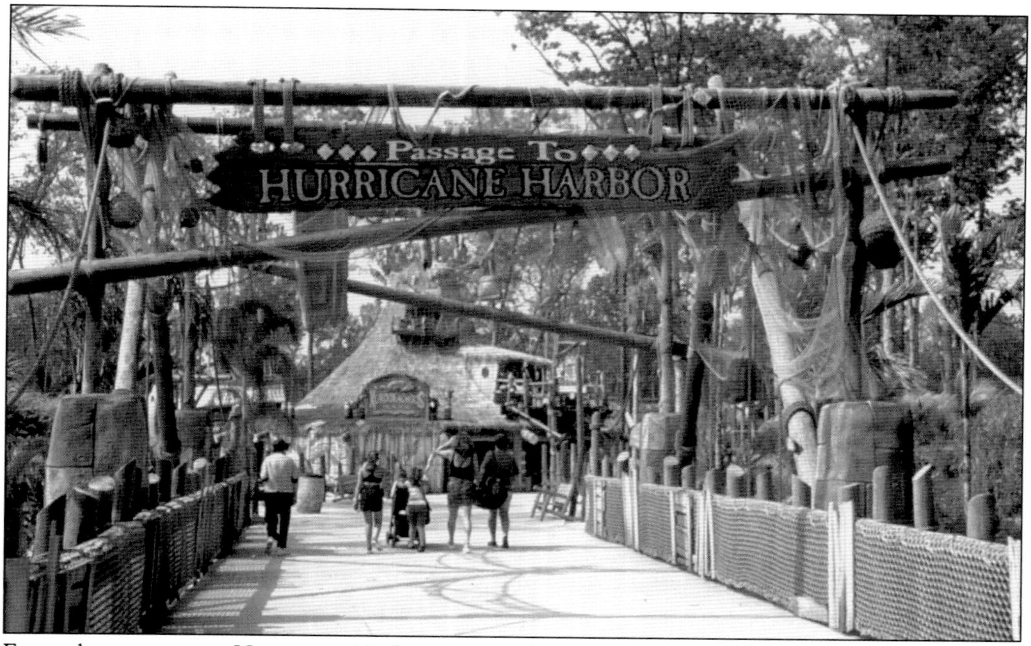

From the entry into Hurricane Harbor, it was clear guests were walking into another world, with highly immersive, themed buildings and rides. The park featured an elaborate backstory of explorer Copernicus T. Potter's discovery of Hurricane Harbor and its friendly natives, the Bada Bings, and their world of resourceful inventions created from indigenous materials and found objects.

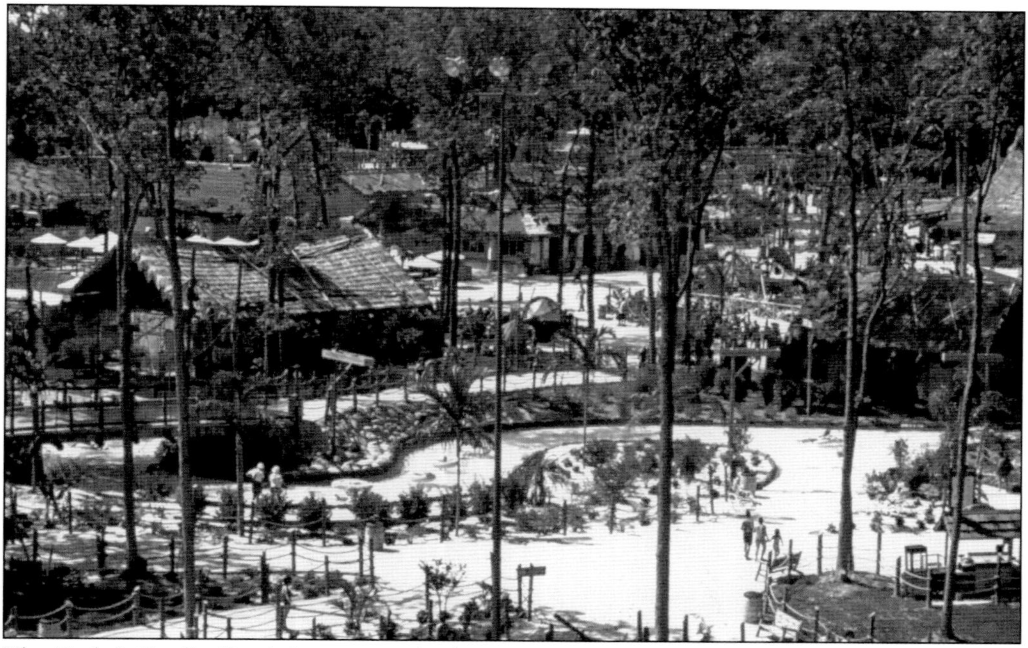

The Taak It Eez Ee Creek lazy river, which was one of the longest ever built, formed an island at the center of Hurricane Harbor. The island was home to the park's shops and guest facilities, with four bridges leading off the island to the water slides and other attractions.

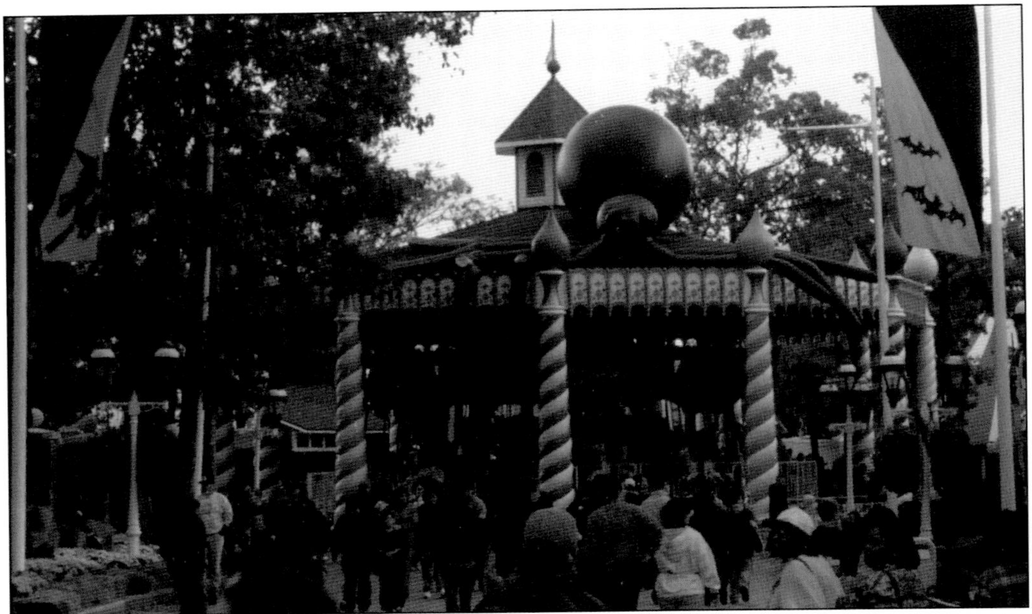

The popular Halloween events at Six Flags Great Adventure have evolved throughout the years, with the October weekends' Fright Fest often being the busiest days of the park's operating season. The park transforms each autumn from theme park to scream park as dozens of ghouls haunt the sinister streets and wicked walkways of Great Adventure.

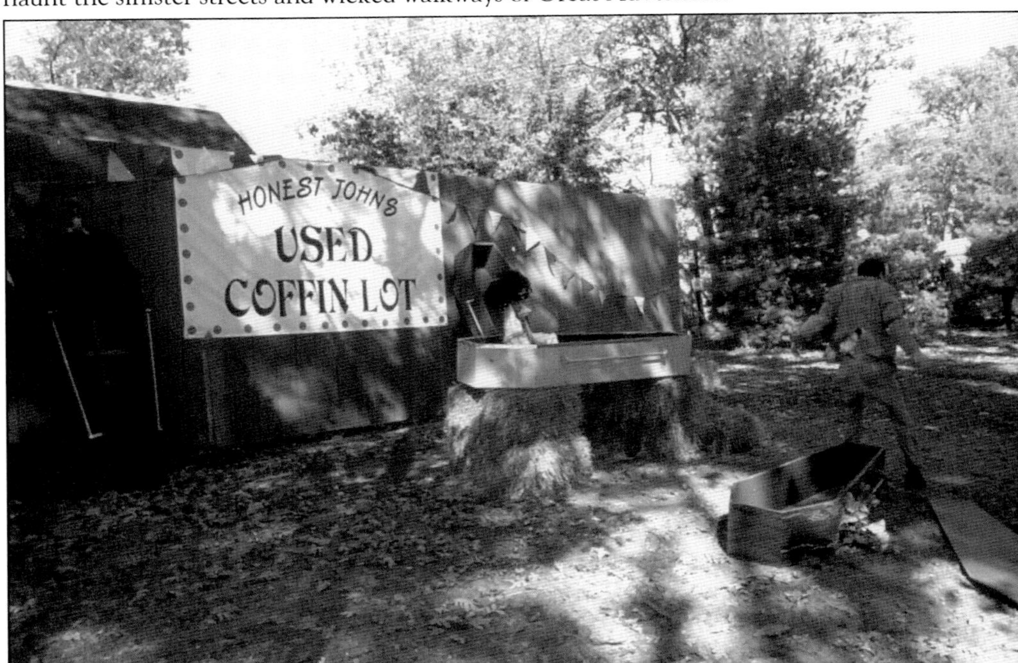

Special Fright Fest attractions like hayrides and Terror Trails have been staged each year, with new twists. The creative team at the park has constantly figured out how to utilize existing props and added new props to keep the attractions fresh and keep guests coming back for more thrills by day and chills by night.

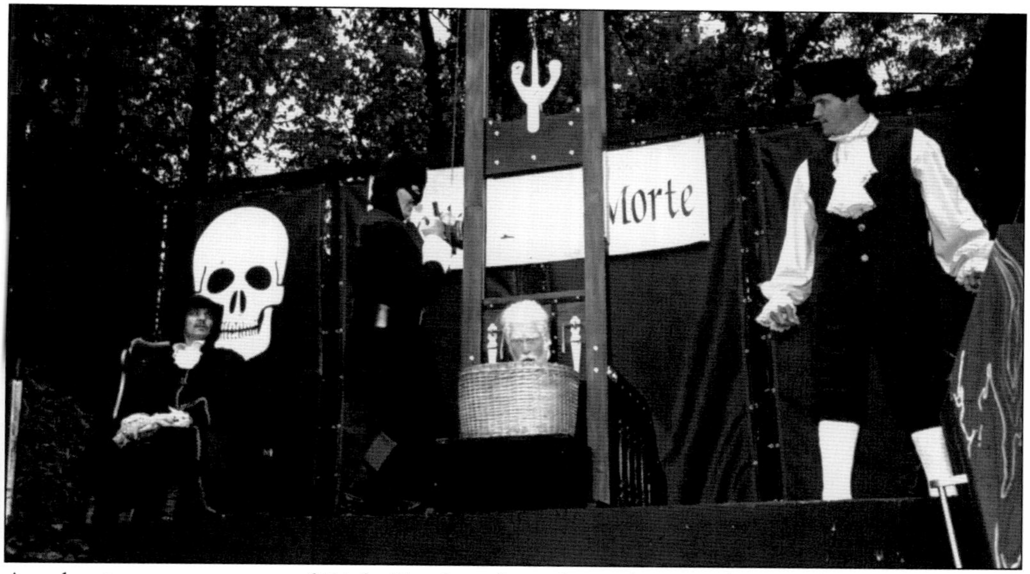

Another important aspect of Fright Fest has always been the great lineup of Halloween shows. Ranging from the not-so-scary, kid-oriented daytime shows to the macabre, like the execution shown here. Most popular of all has been the Dead Man's Party, which takes center stage in front of the Big Wheel.

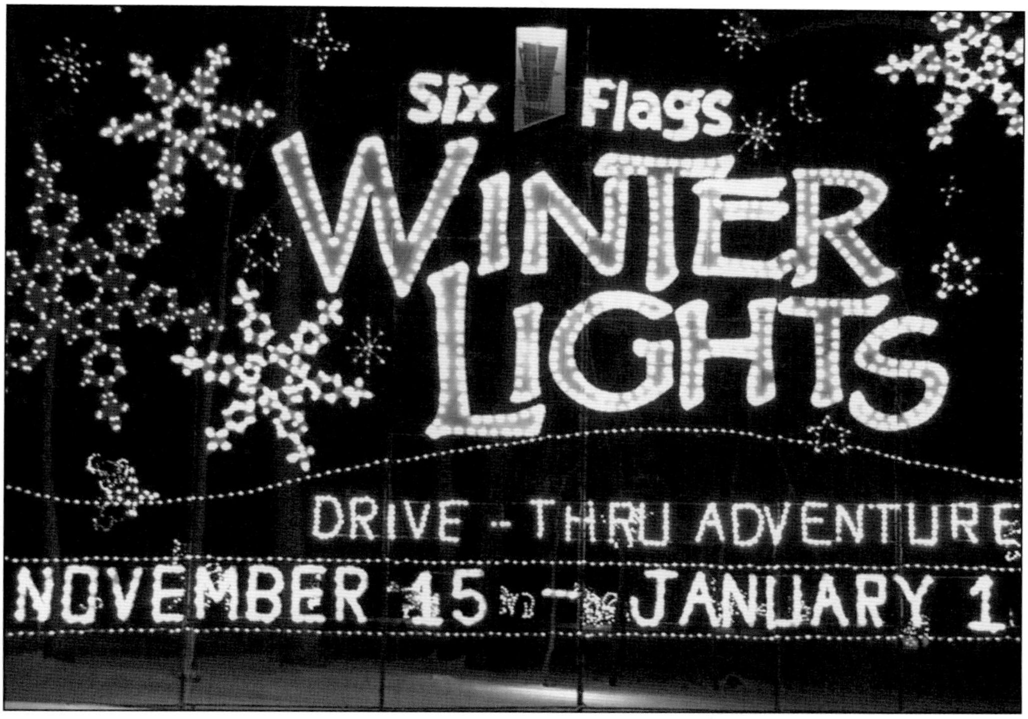

For two seasons, Six Flags presented Winter Lights, a drive-through animated holiday light display winding through the park's property and featuring thousands of lights. Part of the short-lived event was the Twinkle Town village where guests could hear carolers, get hot cocoa, buy gifts, and of course, get their pictures taken with Santa. (GreatAdventureHistory.com collection.)

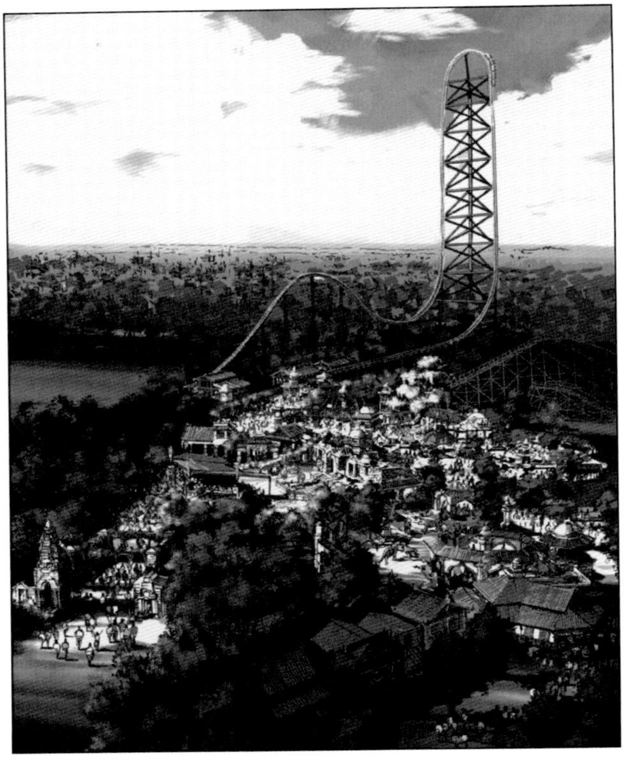

Six Flags Great Adventure has always been a park of record-holding attractions, and in 2005, it went to new heights, introducing Kingda Ka, the world's tallest and fastest roller coaster, launching at 128 miles per hour to climb 456 feet into the sky. Kingda Ka was just part of the new Golden Kingdom, which brought a jungle of fun to the park, complete with beautiful golden tigers.

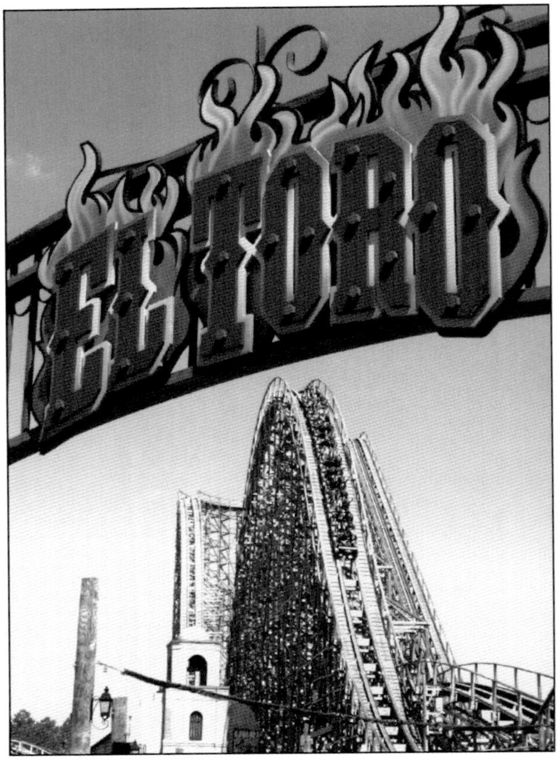

Kingda Ka and the Golden Kingdom were a tough act to follow, but in 2006, Plaza del Carnaval and the amazing El Toro roller coaster were up to the task, bringing the sounds and flavors of Latin America along with a world-class thrill ride to the site that had been part of Frontier Adventures. (GreatAdventureHistory.com collection.)

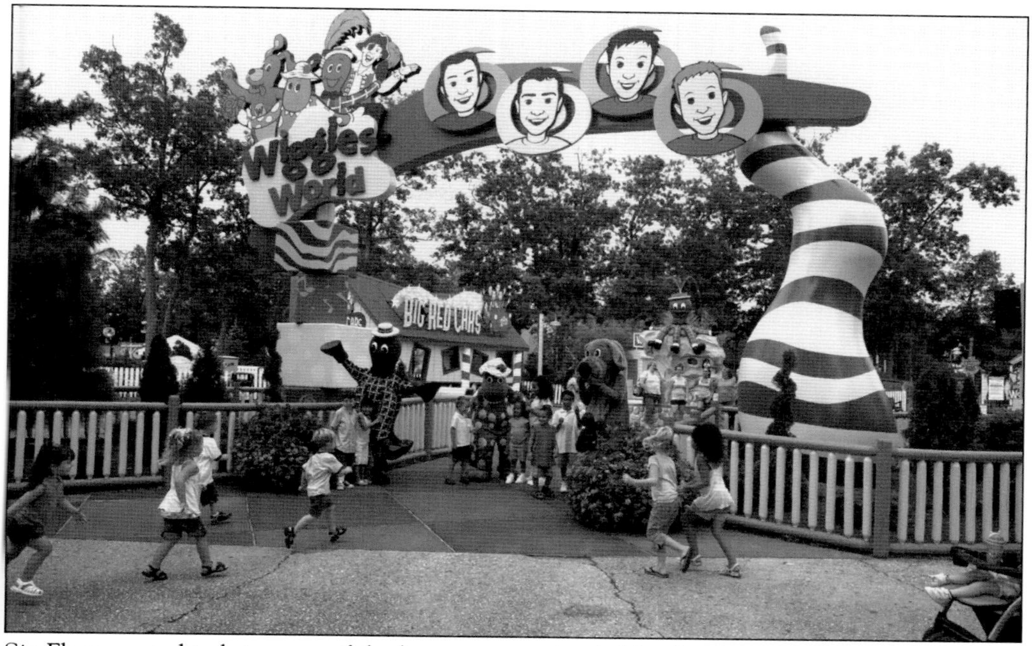

Six Flags wanted to bring one of the hottest names in children's entertainment to the park and built the first Wiggles World–themed area in the United States at Six Flags Great Adventure in 2007. Wiggles World was part of the company's new family focus and efforts to broaden the appeal of the park beyond the thrill seekers.

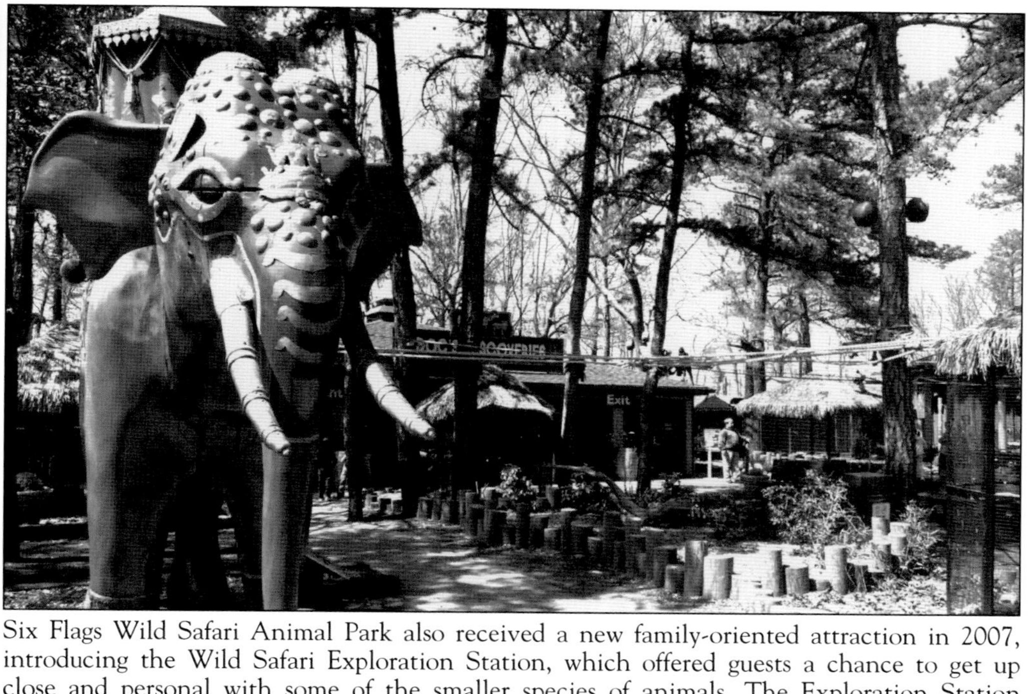

Six Flags Wild Safari Animal Park also received a new family-oriented attraction in 2007, introducing the Wild Safari Exploration Station, which offered guests a chance to get up close and personal with some of the smaller species of animals. The Exploration Station offered more education about the Safari's animals and conservation efforts around the world. (GreatAdventureHistory.com collection.)

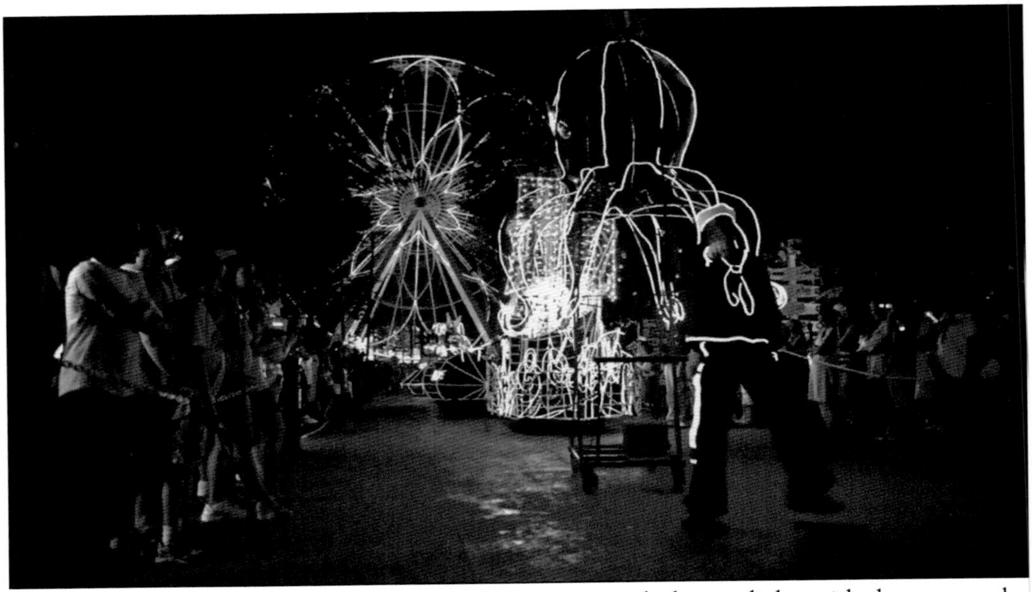

In 2008, guests got to see Six Flags Great Adventure in a whole new light, with the spectacular Glow in the Park Parade taking to the streets on summer nights. The Glow in the Park Parade combined an amazing series of floats made of high-tech lights with cirque-style music and performers.

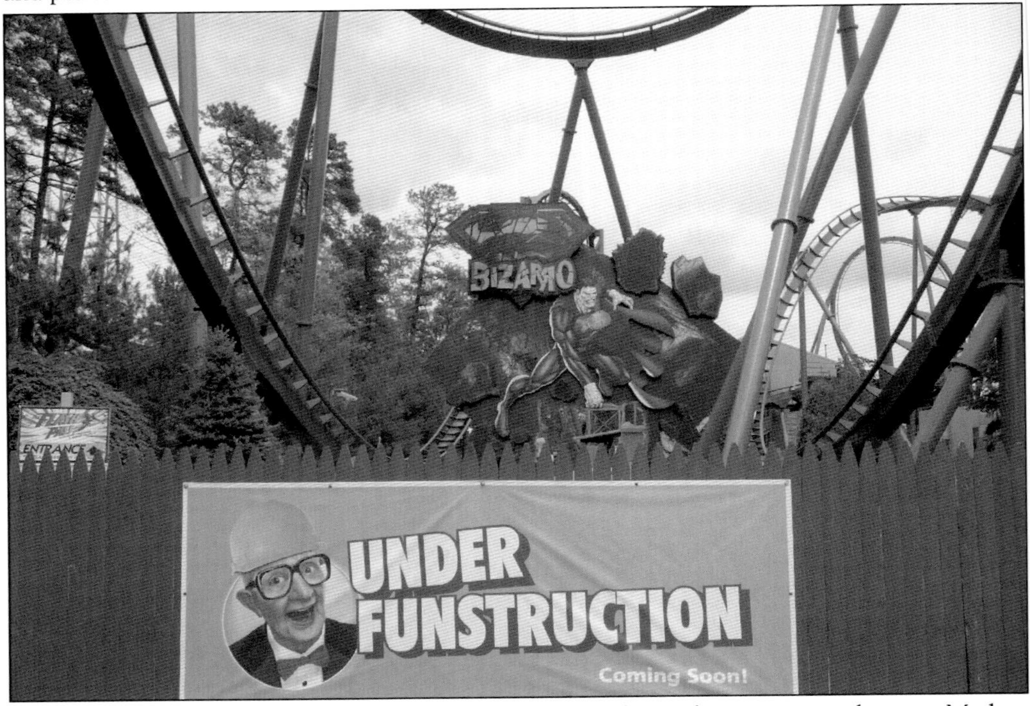

Sometimes a good thing can be made better, and for the ride's 10th anniversary, the great Medusa floorless roller coaster was given a total makeover for the 2009 season, transforming into Bizarro. The redesign introduced new special effects and an onboard audio system, taking riders into a whole new dimension. (GreatAdventureHistory.com collection.)

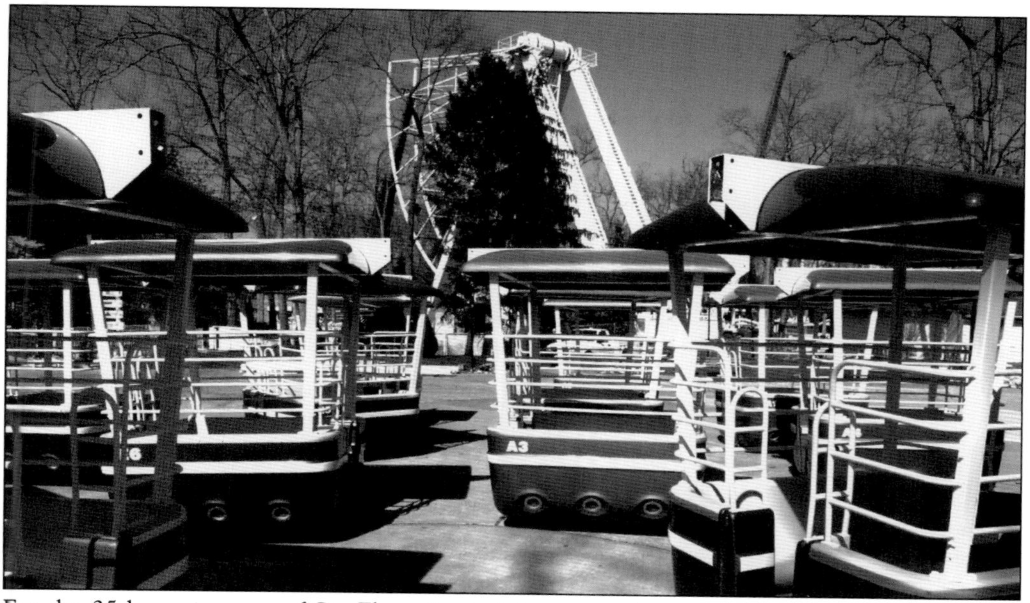

For the 35th anniversary of Six Flags Great Adventure, the park looked to preserve its great history and look to the future. The Big Wheel was given a top-to-bottom restoration that included updating its lighting system with new LEDs, which provided new light shows as well as saving energy. Conserving energy and recycling throughout the park are just part of the park's commitment to the environment. (GreatAdventureHistory.com collection.)

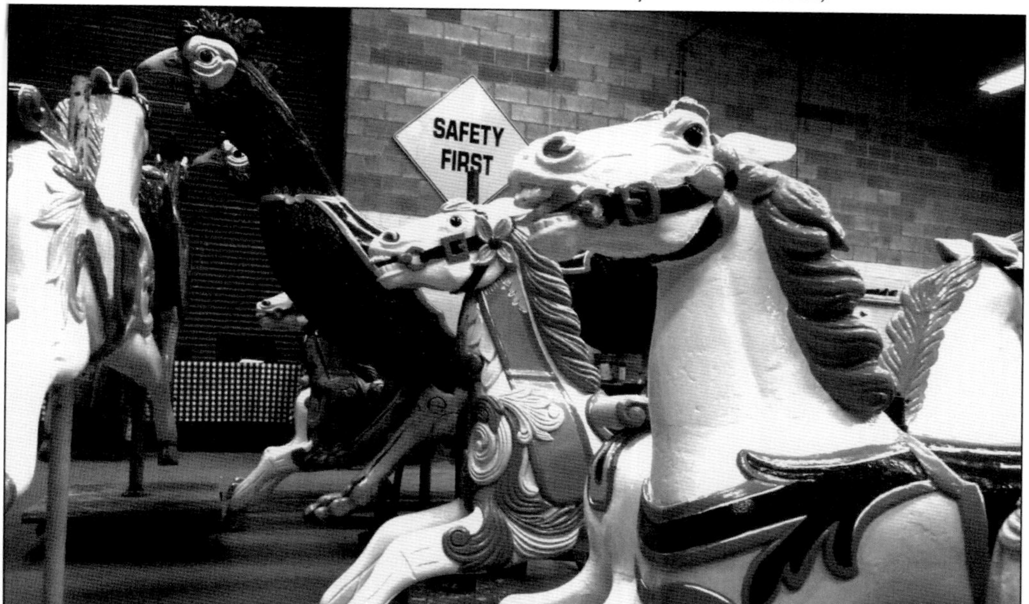

As the oldest ride in the park, the carousel holds a special place in Great Adventure's history, and to celebrate 35 years of memories, a three-year restoration program was started. The horses and cockerels received TLC in the first year, with completion of the rehab set to coincide with the 50th anniversary of the Six Flags family of theme parks in 2011. (GreatAdventureHistory.com collection.)